THE GREAT FLOODS

OF AUGUST, 1829,

IN THE

PROVINCE OF MORAY AND ADJOINING DISTRICTS

SIR THOMAS DICK LAUDER, BART.

OF GRANGE AND FOUNTAINHALL, F.R.S.E.

Produced and published by Moray Books, St Catherines Road, Forres, Morayshire
IV36 1LL, Scotland
Tel: 01309 671181 Fax: 01309 671191 e-mail: moray.books@dial.pipex.com

ISBN 1 901193 20 9

First reprinted edition 1998

Printed in Scotland by Nevisprint Ltd

CONTENTS

THE PUBLISHER'S PREFACE

THOSE for whom reading is as much a pleasure as a modern-day necessity will readily understand that, from time to time, a book is discovered that is genuinely difficult to put down. Sir Thomas Dick Lauder's account of the inundation of vast areas of North-East Scotland in 1829 might seem, at first, an unlikely candidate for such an accolade, but rarely has an historical event been so thoroughly, sympathetically and excitingly recorded.

So great was the interest in the book during the latter half of the nineteenth century, that publishers in London and Scotland were threatening each other with injunctions at law should their rights to the title be infringed in any way. Eventually, the late Mr James Black, founder and proprietor of the now defunct 'Elgin Courant', found the way clear to publish the work, and it ran to at least three editions. In his preface to the third edition, Mr Black comments on the wrangles that had gone on, and somewhat triumphantly includes an Introductory Note penned by Miss C. Dick Lauder, the daughter of Sir Thomas, as that noble family's endorsement of his work. That Introductory Note has been included, in full, in this twentieth century edition because it, like the book itself, provides a fascinating glimpse of the ways in which our forebears thought and conducted their lives.

As to the book itself, any suspicion that the sceptical reader might harbour as to its ability to inform, entertain and enthral, will be banished within moments of beginning to read, in Chapter 1, of the way in which the River Nairn, usually so amiable, carried the machinery of a large mill nine miles downstream on the 3rd of August and, after it had been restored, carried it away for a fifteen-mile excursion on the 27th. Interwoven with such incredible evidence of the floods' power are the human experiences of terror, courage, resourcefulness, resignation and simple godliness, and thus a story emerges of an area and names with which many will be familiar, but of a people whose values and behaviour were utterly different from the norm today.

The present publisher has taken the liberty of adding, where it was thought necessary, footnotes to explain obsolete words. It was also thought helpful, in some instances, to break up some of the longer sentences which, like the comma, were so beloved of the early writers. Apart from these gentle efforts to make the text more suitable to the eye of the modern reader, and the inclusion of the sketches in the vicinity of the relevant text, rather than on separate pages of prints, the book is as originally written.

FORRES, 1998

INTRODUCTORY NOTE TO THE 1873 EDITION

HAVING been asked by the Publisher to write something by way of Preface to this Edition of THE MORAY FLOODS, and, recollecting how much we all felt for his disappointment when prevented bringing it forward some years ago, I am unwilling to refuse his request. I feel, however, that anything I may write cannot in any way enhance the value of this Book, one of the very best of my father's Works. His memory still lives in the hearts of so many who knew him, that it is unnecessary that his daughter should give him the praise which the goodness of his character so truly merited. His genial, kindly, sympathetic nature, made him the joy of the home circle, and of his intimate friends; whilst the brightness and versatility of his talents ensured his being a favourite with all who met him even for the first time in society. He had also a tender heart for the poor, and exerted himself with energy and success in many useful labours of philanthropy.

It may, perhaps, be interesting that I should give my recollections of the time when this Book was first thought of, and of the event which called it forth. For this purpose I have to look along the vista of past years to the time of my happy childhood. Well do I recollect 'The Flood' of Monday, 3rd August, 1829. We, the school-room children of the family, after lessons were over, sat at the window looking out upon the trees bowed by the wind, the glaring sky, and pelting rain, wondering if we should ever get out again. I remember also the excitement caused by the message that the rivers were up "beyond the memory of man." It was not at first intended that we should go out at all; but our pleading looks touched my father, who could never bear to see us disappointed, and we were accordingly sent to equip ourselves in our old pelisses of the previous winter, before covering our heads with boys' caps, for umbrellas were impossible in the wind.

I think we must have looked very like a troop of ragged Highland terriers, as we joyfully followed my father down the garden! And very full of glee we were, until we stood with wonder and awe beside the raging Divie. Then, indeed, our joyous tones were hushed. No sound could be heard but the mighty voice of the waters. One after another, the large trees bent over like willow wands, and on the surface of the flood "were for a moment seen, then gone for ever".

We followed my father further up the river to a place above the Divie Fall, where an incident occurred which has not been recorded in THE FLOODS. The river-walk, at this point, was at a great height above the ordinary course of the stream, but in its flooded condition the river was raging along quite close to it. My two sisters, ignorant, as we all were, that the walk was undermined, were standing on it, gazing with wonder at the river. An English gentleman, one of our visitors, who was out with us, possessed by what seemed to us all a vain fear, called to them, and entreated them to return to where the rest were standing. They did not hear him, and remained gazing on the flood. My father, who had himself no doubts as to the safety of their position, could not, however, bear to see the anxiety of his friend, and shouted to his daughters to come back. They immediately obeyed, and the whole party turned up the bank. Happening just then to look round, I saw the portion of the walk on which my sisters had been standing break away, and fall into the raging torrent. My father's kindness of heart had thus mercifully saved himself a great sorrow.

We now followed my father to the Divie Bridge, and to the junction of the rivers. Here all was indeed changed. The Findhorn, in its ordinary state, received the shallower and more impulsive Divie into the depths of a long dark pool, like a strong man taking into his arms his gleeful child. How different now! The rock, which, with its graceful covering of mingled birch and fir, jutted out, as if presiding at the union of the rivers, was not even to be seen, and far up the bank the rivers met, no longer lovingly, but like contending armies rushing to battle. A stone, put up by my father, still marks the almost incredible point of union.

Darkness alone drove us home that night. Next morning we wandered forth again, retracing our steps of the evening before. Reports of the devastation at Dunphail, and anxiety about its inhabitants, made my father continue his walk up the Divie, and with sorrow we gazed on the destruction there. I remember that, whilst so engaged, the sun, which had been struggling through the clouds, suddenly burst out upon the scene. It seemed, like Noah's bow in the Heavens, to say, "Comfort yourselves; all is over; it shall not be so again."

Urged by the entreaties of his friends, in particular by those of Lord Cockburn, my father undertook to write this book. The task soon became a labour of love. Information poured in from all sides; but my father himself visited all the scenes of devastation reported to him, making frequent expeditions on horseback for days at a time to places he could not otherwise have reached, for rivers had to be forded where bridges had been carried away.

At last the book was finished, but was considered by the Publishers too voluminous for publication, on a subject supposed to be only of local interest. It was a hard task for my father, but, after demurring for a while, he patiently set himself to the work of re-writing and condensing a book which has proved one of his most estimated works, interesting many who knew nothing of the locality.

Of my father's literary productions, two novels and some shorter stories and scientific papers had been published previous to 1829. Of these, my favourite, '*Lochandhu*' is, I believe, the least known.

Subsequent to the publication of THE MORAY FLOODS, my father wrote the '*Highland Rambles*' and the '*Legendary Tales*', a continuation of the former. He edited, besides, some books on natural history, wrote an account of the '*Royal Progress in 1842*', and was engaged on a series of sketches of the Scottish rivers, only three of which had been completed when weakness and suffering compelled him to stop the working of his earnest mind. My father was born in 1784, and died in 1848 at the age of sixty-four.

Having now, though very imperfectly, finished my task, I leave my father's book to speak for itself, feeling sure it will deeply interest the reader.

C. DICK LAUDER.

JULY, 1873.

TO

HENRY COCKBURN, ESQ. OF BONALLY,

ADVOCATE

MY DEAR COCKBURN,

As you are answerable for the infliction of this volume on the public, you must not be surprised that I now claim for it the protection of your name, so universally known and respected; and, at the same time, afford myself an opportunity of acknowledging the many obligations I owe to your long and steady friendship, and of manifesting my admiration of your private virtues, and the pleasure and pride with which I subscribe myself,

MY DEAR COCKBURN,

Your warmly and sincerely attached,

THOs. DICK LAUDER

RELUGAS, *17th June, 1830.*

Portrait of the Author, from the painting by
Robert Scott Lauder, R.S.A.

PRELIMINARY CHAPTER

THE heat in the province of Moray, during the months of May, June, and July, 1829, was unusually great; and, in the earlier part of that period, the drought was so excessive as to kill many of the recently planted shrubs and trees. As the season advanced, the fluctuations of the barometer became very remarkable, but the usual alternations of weather did not always follow these oscillations. It often happened that the results were precisely the reverse of its prognostications, and observers of the instrument began to lose all confidence in it. That these apparent derangements arose from certain electrical changes in the atmosphere, there can be little doubt. The aurora borealis appeared with uncommon brilliancy about the beginning of July, and was frequently seen afterwards, being generally accompanied by windy and unsteady weather, the continued drought having been already interrupted during the previous month by sudden falls of rain, partaking of the character of waterspouts.

A very remarkable instance of one of these occurred on Sunday the 12th of July, at Kean-loch-luichart, a little Highland hamlet, at the head of the lake of that name, in the parish of Contin, in Ross-shire. The innkeeper of Auchanault, having taken shelter under an arch, suddenly beheld a moving mountain of soil, stones, and trees, coming slowly but steadily down the deep worn course of the little stream. He fled in terror. It reached the bridge, where its progress was for a moment arrested when, bursting the feeble barrier that opposed it, on it rushed in dreadful devastation over the plain that bordered the lake below. It was church time. The children left at home were amusing themselves out of doors, and were miraculously preserved by escaping to a hillock ere the ruin reached the spot. An insignificant rivulet, running to the west of the village, was so suddenly swollen, that the people coming from church found great difficulty in passing it. But, as they were on their way towards the larger stream, 300 yards to the eastward, they were alarmed by the fall of the bridge at some distance above the village. In an instant they found themselves between two impassable torrents, and they had barely time to save their lives by crowding to an elevated spot, where they remained till the waters subsided. The whole fury of the flood rushed directly against their devoted houses, and these, and everything they contained, were at once annihilated, as well as their crops, together with the very soil they grew on. After the debacle had passed away, the course of the burn ran through the ruined hearths of this so recently happy a community. This waterspout did not extend beyond two miles on each side of the village, a circumstance that led these simple people to consider their calamity as a visitation of Providence for their landlord's vote in Parliament in favour of Catholic emancipation.

The deluge of rain that produced the flood of the 3rd and 4th of August, fell chiefly on the Monadh-leadh mountains, rising between the south-eastern part of Loch Ness, and Kingussie in Badenoch, and on that part of the Grampian range forming the somewhat independent group of the Cairngorums. The westerly winds, which prevailed for some time previously, seem to have produced a gradual accumulation of vapour, somewhere north of our island; and the column being suddenly impelled by a strong north-easterly blast, it was driven towards the south-west, its right flank almost sweeping the Caithness and Sutherland coasts, until rushing up and across the Moray Firth, it was attracted by the lofty mountains I have mentioned and discharged in torrents perfectly unexampled. The facts which have come to my knowledge amply bear out this hypothesis.

At Kirkwall, in Orkney, there was a violent storm of wind and rain on Monday the 3rd of August. A similar deluge was experienced at Wick, and much damage was done in the parishes of Watten, Halkirk, and Latham. A few miles above the bridge of Wick, a boy was whirled off by the torrent, on a rick of hay, and carried down with great velocity, and was ultimately rescued with much difficulty. In Sutherland and Ross-shire, both lying to the westward of the line I have described, as well as in the country to the north of Loch Ness, little or no injury was sustained. But the river Foyers, deriving its source from the very mountains that first received the column of drifted vapour, was so highly flooded as to destroy Whitebridge, which it did in a very singular manner, the outside walls and parapets being left entire, while the roadway, arch, and all within, totally disappeared.

The rivers Nairn, Findhorn, and Lossie, were all more or less affected by the flood, exactly in proportion as they were more or less connected with the mountains in question. That part of the Spey which is above the line I have marked, was hardly swollen at all, whilst below Kingussie it and its tributaries were elevated to an unexampled height. The Deveron, the Don, the Dee, and the two Esks, were each of them operated upon in a similar ratio.

Many imagined that the fall of rain was not so great as to account for so tremendous a flood, but this was a mistake, arising from the undefined form the rain assumed. For although, at certain times, it fell in heavy drops, yet it was, for the most part, broken by the blast into extremely minute particles. But these came down so thick, that the very air itself seemed to be descending in one mass of water upon the earth. Nothing could withstand it. The best finished windows were ineffectual against it, and every room exposed to the north-east was deluged. The lesser animals, the birds, and especially game of all kinds, were destroyed in great numbers by the rain alone; and the mother partridge, with her progeny and her mate, were found chilled to death amidst the drenching wet. But the question as to the quantity of rain is settled by the accurate observations of Mr. Murdoch, gardener to His Grace the Duke of Gordon, at Huntly Lodge, who informs me that 3 inches of rain fell between five o'clock of the morning of the 3rd, and five o'clock of the morning of the 4th of August. That is to say that, taking the average of the years from 1821 to 1828 inclusive, about one-sixth part of our annual allowance of rain fell within these twenty-four hours; and if such was the fall at so great a distance from the mountains, the deluge that descended on them must have been so enormous, as to lead us rather to wonder that a flood even yet more tremendous in its magnitude and consequences, did not result from it.

That of the 27th of August, which may be called an appendix flood, was also preceded by westerly wind; but, when it changed into the north, it still kept its hold of the west, and consequently the vapour was dispersed over the country to the north of Inverness. It affected the Nairn more than the first flood did, but the other rivers to the south were less raised by it. Its chief influence was on the rivers to the north of the Monadh-leadh group. The Blackwater flooded the whole valley of the Garve, inundated the inn to the depth of four feet, and compelled the shooting party of Messrs. Dilkes and Woomwald to fasten safety ropes for 200 yards to a hill in front, the intervening space being covered with six feet of water. The River Alness did great damage to the estate of Teaninich, and the Beauly flooded the whole of Strathglass. The burn of Moniack worked terrible ruin in the beautiful place of that name, carried away a bridge, and very much alarmed Mr. Fraser's family by paying a most unwelcome visit to the house, and even intruding itself into the chamber of a gentleman who was lying sick of the scarlet fever. The damage at Moniack was valued at above £500, and the burn was equally injurious to Mr. Fraser of Auchnagairn. The River Ness was, in some degree, affected on this occasion. Loch Mickly, in Glen-Urquhart, was considerably raised, and the Mona, that runs into it, presented a grand spectacle where it throws itself over a fall of 100 feet, as it then filled the whole chasm 60 feet wide. The Enrick, which comes from the lake, damaged several cottages, injured a bleachfield and fulling-mill, destroyed a bridge, and it and the Devah, another stream of the same valley, committed great havoc among the crops. The Morriston, and the other rivers on the north side of Loch Ness, were all equally mischievous.

On the south side of Loch Ness, the River Farrigaig was never known to be so high. It inundated Mr. Fraser of Lovat's property to a great extent. It broke through the bulwarks of the mill-stream of Torness, surrounded the house, and entered it by the door and windows. The miller and his family were heard during the night crying for help, which no one could yield them till next morning when they were extricated with very considerable risk. At the summer grazing of Killin, the herdsmen's huts were so instantaneously surrounded, that the inmates were compelled to flee to the best shelter they could find on the cold face of the neighbouring hill, where they remained all night. But they were happy in comparison with one family, who, being too late in attempting to get away, were compelled to sit, man, wife, and children, on two old doors, propped up under the roof, in terror and darkness, till relieved next day. But the most wonderful escape in this district was that of a poor woman, who, in attempting to cross the Calderburn on two narrow planks, below the house of Croachy, was carried off, bridge and all, and hurried down the stream about half a mile. Luckily she was kept floating by the buoyancy of her garments, until she was fortunately rescued by an accidental passenger.

All the facts I have been able to collect, and they have not been few, have conspired to convince me that the flood of the 3rd and 4th of August was considerably greater, and more destructive, than any flood that ever affected the same rivers, so far as recorded, or traditional information is capable of instructing us. I believe this remark will apply to all the rivers I am about to treat of, but as to the Findhorn and the Spey, the fact is unquestionably established. As the rise was less on former occasions, so the reign of terror was comparatively short, whereas the late flood was fearfully enduring. And where is there even a legend that tells of any of these rivers having ever before worked ruin so universal, or produced misery so extensive? Nor is this wonderful. Any given quantity of rain must now produce a much greater flood than it could have done before the country became so highly improved. Formerly the rain drops were either evaporated on the hill side, or were sucked up by an arid or a spongy soil, before so many of them could coalesce as to form a rill. But when we consider the number of open cuts made to dry hill pastures, the numerous bogs reclaimed by drainage, the ditches of enclosure recently constructed and the long lines of roads formed with side drains, back drains, and cross conduits, we shall find that, of late years, the country has been covered with a perfect network of courses to catch and to concentrate the rain-drops as they fall, and to hurry them off in accumulated tribute to the next stream.

The very contemplation of the task I have undertaken is deeply distressing. Nor is it without its difficulties. The united line of the rivers I have to travel over cannot be less in extent than from 500 to 600 miles. Along the whole of this the march of ruin has been traced. Were I to follow it with minute description, I should swell this work to an infinitely greater bulk than is usually permitted to such subjects. I must therefore pass slightly over many circumstances that are too deeply traced on the minds of those who were connected with them, to be ever forgotten; whilst to others I must allow larger limits than they may at first sight appear to be entitled to, that the meagreness of narration may not prove fatal to the interest. Having visited the greater part of the flooded districts in person, I shall write about them very much from my own observation, aided, as it has been, by the ample oral and written information I have obtained; and, in some cases, I shall, perhaps, bring forward the witnesses to tell their own story, rather than unravel its threads to interweave them with my own, at the risk of marring the texture of both.

As I conceive the present to be a work of too popular a nature to be loaded with geological details, I shall confine my remarks on this subject chiefly to the changes produced by rivers in their channels and courses. For the same reason, I must reserve to myself a licence to notice such scraps of an historical, or traditional nature, as chance may have thrown in my way.

I shall begin with the river Nairn, and shall follow its course from the mountains to the sea, and so on with the Findhorn, and the other rivers in succession. When I come to any important tributary stream, I shall discuss it in the same order, before pursuing my way down that to which it unites itself.

The eye-sketch of the rivers has no pretensions to geographical accuracy, and is on a scale too small to admit of the insertion of all the places noticed, but enough will be found to render the narration more intelligible. The etchings with which the work is illustrated were reduced from my own sketches by Mr. Alexander, the Artist, who has kindly added some interesting subjects from drawings made by himself at the time. The view of Dunphail is from a sketch by Mrs. Cumming Bruce.

CHAPTER 1

THE RIVER NAIRN, FROM THE HILLS TO BELOW GEDDES

THE River Nairn, running through a straight line of country, of somewhat more than thirty miles in extent, but of much longer course in its sinuosities, drains off the waters from a small part of the Monadh-leadh group. The scenery of its upper district is of a bold, high-land character, its valley being of considerable width, chiefly cultivated and smiling, and bounded by birch-fringed hills, grandly massed, and everywhere exhibiting singularly picturesque outlines.

The rain in this upper country began on Sunday evening, the 2nd, and continued, with little or no intermission, till Tuesday the 4th. The Nairn, and the other streams of the valley, rushed from the mountains, filled with gravel and stones, and committed great havoc on many farms, especially on that of Mains of Aberarder, where seven hands were able to reap, in one day, all that remained of a crop for which £150 of rent was payable. The fulling-mill of Faillie was the sport of both floods. The first carried a huge, heavy mass of machinery down to Cantray, nine miles below, whence it was, with much labour, brought back to its high-land home; but it was hardly well established there, when the flood of the 27th bore it away on a second expedition, and landed it at Kilravock, after a voyage of eleven miles.

Colonel Mackintosh of Farr suffered considerably from the Fernack, a large tributary of the Nairn. Some years ago he cut a straight channel for the river, for above a mile in length; and it may be useful to those exposed to such devastations, to know that he succeeded in securing the banks of it by felling alder trees, and applying them with the bole part towards the bank, and the branches protruding obliquely in the direction of the stream, layer over layer, the whole being secured by placing very large stones above them. Every rise of the water deposits sand along this work, till a sodded bank is naturally formed, so smooth and solid as perfectly to resist the current. No part of this yielded before the recent floods, and all the damage Colonel Mackintosh received from them was occasioned by a breach made by the river at a point considerably above the entrance to the new cut.

Two bridges were carried away on the Parliamentary line of road; one at Dunmaglass, and the other, of two arches, over the burn of Aultrouagh, that joins the Nairn from the right. The cause of failure of this last bridge was want of size and accuracy of fitting of the stones, where strength to resist the force of the torrent was most requisite.

The road from Farr to Craggy leads along the base of some alluvial hills, about 100 feet high, very extensive, and very curious. They lie above the primitive rocks, here showing themselves in red granitic masses, rising at intervals through the level plain where the river flows. These hills are evidently the remains of a vast alluvial plain, cut away through the course of ages by the Nairn and its tributaries. The plain itself was probably the result of the deposits of a great lake that covered this upper country of Strathnairn, until gradually drained off by the natural excavation of the ravine of Daviot.

The burn of Craggy comes in from the right. The little inn of that name, standing very picturesquely, and apparently beyond all danger, on the top of a green alluvial bank amidst irregularly dropped birches, and surrounded by birch-covered knolls, formed, with its bridge below it, a very beautiful scene. But the flood of the 27th carried away the bridge, cut the bank into a high, perpendicular precipice, and was only prevented from undermining and bringing down the inn by the accidental fall of a tree, with a quantity of soil attached to its roots, which turned the force of the torrent, proving the beneficial effects of this description of guard when applied in the proper place.

The mill of Clava, on the right bank, was destroyed by the first flood, and was rebuilt and repaired exactly in time to be again demolished by the flood of the 27th. The plain of Clava may be almost denominated the Scottish Stonehenge, being covered with Druidical circles of great magnitude. The largest of these, like several of the others, consists of one external circle of stones, with a smaller concentric circle within it enclosing, and in some degree supporting, a great cairn. This was lately opened by direction, and under the superintendence, of Mrs Campbell, resident at Kilravock Castle, and a curious circular apartment was discovered, measuring 12 feet in diameter, the wall converging to the centre in a rude dome (Plate 1),

PLATE 1. INTERIOR OF CAIRN OF DRUIDICAL CIRCLE AT CLAVA

about 12 feet high, the foundation being formed of fourteen large stones, surmounted by courses of uncemented masonry, each stone placed immediately over that below it, and not over the division between two, as is commonly the case in mason work. A passage leads inwards from the south, eighteen feet long, two feet wide, and having eight large foundation stones on either side. This cell distinguishes the cairn dedicated to religious purposes from that which was monumental or sepulchral. The largest of the standing stones of the exterior circle measures about 9½ feet high, by 1 foot thick, and 4 feet broad.

A mile farther down the valley, and on the same side, we found a huge cubical boulder of conglomerate, resting on the gneiss, but within thirty horizontal yards of the out-crop of a stratum of what may be supposed its native rock. It stands in an ancient river-bed, about 100 feet above the present channel of the Nairn. It is about 24 feet square by 14 feet high, and, allowing it a specific gravity equal to 2½ that of water, its weight may be estimated at about 560 tons. It is called *Clach-mhor-a'-chruaidh-ghorston*, or the Great Stone of the rough ground (Plate 2).

PLATE 2. *CLACH-MHOR-A'-CHRUAIDH-GHORSTON* - THE BIG STONE OF THE ROUGH GROUND

The damage done on the estate of Cantray is estimated at £1200, exclusive of the destruction of crops, which was very great. About fifteen acres of valuable land have been entirely swept away. Both floods filled the garden belonging to the mansion-house; and after undermining the eastern wall, the water made its escape by throwing down many roods of the masonry, leaving the beds covered with deposits of sand. The houses of the miller and gardener were inundated and ruined.

The greater part of the low grounds of Holm, together with the offices and mills, were flooded. The horses and cattle were extricated from their stalls, where the water was three feet deep, while the rats and moles were swimming about among the buildings. The damage done to the crops was very considerable. The flower-garden, being close to the river's bank, was saved by very great exertion; but the shrubbery, extending nearly a mile along the margin of the stream, was very much injured. A little above the private bridge of approach, a breach was made quite through the screen of trees and shrubs; and the handsome arch of fifty-five feet span, having been shaken by the first flood, was entirely carried away by that of the 27th (Plate 3). The expansion of the water here was greatly more than 100 yards. It rose high on a dry-stone wall dividing the Holm and Kilravock estates; and it had no sooner touched its foundation, than the sods on the top of it became as it were alive with mice, all forcing their way out, to escape as fast as they could from the inundation that threatened their citadel.

PLATE 3. BRIDGE OF HOLM

It is a singular fact that, as the salmon fishing on the Findhorn was utterly ruined for the season by the flood, so that on the Nairn was proportionably improved. This, as regards Holm, may have partly arisen from the demolition of certain obstacles below. But the chief cause undoubtedly was that the fish, being scared from the Findhorn by the dirty and troubled state in which its waters so long remained, sought their way into the Nairn, which sooner cleared itself. The salmon-angling at Holm is seldom very successful; but after the flood, and before the end of the season, Colonel Rose, the proprietor, killed between seventy and eighty fish with the rod.

The stretch of valley occupied by the residences of Cantray, Holm, and Kilravock, has something peculiarly smiling in its aspect; but its appearance, when converted into a moving lake, was very appalling. The old castle of Kilravock, rearing its weather-beaten front and grey tower above its rocky and wooded bank, looked like the wizard enchanter by whose spell the metamorphosis had been wrought. The view from its bartizan must have been extremely grand. Long as it has stood the emblem of the ancient family of Rose, to which it has immemorially belonged, I doubt whether it ever saw so wide a deluge. I grieve to say that the injury done to the property attached to it is very great. At one point, immediately below the beautiful garden, the river cut up the ground terribly, and varied considerably from its former channel; and a little way farther down it carried above two acres of a thriving wood of deciduous trees, of thirty years' growth, entirely away.

The bridge of Kilravock is one of the old military school of architecture, with a very steep ascent from the low right to the high left bank. Though it suffered some scars, it resisted the flood like a veteran warrior, as all these bridges do when not modernised. Some of them standing in positions where both banks are low, are formed with steep ascents from either end towards the centre. In both these cases the bridges are quite secure in floods, from the superabundant water being allowed to escape over the low end or ends. But let the approach or approaches to the bridges be modernised, by raising the wing-walls, and banking up the roadway, as has unfortunately been done in some instances, and the result must be destruction; for the flood-water being compelled to pass through an arch which the builders never intended should contain it, the bridge or its approaches must give way before its pressure.

John Pryse, one of Lord Cawdor's labourers, was sent in the forenoon of the 27th with a cart, drawn by a very active mare, to carry to Inverness the baggage of Lord Henry Thynne and Sir Rowland Hill, who had been on a sporting visit at Cawdor Castle. On his return, Pryse reached the inn of Clephanton, a quarter of a mile north of the bridge of Kilravock, about eight o'clock in the evening, and was there told by the landlady that the river was so much out over the level ground to the south of the bridge, as to render it madness to attempt to cross. But, having afterwards held a consultation with the hostler, it was determined that there could be no harm in going down to look at the river. Pryse was quite willing to believe there was no danger, for he was completely soaked with the heavy rain, and therefore felt extremely desirous to get home. They passed the bridge without interruption; but, on reaching the lower end of it, they found the road covered with water, though, from its muddy state and the darkness of the night, it was impossible to tell either the depth or the extent of the angry flood that rolled before them. But Pryse said he knew the direction of the road, which was somewhat elevated above the corn-land on either side of it; and, trusting to that knowledge, he was determined to attempt the adventure. The hostler waited at the end of the bridge to watch how he might succeed. Pryse boldly entered the water, but the cart had not gone many yards when it, and mare, and man, disappeared at once from the terrified eyes of the hostler, who, without waiting for further information, ran back in horror to the inn, screaming for help.

When the landlord and others got down to the bridge, they were in some degree relieved by hearing the cries of Pryse, which at least assured them that he was still alive, and on some place of temporary safety. A hoarse and short conversation maintained with him among the roar of the elements, informed them that he was sitting in his cart, which had been providentially arrested at some distance below the bridge; that the water was up to his middle, and that he had extricated his mare from the shafts by cutting away the harness. He implored them for help, as he every moment dreaded that the force of the water would sweep away the cart into the main stream where his destruction must be certain and immediate. Unremitting were the exertions made by those on the bridge to save him by means of ropes, and by attempts to reach him by means of wading; but the darkness of the night, and the depth and fury of the torrent, rendered all their efforts unavailable, until three o'clock in the morning, when the river had so far subsided that he was rescued without much difficulty, after having been seven hours in the water. It was then discovered that the whole of the level half-moon *haugh* of Culbeg, of twenty-five acres in extent, had been flooded; and, when the water ebbed away, it appeared that the mare had been interrupted in her passage along the road by some great trees stranded there, and that, in trying to get round them, she had turned off into the corn field, and was carried down by the deep and strong current, till stopped by a flow-bank about four feet high. Had they gone a yard or two farther, they must have been inevitably swept through a breach in the bank, directly into the main current of the river. The mare, after being released, swam away, till she fortunately grounded on a hillock, where she had the wisdom and patience to remain stationary till her master was relieved.

The Haugh of Culbeg had the whole of its crop completely annihilated. An elevated bank bounds the half-moon on its straight side, and also marks the boundary between the estates of Kilravock and Cawdor at this point, having been probably declared so at the time the river ran along its base. Some generations ago, the proprietor of Kilravock besought him of Cawdor to permit his tenant's house of Culbeg to be built on the top of the bank. The boon was refused, and its refusal had nearly proved fatal to the present worthy farmer, James Mackintosh, and his family, who narrowly escaped destruction on the late occasion. I visited this poor man, now above seventy-three years of age, and who, to add to his other misfortunes, is deaf, a circumstance that rendered our conversation loud and long. He took me into his house, a few yards from the foot of the bank I have mentioned. It still exhibited wreck and desolation. The very smell of it was like that of a house newly disinterred after being buried for a century. The old man, drenched and woe-begone, looked down from the bank on the utter ruin of his farm, with the expectation of seeing his house and all that it contained borne away by the billows. For two days were he and his family kept out of their dwelling. At length, circumstances permitted them to return to it, and, thanking God for their personal safety, they set themselves to put matters about the premises in order.

They were beginning to recover a little from their panic, when the yet more terrible flood of the evening of the 27th visited their habitation, and filled the rooms to the height of five feet, as I ascertained from the stain it had left on the plaster. Being more quickly alarmed on this occasion, their flight was more precipitate. "But," said Mr. Mackintosh to me, as we stood on his damp and disconsolate floor, "I minded me o' something I wad ha'e done ill wanting; and so I wade back again, and crap in at that window there, and after grapin' aboot and gettin' a haud o' what I was seekin', I was gawin' to creep oot again, when I bethought me o' my specks." "Specks!" roared I into his ear, "how could you risk your life for a pair of spectacles?" "Trouth, Sir," replied he, seriously, "I couldna ha' read my Bible without them, and, mair nor that, they were silver specks, and they were specks sent me hame in a praisant fae my son, the Yepiscopal meenister in Canada." This was unanswerable, and I was glad to learn that the result of his boldness was the salvation of his "specks," as well as of the purse or pocket-book into which I presume to interpret what he called "the thing he wad ha'e done ill wantin'." Not a particle of corn was spared to him, and even the straw was so completely ruined that he was compelled to sell off his live stock and to give up the farm. As he told me himself, "he was three days on the hill looking over this disagreeable affair;" yet I heard no murmur of complaint escape him, and all his talk was of thanks to God for the preservation of himself and his family.

Immediately below Culbeg, the river made a breach through the farm of Little Budzeate, following the line of an ancient course, and entirely abandoning that where it recently ran. I learned from the farmer who witnessed this operation that, after the stream began to run in the new line, it commenced cutting at the point where it fell over the bank to rejoin the river, and so it continued to work backwards gradually, but expeditiously. This is invariably the process in all similar cases.

The farm of Rosefield, on the right bank, contains about fifty arable acres, of which above one-third have been carried away entirely, or destroyed beyond all hope of redemption, by deposits of gravel and stones. The crops and grass were utterly ruined; a number of expensive works annihilated; the lime heaps for manure swept away, together with the whole corn of last year; the lower storey of the house was flooded, and the whole farm, now in a state of chaos, lies at the mercy of every partial rise of the river. The farm of Milton of Kildrummie; on the left bank, also suffered severely; the mill was damaged, its run destroyed, and the dwelling-house and out-houses rendered uninhabitable. The crop ruined on the estate of Kilravock cannot be estimated at less than £500, and the actual damage done to the property has been calculated by the factor at £2400. Lord Cawdor's loss of soil, and other injury done to his estate along this part of the Nairn, may be set down at not less than £2000; and that of Mr. Mackintosh of Geddes is given in at £1200. The inundation here spread far over the rich plain on the right bank, flooding some of the farm houses that were 400 or 500 yards from the usual margin of the river, and ruining the crops to an extent that defies calculation.

CHAPTER 2

The River Nairn, from Broadley to the sea

AFTER quitting the extensive arable plain noticed at the conclusion of the last chapter, the Nairn runs for about three-quarters of a mile through a comparatively narrow pass, whence it expands into a second plain, a little below the farm of Broadley. At Firhall, on the left, the offices were most substantially built on the summit of a bank, about thirty feet high, and at the distance of about thirty horizontal yards from the edge of the river. The flood attacked the base of this bank, and cut it entirely back, until it undermined the buildings, and carried away the thrashing-mill, and the gable of a lofty barn (Plate 4). It also swept off great part of a very thriving plantation of well-grown timber trees from below the offices. Mr. Mackintosh of Firhall's damage is estimated at £400. That of Mr. Robertson of Househill, on the right bank, is very considerable, but it has not been ascertained. At Mr. Cant's, Mills of Millfield, on the left bank, the flood made a breach to the right, rushed down a new course at a lower level, and so left the mills entirely without water, to restore which cost above £50.

PLATE 4. OFFICES AT FIRHALL

A little way below the mills, the washing-green of the Burgh of Nairn presents a very mutilated and deplorable appearance, about two acres of it having been carried away, and a mere fragment left. The inundation between Househill and Nairn was not much less than a mile in length, by half a mile in breadth; but the force of the water was not great, and the damage done to the grain was chiefly in destroying its quality, by chilling its roots, and arresting the process of filling. At a point on the left bank of the river, above the bridge, called the Constabulary, a large tree, rooted in the crevices of the sandstone, was torn down by the flood of the 27th. Some fragments of the rock were dislodged by its fall; and so great was the violence of the stream, that one of them, 14 feet long by 3 feet wide, and 1 foot thick, was carried above 200 yards down the river, and some of the others to a still greater distance.

On the evening of Saturday the 1st of August, the Rev. James Grant, minister of Nairn, observed a dark cloud hovering over the sea in a straight line between Cromarty and Findhorn. It soon assumed the shape of a huge black column, with its base resting on the surface of the waters, and its top apparently reaching the clouds. It remained for a considerable time, during which he particularly remarked its circumgyrations to be very distinct. It then became lighter and bluer in colour, until it gradually disappeared. This ascending waterspout was also seen by Dr. Smith and others. The morning of the 3rd was ushered in by heavy rain at Nairn, and in the afternoon the gale from the north became tremendous, and the loitering fisher-men cast many an eye towards the Firth, where the lowering sky seemed as if stooping to mingle its waters with those of the sea, and where both were so lashed up together by the furious blast, that it became difficult to tell the precise boundary between them. About six o'clock in the evening, a sail was descried off the sand-hills to the north-east of Nairn. She seemed to struggle forth from the dark mantle of mist obscuring the horizon in that direction. It was a schooner-rigged vessel, and she came staggering along before the wind as if in sore distress, with her mainsail torn and flying before her. To the weather-beaten men of the sea, who anxiously watched her motions from the pier, she at first seemed as if endeavouring to make the harbour of Nairn, or run aground on the back shore, as the only remaining chance of safety; but as she neared, it became obvious to every experienced eye that, whatever were the wishes of those on board, they were utterly unable to carry them into effect, from her water-logged and unmanageable condition. Terrific as was the storm, yet there were hearts there tender as those of women for the miseries of others, and firm as the toughest oak when danger was to be grappled with, who would have sprung to brave the tempest in any cause of humanity. But to launch a boat in such a sea was impossible. Nor could their well-meant succour have availed, even if they could have passed beyond the overwhelming surf that broke upon the shore. Opposite to Nairn there is generally a strong current setting from the east towards Delnies, and Whitenesshead, to the westward. Already had the fated vessel been driven into this current, and notwithstanding the furious northern blast, she was hurried rapidly on, like the floating carcass of some drowned creature devoid of voluntary action; and after being carried for a time as if towards Cromarty, she was seen to sink almost instantaneously, leaving only a few feet of one of her masts above water, as a frail and transient monument to mark the spot where the last despairing shriek of the crew had been stifled by the waves. A subdued exclamation of horror burst from those who witnessed the spectacle. Each felt that such might one day be his own fate, and with compressed lips, contracted brows, and moistened eyes, they slowly separated to return to their homes.

Towards the afternoon of the 3rd, the Nairn was much swollen, and it continued to increase till the forenoon of next day, when its height surpassed anything ever witnessed before. The aggregate breadth of the three arches of the bridge of the Nairn is 120 feet, and, immediately below it, the rise was nine feet above the ordinary level. Numerous bulwark frames and many large trees were seen hurrying down to the sea, and the force and fury of the stream were alarming. The harbour, a work of recent construction, was formed by cutting a new course for the river straight from the bridge to the sea, in a line where it must have flowed at one period, until it was gradually forced eastward, into the diagonal direction it lately followed, by depositions of sand drifted by the winds from the country to the westward. The new embouchure was regularly shaped into a harbour, and faced with stone piers. These were much undermined by the flood of the 3rd and 4th, though not actually thrown down to any great extent, and the channel was found to be infinitely too narrow for the fearful column of water that strained through it. Immediately below the bridge, on the left bank, were two stone bulwarks, eleven feet high, and very strong, erected to defend the ground on which the lower part of the town stands. The flood made a breach through one of these, levelling and scattering its materials and, attacking the right bank at the same time, it cut away a considerable portion of the flat ground called The Maggot.

Such were the injuries done to the burgh of Nairn by the first flood; and whilst its good burghers were musing over them, they were astonished to behold the return of the Duke of Gordon coach, which had left them only two hours before on its way to Aberdeen; and learning that the cause was the fall of the bridge of Findhorn, they thanked their stars that they had so little to complain of.

But their turn was yet to come. The 27th was also a day of tempest and incessant rain, though by no means so stormy as the 3rd. But owing to the deluge that fell higher up the country, the river rose more rapidly, and six inches higher than it then did. About three o'clock in the afternoon, the brig '*Mariner*,' of Sunderland, of eighty-three tons, was broken from her moorings at the pier by the weight of the stream. She heeled round, and striking the stone-work, her sternpost and rudder were stove in, and she partially filled with water. In the evening the piers, especially those on the right bank, began to give way. Being founded in the sand, the lower courses of the stones were dislodged, and ledge after ledge dropped successively into the stream.

The dawn of day discovered a very ruinous state of matters at Nairn. The river, though still very high, had now begun to subside. Besides the ruin of one arch of thirty feet span, the whole fabric of the bridge was much shaken, and the repairs are calculated at £500. The wretched nature of its foundations had been exhibited for some time, by the stream deepening the channel in consequence of the new cut for the harbour below; and if great exertions had not been used to repair the damage it sustained by the first flood, it must have been entirely swept away on this second occasion. The stone embankments a little further down appear to have done it harm by impeding the escape of the water, and creating an accumulated pressure on the piers. These impediments are now, fortunately, pretty well demolished and removed by the action of the stream.

PLATE 5. MOUTH OF NAIRN HARBOUR

The harbour presented a truly lamentable sight. The whole of the piers of its eastern side were gone, as well as much of the artificial bank behind them: and, on the western side, a gap was opened in the solid masonry at the lower end of the wharf, and the whole pier beyond carried quite away seaward except a heap of fallen stones at the further extremity, and the exposed ground behind was cut abruptly out into a bay, practically illustrating the impropriety of attempting to impose too great confinement on any such stream as the Nairn, or to build along its banks without a proper foundation. I am informed that those employed to erect the piers, being strangers to the river they had to deal with, having only seen it when low, proposed to make the channel considerably narrower than the breadth at which they afterwards finished it, and laughed at the idea of its being necessary to face it up with masonry as far as the bridge. But an old blind fisherman of Nairn, on hearing of the proposed dimensions of the harbour, predicted the very result that has now taken place. The wharf, being founded on rock, stands as secure as if nothing had happened. Where such a foundation is not to be had, the best facing for the piers of the Nairn, or any similar harbour, would be huge posts and framing beams, covered in front with strong wood-work, substantially fitted and secured, and strengthened behind with triangular bearers or counterforts, backed by heavy stones or other weighty materials. I have great doubts of the wisdom of bringing the river through the harbour at all. The object, of course, was to clear it out; but might it not be likely to deposit more at one time than it carries away at others? Then the risk to which the craft are exposed by every small rise of the river is a serious objection. It appears to me that the scouring of the harbour might have been better provided for by a sluice, through which a regulated quantity of water might have been at any time allowed to pass from the river. The brig '*Mariner*' furnished a sad illustration of these remarks. Being filled with water, and partially sunk, she toppled over and, her mooring-posts giving way, she drifted down to the mouth of the harbour, where I saw her lying a total wreck. Nothing could be more cheerless and depressing than the view of the harbour (Plate 5) looking seaward, with its defences entirely gone, and every successive surge washing down fresh portions of the raw banks; the hull of the wrecked vessel lying in the throat of the channel; and at every stroke of the tide, spouting up the water into the air, through some hole in her timbers.

PLATE 6. SALMON FISHING PORT AT NAIRN

One very remarkable feature in the surrounding scene, was a fishing-hut, about twelve feet long, standing on a beach in the middle of the river, constructed of four posts, with bearers stretched between them at top and bottom, and covered, roof and all, with outside planks. While the bridge, the pier, the vessel, nay the very rocks, were yielding to the furious force of the deluge, this ark stood unmoved in the midst of the waters of both floods, uninjured (Plate 6) except that it was swayed a little from the perpendicular. No building of stone and lime could have stood in the same place. Its preservation, therefore, is worthy of record, as a valuable fact, to prove how much mere posts and planks will resist in such a situation. It stands as a useful instructor to the burghers of Nairn for the restoration of their harbour, the damage done to which is calculated at £2500.

CHAPTER 3

THE RIVER FINDHORN, FROM THE MOUNTAINS TO DULSIE BRIDGE

THE River Findhorn rises from a wide morass, covering the flat summit of a mountain in the midst of the Monadh-leadh group, and runs through a direct line of country of not less than sixty miles, its sinuosities being about thirty more. Perhaps no river of the same size in Great Britain possesses so exquisite, so continued, and yet so varied, a range of scenery as it does, from within a few miles of its source till it approaches the sea-port to which it gives its name. After leaving its bleak parent hill, it runs through a deep ravine in the primitive rocks, whence it enters a beautiful pastoral glen and valley, bounded by steep and high mountains with occasional rocky faces, but generally covered with a rich and valuable herbage. From all I could learn, the rain on the 2nd, 3rd, and 4th of August was without parallel in these regions. The damage done by the river and its tributaries was immense; but the manner in which the destruction was scattered renders it impossible to attempt any detail of it. I may mention, however, that the wool-house of Laggan, with the whole shearing of wool, was carried off.

Lower down, where the valley becomes generally cultivated, the estates of Dalmigavie, on the right bank, and Killochie, on the left, suffered severely. These are small Highland properties, and the farms poor; but the calamity is not lessened by such considerations; on the contrary, the catalogue of human misery is greatly swelled by these very circumstances, where, in many instances, nearly the whole crops of corn and potatoes were destroyed. The property of Mr. Mackintosh of Balnespick has been injured very extensively. At the farm of Clunes the burn burst through the garden; and the Findhorn, abandoning its course altogether, cut an entirely new channel for itself, for at least a quarter of a mile in length, and at the distance of not less than 200 yards from its former run, isolating a fine alluvial field, and utterly ruining its surface. To judge of the injury a Highland estate has received merely by counting the number of acres lost and estimating their value, would be very erroneous. Much depends on the shape and situation of the ground carried away. A few acres cut off a compact and extensive arable farm make but the loss of so many acres, at a certain given price per acre. But in these Highland districts, half of a small field being swept away may render the remainder of it altogether useless; and one or two instances of this kind occurring on the same farm may make it quite untenable. The number of acres carried off from the estates I have mentioned was very considerable. The river indeed filled the valley, though, in some places, not much less than half a mile wide; and the tributary burns destroyed all the small bridges and conduits on the district roads. The little burn of Aultaneachgra, coming in from the left, did a world of mischief in a small space, filling up and ruining the dams and water-courses of its carding and meal mills, injuring the houses and machinery, and leaving all in a state of silent, melancholy, and motionless ruin. Where the burn joins the river the valley was one sea, and at least twenty acres of crop and land were ruined or carried off. A little below this point the side of a wooded hill, 80 or 100 feet high, slid down at once, owing to the soaking rain loosening the soil behind; and the great public road was covered with the debris, and with large trees, many of them in the growing position. It is worth remarking that the materials of this hill were naturally quite dry.

We now come to the site of the old Bridge of Corrybrugh, or, as more commonly called, the Bridge of Freeburn. It consisted of three large arches, and nothing now remains but the ruins of the two land abutments. A horizontal crack in the masonry, running quite back into the north-east wing-wall (Plate 7), from the fractured arch, manifestly shows that the mass above was lifted up like the lid of a chest, and then dropped into its place again after the fall of the arch.

PLATE 7. BRIDGE OF CORRYBRUGH, OVER THE FINDHORN

The people told me that the arches were quite full, and the crack bears witness that at least the arch next to it was raised in the air by the upward force of the flood. Though the space the Findhorn filled here was not less than 200 yards, yet it was 17 feet above its usual level. But it is probable that the river was much higher in the middle; for, in violent floods, the fury of a stream is so great, that, in whatsoever direction it sets, the water is raised many feet above the other parts of the same cross section. The middle arch of the bridge fell early in the night between the 3rd and 4th, and the others towards morning. A poor woman, whose daughter had crossed the river on some errand, was driven almost distracted by the belief that she was lost, but was happily relieved when the subsidence of the stream admitted of the girl's return. It was gratifying to see the activity of the agents of the Parliamentary Commissioners for Highland Roads and Bridges, who had already nearly completed a substantial wooden bridge, a little below the ruins, to act as a temporary passage for the great Highland road over this rapid stream. Its structure seemed to be a good deal like that of Caesar's famous bridge over the Rhine. Though the scenery here is by no means ugly, yet, unfortunately for travellers, it is the only part of the whole river that is not highly romantic, till it reaches the cultivated plain of Forres.

The estate of Tomatin, on the left bank, was chiefly injured in crop and grass. The flood covered the greater part of the extended flat where the house stands; but though it threatened the mansion, it did little harm.

The landlord of the inn told me that there were showers on Sunday the 2nd, and during the night; but that "the serious rain," as he called it, did not come on until Monday morning, about eight o'clock, when "the water fell from the heavens more tremendously than he had ever seen it fall in his life before." Here, as elsewhere, it was accompanied by a violent north-east wind, and it continued till about four o'clock on Tuesday evening. The Findhorn and its tributaries were all up by twelve o'clock on Monday; but the flood did not reach its height till early on the morning of Tuesday, when it continued till twelve o'clock, without diminution. So tremendous was the rain that it penetrated by every door, window, and chimney in the house, and even through places where no crevice was suspected. The floors of the lower rooms were actually covered with three inches of water from the rain alone; and the servants were employed during the greater part of Monday and Tuesday in carrying it out in tubs and buckets. The cattle in their stalls were standing knee-deep in water, from the deluge that poured on them through the roofs; and the poor animals were nearly starved, for the people who were sent to cut a few bunches of green corn, that they might not be altogether without food, were actually unable to remain out under the fearful torrent that fell from the sky. The landlord told me that he lost many acres of land from his extensive grazing farm, by the operation of the burn of Freeburn; of these, however, not more than six or eight were arable. Two fine bridges, near the inn, were carried away by tributary streams.

Below Freeburn, the valley expands to so great a width that it may be called a plain, the dimensions of which may be 2½ miles long, by ⅔ of a mile broad. The lower end of it is blocked up by the hill of Pollochock, or the Barns. From the marks of terraces appearing along the bases of the hills on both sides (Plate 8), I am disposed to think this must have been an ancient lake; and if so, the late floods restored it to its pristine character whilst they endured. The river changed its course in several places here, ruined the crop on Mackintosh of Mackintosh's farms of Invering, carried about eight acres of land entirely away, and damaged and scarified about twenty acres more. I had William Clarke, the Tomatin gamekeeper, with me as a guide. He is a native of this valley, and his natural shrewdness has been sharpened up by his long service in the 42nd Regiment, in which, after seeing enough both of life and death, he lost an eye. From him I learned that the Loch of Moy, which discharges itself into the Findhorn from the left, by the burn of Fuantack, was much affected by the flood. The late Sir Æneas Mackintosh reduced the level of the lake by cutting a canal, at the expense of £1000. But the burn of Dalmigarry, rushing furiously from the hills, on the late occasion, filled up the canal with debris, stopped the vent of the lake, raised it about thirteen feet, and inundated the sunk storey of Moyhall. If the veteran gamekeeper is correct, the levels hereabouts are very remarkable. Were it possible to erect a bulwark eighteen feet high, so as to arrest the Findhorn where it now leaves the plain, its waters, it is said, would be forced up the Fuantack, through the Loch of Moy, and so down into the River Nairn; and it appears probable that such may have been the run of the water when the ancient lake existed.

PLATE 8. VALLEY OF THE FINDHORN BELOW FREEBURN, AND ABOVE THE STREENS, SUPPOSED AN OLD LAKE BED

The hill of the Barns forms the upper boundary of the highly interesting pastoral district called the Streens, the entrance to which, at Eanack, is one of the most romantic passes that can be imagined. We had now a range of eight miles of very uncommon scenery before us. The glen is everywhere extremely narrow, and it has the appearance of being still more so than it really is, from the height and steep acclivity of the mountain faces forming its boundary wall on either side. From these, picturesque rocks are frequently seen to jut out, and in many places they are seared with tributary ravines, tufted here and there with birches, which, except in such accidental spots, are kept under by the browsing of animals, "being," as Clarke told me, "very *wishful* to grow if the sheep and cattle wad but let them." The course of the glen, too, is winding, every turn opening on a new scene, where the simple buildings of a little farm appear perched on some knoll. A mere track runs, like those of Switzerland, winding along the mountain sides, and crossing the glen so often that we forded the Findhorn no less than five times during our passage through the district.

Immediately within the pass, and on the right bank, stand the bare ruins of the interesting little mansion-house of Pollochock. Macqueen, the laird of this little property, is said to have been nearer seven than six feet high, proportionably built, and active as a roe-buck. Though he was alive within half a century, it is said that in his youth he killed the last wolf that infested this district*. The prevailing story is this:-

A poor woman, crossing the mountains with two children, was assailed by the wolf, and her infants devoured, and she escaped with difficulty to Moyhall. The chief of Mackintosh no sooner heard of the tragical fate of the babes, than, moved by pity and rage, he dispatched orders to his clan and vassals to assemble the next day at twelve o'clock to proceed in a body to destroy the wolf. Pollochock was one of those vassals, and being then in the vigour of youth, and possessed of gigantic strength and determined courage, his appearance was eagerly looked for to take a lead in the enterprise. But the hour came, and all were assembled except him to whom they most trusted. Unwilling to go without him the impatient chief fretted and fumed through the hall; till at length, about an hour after the appointed time, in stalked Pollochock, dressed in his full Highland attire; "I am little used to wait thus for any man," exclaimed the chafed chieftain, "and still less for thee, Pollochock, especially when such game is a-foot as we are boune after!" "What sort o' game are ye after, Mackintosh?" said Pollochock simply, and not quite understanding his allusion. "The wolf, sir," replied Mackintosh; "did not my messenger instruct you?" "Ou aye, that's true," answered Pollochock, with a good humoured smile; "troth I had forgotten. But an that be a'," continued he, groping with his right hand among the ample folds of his plaid, "there's the wolf's head!" Exclamations of astonishment and admiration burst from

**Wolves are believed to have been extirpated in Scotland about the year 1680, but there is reason to suppose that they partially existed in remote districts considerably after that period.*

chief and clansmen as he held out the grim and bloody head of the monster at arm's length, for the gratification of those who crowded around him. "As I came through the slochk*, by east the hill there," said he, as if talking of some everyday occurrence, "I forgathered wi' the beast. My long dog there turned him. I buckled wi' him, and dirkit him, and syne whuttled his craig, and brought awa' his countenance, for fear he might come alive again; for they are very precarious creatures." "My noble Pollochock!" cried the chief in ecstasy; "the deed was worthy of thee! In memorial of thy hardihood, I here bestow upon thee Seannachan, to yield meal for thy good greyhound in all time coming."

Seannachan, or 'the old field,' is directly opposite to Pollochock. The ten acres of which it consisted were entirely destroyed by the flood. The tenant was a drover, who, having failed in business, retired to this small spot, which was barely enough to keep body and soul together. Despair came upon him with this fresh ruin; he took to his bed, and, at the time I was there, he was supposed to be dying.

The spouts of rain on the 3rd and 4th converted every dry scar on the mountain faces into a torrent, which soon cut it into a ravine, and covered an acre or two of the slope below with huge stones and heaps of gravel, to the depth of many feet. In two places, where the hill-side was formerly quite entire, it was torn open, and fragments of detached rocks, eight or ten tons in weight, were thus dislodged and thrown down. How sublime must the scenery of the glen have appeared, when the river was roaring furiously over the whole of the level bottom, the rocks and hills everywhere sheeted with cataracts, whilst these huge masses were tumbling headlong from their beds, with a thunder even louder than that of the river!

We now come to Lord Cawdor's property; and, a little further down, I stopped at the farm-house of Cuilliachan, situated on a rising ground. It is tenanted by Mr. Mackintosh, usually called Cuilliachan, who, though he lives very much in the aboriginal style, has yet met me more than once at his door with a hearty welcome. He is now a very old man; but a few years ago he could breast a hill without either stocking or shoe to his foot and without drawing his breath one degree beyond an ordinary inspiration. He has long been considered as a sort of viceroy in this romantic territory. He told me he well remembered the great flood of 1782. I insisted that it must have been the still greater flood of 1768 that he meant. But whether it was 1768, as I suspect, or 1782, as he asserted, he positively declared that any thing like the rain or the flood of the 3rd and 4th August last he had never seen. "No! nor any one," as he added, "of the oldest people in the glen!" an addition, by the way, that was quite unnecessary, as there could scarcely be any older than himself.

* *Hollow or ravine.*

He assured me that the flood of the 3rd and 4th was at least five or six feet higher than any flood he had ever seen in his native Findhorn; which, considering that the river filled the whole width of the glen, there 200 or 300 yards wide, was an amazing difference. Yet old people are not wont to exaggerate modern events at the expense of those of the olden time. From his own observations, he was inclined to think that on the recent occasion the flood in the Streens was from 15 to 25 feet above ordinary level, according to the width of the different places measured.

Cuilliachan's own farm suffered very much. His crop of twenty acres was annihilated, his garden nearly carried away, and the whole surface of his land more or less injured.

It was melancholy to behold the devastation committed by the flood on every little farm we passed, some of which were really altogether ruined by the annihilation of half their arable land. That of Dalless, for instance, lost no less than seventeen acres. The river having filled the glen from side to side, the whole crop in the bottom was necessarily destroyed, and misery and wretchedness everywhere appeared. The farm of Easter Tchirfogrein, or, 'The place hid from the sun' on the right bank, was so called, with the usual accuracy of Gaelic definition, because the height and acclivity of the mountains hardly ever permitted the orb of day to look upon the house, which, with its offices, stood on a level haugh 12 feet above the usual surface of the river, and 80 or 100 horizontal yards from the edge of it. From the northern mountain side where we rode, Cuilliachan descried William Fraser, son of the widow who held this farm, and raising a shout that did ample credit to the soundness of his veteran lungs by making the whole glen ring again, he called him to come across the river, which the poor fellow instantly waded, and gave me his whole melancholy story.

PLATE 9. EASTER TCHIRFOGREIN

On the evening of Monday the 3rd, the river rose and came down roaring tremendously. It soon overtopped the bank and, speedily covering the level ground above, surrounded the houses with three feet deep of water by the time it became dark. Meanwhile, the stream was rapidly, though invisibly, sweeping away the alluvial plain they stood on. Becoming alarmed at length, he and his brother quickly got out their sister and their poor old mother, who, to use his own expression, "could do naething for hersel'" and carried them through the water to the hill-side. They had no sooner reached it, than, "amidst the gloom of the night and the glare of the water", they saw their dwelling-house and other buildings, one by one, disappear. Luckily they had got out their cattle but, excepting their lives, and the clothes on their backs, everything else was lost. Next morning, the only vestige remaining of their residence was the one end of a cow-house (Plate 9). Their whole crop was gone; five or six acres of their arable land had disappeared, and the rest was ruined by deep deposits of sand and gravel. Cuilliachan told me that this was one of the best plenished houses in the whole Streens. The great store-chest, full of meal, by some accident floated across the river, and having settled on an opposite bank, it was descried by Fraser in the morning. For some time he looked at it with longing eyes; but a remorseless eddy at length displacing it, he had the mortification to see it sweep away. It was seen at the mouth of the Findhorn, about twenty-seven miles below, after having run through the perilous gauntlet of rocks that lined its way thither, with only an inch in thickness of the outer part of the meal moistened. I am sorry to say, however, that the chest and its contents never reached the owner; yet whilst I state this, it is gratifying to assert that this is the only instance of dishonesty I have to record.

But I have not yet done with these poor Frasers, who took refuge where they had lived a short time before at the farm of Knockandhu, to the eastward. The house here stood about 21 yards from the edge of a bank 80 or 100 feet high above the Findhorn. Here, at least, they deemed themselves secure. But down came the river in the flood of the 27th, and finding the base of this lofty bank already scarified, it attacked, undermined, and tumbled it down in enormous masses, with a noise like volleys of artillery, and the level at top disappeared so rapidly that the poor people were again compelled to flee in the greatest alarm. As it happened, the flood subsided, and the houses were not hurled over; but they were left near the brink of a raw, red, perpendicular precipice, presenting a most alarming appearance when viewed, as I saw it, from the opposite side (Plate 10).

The farms of Dalbuie and Banchar had about 10 acres of valuable land carried off. The river completely sanded up its channel there, and dug out an entirely new course for a great distance, removing the whole surface of the intervening haugh, one of the most beautiful

PLATE 10. KNOCKANDHU

in the Streens. These may serve as samples of the ruin created in this once beautiful and happy district. The rent of Lord Cawdor's part of it was about £278. But at least 40 arable acres have been snatched from it by the river, and much of the rest of it destroyed. The factor considers that twenty times the sum would do little towards producing anything like security to the property that remains, along an extent of more than five miles, where the narrow grounds are more or less damaged all the way. But, indeed, the difficulty of access, and want of materials, must forbid any attempt at general protection. From the complete loss of their winter provender, the poor tenants were compelled to sell off their cattle. Though the sum-total of their damage would not appear great, yet it has been ruinous to them; and the loss sustained by the landlord has been estimated at about £6000.

The farms on the Lethen estate, between the Streens and Dulsie Bridge, were cut up in a similar way. About 17 acres were ruined or carried off from three of them, of no great size.

CHAPTER 4

THE FINDHORN, FROM DULSIE BRIDGE TO RANDOLPH'S BRIDGE

THE old military Bridge of Dulsie, consisting of one bold and lofty arch of forty-six feet spanning the yawning chasm, and a smaller subsidiary that carries the roadway from a high rock onwards to the north bank, is highly picturesque and surrounded by scenery of the wildest character. The rock here, and for eight or ten miles downwards, is a beautiful red porphyritic granite; and the whole river's course is of the most romantic character. The flood was very grand at Dulsie Bridge, where the column of water was so confined that it filled the smaller arch altogether, and rose, in the great arch, to within three feet of the key-stone. It was thus no less than *forty feet perpendicular above the usual level* (Plate 11). The foundations of the piers have suffered considerably, but a smaller sum than £10 would make this venerable bridge quite secure; and it is to be hoped that the Parliamentary Commissioners, under whose charge it is, will not, for so trifling a consideration, allow the country to be robbed of so useful a passage across a dangerous stream.

PLATE 11. DULSIE BRIDGE - A LINE SHOWS THE FLOOD LEVEL 40 FEET PERPENDICULAR ABOVE THE USUAL LEVEL

The Drumlochan Burn comes in from the right, and its branches carried away two bridges of twenty feet span. In its ordinary state this burn is hardly sufficient to keep the saw-mill going; but, during the flood, the column of water was 10 feet deep by 40 feet broad. At one place it carried away nearly an acre of land.

At Ferness, about two miles below Dulsie Bridge, the river sweeps for three miles round a high peninsula, through some of the wildest scenery imaginable, between lofty and precipitous rocks, towering, in some places, into castellated shapes, where the natural pine shoots out its tortuous and scaly form, mingled with the birch and other trees. In the midst of a beautiful holm, which the river embraces before it enters this romantic part of its course, stands a lonely cairn with a rudely-sculptured obelisk rising from it. Tradition tells us that this is the grave of two lovers; the hero a Dane, and the lady the daughter of the prince of the country. The father refused his daughter's hand to one who was his natural enemy. They fled together on the same horse, were pursued to the wooded hill of Dulsie where they had taken refuge and, being driven from thence, they were drowned in a desperate attempt to ford the river. Their bodies were found on this haugh, locked in each other's arms, and they were buried under this cairn. The tomb of these unfortunate lovers was respected by the flood, though the haugh itself suffered very considerable loss. This solitary spot is perfectly beautiful.

Immediately below Ferness, but on the left bank, there was a low flat peninsula, the neck of which was formerly cut through for the run of a sawmill, removed a good many years ago. The flood found its way into this old cut, and completely annihilated the whole peninsula. The tenant of Daltraw had his cattle pasturing in it. They were soon surrounded by streams so powerful as to render all hope of saving them perfectly vain. But, to the surprise of every one, they were all found safe on the bank in the morning, though nobody could tell how they got out. Some time after the flood, a blanket, and a piece of home-made cloth, thirty yards in length, part of the plenishing of poor Widow Fraser's house at Tchirfogrein, were found embedded in the sand near Ferness.

The glebe of Ardclach lost one acre of land. The church and churchyard lie hid in a low dell, embraced by the river, surrounded by lofty and richly wooded banks, and closed in below by a bold, bare, projecting rock. The regurgitation of the water floated gently over the lower part of the churchyard, but gave no disturbance to the dust that moulders there. All Sir James Montgomery Cunninghame's farms, along the right bank, suffered in loss of soil as well as in destruction of crop.

The bridge of Ferness, built of solid granite by the Parliamentary Commissioners, and consisting of three arches of 36, 55, and 30 feet span, is founded on the solid rock, and rises from a low haugh on the right to a high bank on the left. Sir James's gardener tells me that he went down to look at the river there about four o'clock in the morning of the 4th; and, although he found it much larger than when he left it the previous evening, he saw enough to convince him that it had been still higher during the night. It is a fact worth remarking that this partial subsidence was observed in all the flooded rivers. But, about five o'clock, it increased, and so rapidly that every five minutes made a visible change. It went on to rise in this way till about seven o'clock, when the haugh on the right bank was covered, and the arches were not only completely filled, but the water was level with the top of the parapet, 27 feet above the ordinary level; and, indeed, if a few yards of the parapets towards the left and highest bank had not appeared, no one could have suspected that there was a bridge there at all. Grouped with some cottages and some other trees at a point about 150 yards above the bridge, grew one of the most beautiful ashes I ever beheld. It had a tall triple stem, supporting a perfect grove of foliage. The largest of its three divisions was 12½ feet in circumference, the next 7½ feet, and the smallest about 7 feet. This noble tree was covered to a considerable height by the water; but the gardener had no apprehension for its safety, when all at once it fell with a fearful crash, breaking a number of its branches by the very force and weight with which they struck the surface of the water, and throwing up the agitated element to a great height. Down it went out of sight, with an enormous bank of gravel, torn away and retained by the long and multiplied reticulations of its roots. As it got rid of a part of this dead weight, and rapidly approached the bridge, its branches rose for a moment, with great majesty, some 40 or 50 feet above the water, and fell backwards in such a manner as to bring the root forward. In an instant it was sucked into the vortex of the centre arch. The branches and smaller limbs were ground to pieces with a noise like thunder, mingled with that of the explosions of gunpowder. For three or four minutes it stuck, "groaning and bellowing," as if from torture, and then appeared darting below the lower side of the bridge, shorn of its mighty honours. When the river subsided, the bridge of Ferness, to the astonishment of every one, emerged from the flood with no other damage than the loss of a part of its southern wing-walls and roadway, estimated at about £100. But the preservation of the arches and the body of the bridge must ever occasion it to be regarded as a miracle of masonry.

The bridge over the eastern branch of the burn of Easter Logie, on the Parliamentary road from Forres to Grantown, was so destroyed as to require rebuilding.

Coming to the Relugas property, on the right bank, we have a striking example of the power of water. The march-ditch was cut in a direct line from the hill towards the river, passing in its way thither alternately along broad plains and down steep banks. At one place, immediately above where the public road now runs, it was carried past *Cumin's Cairn*, rising on the verge of a steeply inclined bank of 70 or 80 feet high. This heap of stones was raised over the body of a man of the name of Cumin, who, having hanged himself in his barn in the beginning of the eighteenth century, that is to say, about one hundred years before the time I now speak of, was buried on the march, according to the custom observed with suicides. The moment the ditch was opened down the face of the bank, it collected the water of every shower of rain; and, being thereby converted into a temporary cataract, a gully of immense magnitude was cut in the alluvial matter in the course of a year or two. The bottom of this soon formed itself into an inclined plane, of above 100 yards in length, after which the water ceased to have any effect on it. This sufficiently illustrates the law governing all streams in their operations on the face of the earth, which have all a tendency, by deepening one place and filling up another, to reduce their channels to inclined planes. After a flood, which brought down a good deal of the loose material on the sides of the gully, a boy, tending cattle, observed something like long red hair streaming in the breeze near the top of the broken bank. On climbing up to investigate the matter, what was his horror and dread when he discovered that the hair was attached to a ghastly human head! He fled home in terror, and the people crowded out to see the wonder. There they found the corpse of Cumin, so entire that, if any one could have known him alive, he must have perfectly recognised his features. The head protruded horizontally from the bank, and the exudation from the body had tinged the sand beneath it of a black colour to a considerable depth. The cause of the preservation of the body was manifestly the dry ferruginous sand it was buried in. The rope was found about his neck, and attached to the fatal beam. During the night following the discovery of the body, the man's descendants carried all off, and buried them in the churchyard of Edinkillie.

The bridge of Daltlich is a fine bold arch, of 82 feet span, springing from a rock on the right bank on the Estate of Relugas, and landing on another on the farm from which it takes its name. From the ordinary level of the water, to the top of the parapet, the height is 44 feet, of which the flood rose 31 feet. The river's banks are so well defended by rocks, as they are traced downwards, that little damage was done either on Lord Moray's property of Downduff, on the left bank, or on that of Relugas on the right, except by the tearing away of beautiful trees, till we reach the Haugh of Randolph, or Rannoch, as it is vulgarly called, one end of which lost a portion of the soil. But this is a part of the river that demands particular notice.

The field is named from a narrow passage between the rocks, not more than eight feet wide, but of immense depth (Plate 12), through which the whole river runs in the ordinary state of its waters. This is called Randolph's Bridge, from Earl Randolph, the Regent, having had a bridge here for crossing from his castle of Tarnawa. The bridge was of wood, and consequently it was swept away twenty times in a year; but, from long custom, or some other cause, the Earl of Moray conceived himself bound to restore it after every demolition, till after the building of the bridge of Daltlich, when it was finally condemned as productive of numerous accidents. It was here that the desperate skirmish of *'The lost Standard'* was fought between Randolph and the Cumins.

PLATE 12. BRIG OF RANNOCH - A LINE SHOWS THE FLOOD LEVEL 50 FEET PERPENDICULAR ABOVE THE USUAL LEVEL

Cumin of Raites,* the ruins of whose castle still stand on the north side of the hill of Urquenay, had gone with numerous followers to assist his kinsman Cumin of Inverlochy, in a feud which then occupied him. They were on the eve of a great battle, when a hot-footed messenger arrived to tell Raites that Randolph was preparing for hostilities against him, and earnestly urging his immediate return. "With the help of God", said Raites, "I will fight *this* battle and *that*

* *By a charter, dated Elgin, 2nd November, 1494, to John Calder, son to William, Thane of Calder, we find "the half of the towne of Rate, in Nairne," among a great many other lands.*

too". Fortune was unpropitious; they were defeated, and the chief of Inverlochy was slain. Raites snatched up a spear ere he quitted the field, broke it, and besmeared that and his battle-axe with the blood of his dying relation; and, on his return, he sent this ensanguined, fiery cross, surmounting his battle-axe, through the clan as an imperative summons to war. The place of meeting was that immense Druidical cairn called *Cairnbar,* on the western summit of the high hill separating Daltlich from Lethen. The private password was, *"Live or die like a Cumin".*

Raites, Gorm, Dunearn, and Dunlugas (or the Doune of Relugas), blazed forth their beacon-fires. Every clansman hurried to Cairnbar, and their ranks being quickly formed, their dauntless chief led them down the gentle slope towards Tarnawa, in full hope of surprising his enemy. All was still, not a movement indicated opposition till they reached Bogenkatt (now Whitemire), when Randolph, who had kept himself informed of all their motions, suddenly issued upon them from the ravine, with his men arranged in perfect order. Raites, seeing the ambush he had hurried into, endeavoured to fall back; but his error was irreparable. Randolph attacked his little army whilst in confusion, routed them, and Raites fell bravely fighting. He was buried on the field of battle by Randolph, who, as his followers were heaping the cairn over the remains of his enemy, exclaimed, "There have I buried the *plague* of Moray!" - a speech which has given rise to a very extraordinary superstitious belief among the vulgar, that the *disease* has been actually buried there, and that, if the secret recesses of that grey cairn were laid open, it would burst forth, and spread death throughout the country.

The defeat of the Cumins would have become a complete rout, but for the gallant conduct of Allister Bane, son of old Cumin of Dunphail, who collected and re-animated the fugitives, checked the enemy's pursuit, retreated in tolerable order towards Clune, and drew up his men on a rising ground where the farm house now stands, inaccessible to cavalry and, on three sides, difficult of assault for foot soldiers. Here, for a short time, he put a stop to the slaughter; but, seeing himself likely to be surrounded in his position, he called out, "Let those who fear not to die follow Allister Bane!" and, waving his sword over his head, and rushing furiously upon his enemy, his clansmen poured after him with enthusiastic cries, and in a moment they hewed for themselves an opening through their foes, and continued their retreat, with little loss, in the direction of Dunphail, till they reached the *Rait Cuack* of Ern (the narrow pass on the Findhorn), which they found pre-occupied by a strong detachment of Randolph's troops, who were posted on the opposite bank.

As the enemy were fast advancing on them behind, Allister Bane himself kept command of the rear that he might hold them in check, whilst he ordered Cumin of Drummine to take the ford a little way above with his men, and to endeavour to dispossess the enemy of the pass. The river was instantly forded by Drummine's small body, and a desperate struggle ensued upon the rocks, and on the banks, between them and Randolph's detachment; whilst those of the enemy who had hotly followed the pursuit were pressing in numbers on the harassed Cumins from behind. They fell in numbers, covered with glorious wounds. The gallant Allister Bane fought manfully, and humanely aided the wounded in escaping through the shallow; whilst the ferocious followers of Randolph pushed them back with their long spears, and thrust down into the water the heads of those who were already gasping in death. At length, driven to desperation, he flung his standard across the narrow chasm among the combatants and, calling out "Let the bravest keep it", he leaped the yawning gulph, cut his way desperately through the thickest of his enemies, with a few followers, and escaped towards the fastnesses of his father's domains.

It was by crossing this narrow and secret pass that Sir Andrew Murray retreated, undiscovered, from King Edward the Third's army, when that monarch came to relieve Lochindorbe Castle. Wyntoun describes the *carte de pays* with his usual accuracy, and then goes on to say:-

"Thai had wyth thaim ane
That kennyd hame a by way,
That swyn down betwixt Craggys lay
Throw that strayte rode; that I de wys*
Thai gat welle fra thare Innymys,
And left nothir man na lad."

WYNTOUN, Book 8.

Although the opening at Randolph's Bridge expands as the rocks rise upwards, till the width is perhaps not less than 70 or 80 feet above, yet, from the sudden turn the river takes as it enters this passage, the stream was so checked in its progress, that the flood actually rose over the very top of the rocks, 46 feet above the usual height, and inundated the level part of Rannoch Haugh that lies over them, to the depth of 4 feet, *making a total perpendicular rise, at this point, of no less than 50 feet*. I shall afterwards have occasion to describe the appearance of the flood itself at this place, from my own observation.

* *It is remarkable that the Gaelic words Rait Cuack are here literally translated by the historic poet.*

CHAPTER 5

THE RIVER DIVIE, WITH ITS TRIBUTARY THE DORBACK, TO DUNPHAIL

ACCORDING to the arrangement proposed in the Preliminary Chapter, I now proceed to describe the ravages of the River Divie, which falls into the Findhorn immediately below the house of Relugas. It has its origin in the hills, dividing the district of Braemoray from that of Strathspey, and is formed from the combination of a number of small streams. Its scenery, for a stretch of 6 or 7 miles from the spot where it leaps into its glen in a wild waterfall, to its junction with the Findhorn, is exquisitely beautiful. The estate of Dunphail, belonging to Mr. Cumming Bruce, stretches nearly to its upper extremity 5 or 6 miles above the fall; and he has, or, I should rather say, he had, a range of small farms all along its course, the haugh lands of which were entirely swept away by the flood. Immediately above the point where the Dorback falls in, the Divie carried away a beautiful bridge of one arch, which had been there for the better part of a century. The flood broke quite over the parapets, yet still the arch stood, till about a quarter of an hour afterwards, when some very large trees came down with the stream, stuck within it for a time, and, the pressure accumulating above, it was carried off en masse, and actually hurried for some distance down the river, before it went to pieces and sank* (Plate 13).

PLATE 13. RUINS OF BRIDGE ON THE DIVIE

* *This extraordinary fact was established by the evidence of an eye-witness, whose testimony is unquestionable; nor was this a solitary instance of so wonderful a proof of the power of the flood.*

The Dorback runs from the wild lake of Lochindorbe, remarkable for the extensive ruins of its insulated castle which was of sufficient importance in the fourteenth century to draw Edward III out of his way in order to raise the siege of it, as already noticed. The Dorback has a number of tributary burns. One of these comes out of a small lake in which there is a floating island of some 10 or 15 yards square, that shifts its position from one side to the other, according as the winds may blow, and yet is sufficiently tenacious to support the weight of one or two people. This branch destroyed a bridge on the Grantown road, and another burn tore down the smaller bridge of Dava, swept away the garden of the inn, and the whole crop and soil of the farm attached to it.

Lord Moray's estate of Braemoray has had the whole of its low land utterly annihilated by the Dorback, and the green slopes of the hills have been converted into naked precipices. The farm of Kerrow alone lost about 30 acres, together with a recently erected meal-mill, not a vestige of which was left. The adjacent farm, occupied by Francis Gibb, lost 15 acres. Gibb, observing that the flood was making rapid encroachments on a hill, on the brow of which he had some bee-hives, determined to attempt removing them. He had succeeded in taking them all away but one, the removal of which was rendered extremely hazardous from its proximity to the brink of the falling precipice. He approached it with much caution, and with a light step. His weight was too much for the crumbling ground. It cracked for several yards behind him. But he had already seized on the bee-hive, and with one vigorous spring he cleared the opening chasm with it; and, ere he turned to look, the whole mass was quenching its smoking fragments in the flood far below. An old woman's house, standing on the side of this hill at a considerable distance from the river, was left by its operations on the verge of a frightful precipice. The farm of Tomdow lost 10 acres. The tenants on this upland property had lately begun to exhibit great industry and enterprise in cleaning and liming their land. Their crops promised amply to reward their labour when, in this one night, all their golden hopes perished. I cannot estimate their damage, but that of their landlord amounts to £1800.

The damage done on Mr. Cumming Bruce's part of the Dorback is of the same character and comparative extent. At the Ess, or Waterfall of the Dorback, where the river runs through a ravine of 30 feet wide, the flood was 30 feet high. The inundation above this point was great in consequence of the stoppage, and dreadful ruin was produced when it came to run off. But the operations of the river lower down demand longer detail.

Immediately opposite to a place which has the whimsical appellation of The Stinking Stripes, probably from some chalybeate spring in the vicinity, and in front of a handsome newly erected cottage, there is an isthmus composed of a clayey gravel, against the neck of which the river ran headlong for time immemorial, until it reduced it to about a dozen yards in thickness. Coming from the south, the stream, after impinging on this neck, started eastwards at a right angle, swept round a conical shaped hill (Plates 14 and 15), of about 70 feet high, and returned to the north side after a circuitous course of 730 yards. The level of the stream, on the south side of the neck of the peninsula, was about 22 feet above that of the stream on the north side; and the bank between rose only about 6 feet higher than the upper stream. I have, therefore, watched this part of the Dorback with much interest for some years, in the hope of seeing it burst directly through the neck, leave its circuitous channel high and dry, and so illustrate many geological facts existing in this and other districts. The floods of August did much towards effecting this. That of the 3rd, having breached completely over the narrow neck, notwithstanding its great expansion over the haugh above, and having established a fall into the stream below, it began so to cut backwards, that, if the flood had continued many hours longer, the change would have been certainly wrought on that occasion. But, what was much to be regretted, it cut away above a third of the conical hill, the interesting memorial of one of our traditional stories. I shall give this tale as I had it from Mr. Cumming Bruce.

PLATE 14. THOMAS-A-RHYMER'S HILL, FROM THE WEST

The last wolves existing in this district had their den in a deep sandy ravine under the Knock of Braemoray, near the source of the Burn of Newton. Two brothers, residing at the little place of Falkirk, boldly undertook to watch the old ones out, and to kill their young; and, as every one had suffered more or less from their depredations, the excitement to learn the result of so perilous an enterprise was universal. Having seen the parent animals quit their den in search of prey, the one brother stationed himself as a sentinel to give the alarm in case the wolves should return, whilst the other threw off his plaid and, armed with his dirk alone, crawled in to dispatch the cubs. He had not been long in the den, when the wolves were seen by the watchman hastening back to the ravine. A sudden panic seized the wretched man, and he fled, without giving the promised warning, and never stopped till he had crossed the Divie two miles off. There, conscience stricken for his cowardice, he wounded himself in various places with his dirk, and, on reaching Falkirk, he told the people, who eagerly collected to hear the result of the adventure, that the wolves had surprised them in the den, that his brother was killed, and that he had miraculously escaped, wounded as he was. A shout of vengeance rent the air, and each man, catching up whatever weapon he could lay hands on, the whole gathering set out, determined at all hazards to recover the mutilated remains of their lost friend.

PLATE 15. THOMAS-A-RHYMER'S HILL, FROM THE EAST

But what was their astonishment, when, on reaching the Hill of Bogney, they beheld the mangled and bloody form of him they supposed dead, dragging itself towards them. For a moment they were awed by a superstitious fear, but they soon learned the history of his escape. He had found little difficulty in killing the cubs, and he was in the act of making his way out when the mouth of the hole was darkened, and the she-wolf was upon him. With one lucky thrust of his dirk he dispatched her at once, but his contest with her grim companion was long and severe, and although he fought in that narrow place, and from behind the body of the brute he had killed, he was nearly torn to pieces before he succeeded in depriving his ferocious enemy of life. The indignation of the people against the dastard brother on thus beholding his falsehood and cowardice made manifest, knew no bounds. They dragged him before the laird, who, on hearing the case, adjudged him to be forthwith hanged on the summit of the conical hill; a sentence that was immediately put in execution. The hill is called Thomas Rhymer's Hill, but for what reason I could never make out.

Anxious to save this interesting memorial, and also to divert the stream from cutting the banks where the new cottage stands, Mr. Cumming Bruce came to the resolution of assisting the operations of nature by opening a passage for the river through the neck of the peninsula. Accordingly, on the 2nd November, six men went to work at eight o'clock in the morning, and by two o'clock in the afternoon they had effected a cut 10 yards long, 3½ feet wide, from 6 to 8 feet deep, and with a fall of about 4 feet from one end to the other. The river was of its average size at the time, and a dam of a foot thick, and just of sufficient height to retain the water, was left, like the last pin that supports a vessel about to be launched. A little after four o'clock, our party reached the spot. The order was given. A man sprang into the trench and, with one blow of a pick-axe, the frail barrier yielded to the pressure above, burst at once, and the exulting river would have swept the man before it, had he not escaped with wonderful agility down the trench with the water at his heels.

PLATE 16. NEW CUT OF THE DORBACK, IMMEDIATELY AFTER THE RIVER WAS LET THROUGH

Nothing could be more interesting or striking than this event, where the effect of a single blow was, in one moment, to produce so great a change in nature's works - a change which, though wrought by a single hand, was in itself, and in its consequences, so vast and so uncontrollable that, if thousands of men had been on the spot, they could not have turned that river back again. On swept its devouring column, with the low hissing sound of a serpent, but with the force and swiftness of the eagle sweeping to its prey. To resist shouting was impossible. We joined in one hearty hurrah! (Plate 16). And, when our voices sank, we heard the deadened roar of the river as it poured over the clayey bank in a fall of fifteen feet, carrying everything before it, and damming back its own astonished waters, which it met and caught, after the long circuit round the Rhymer's Hill, filling them with the liquid yellow mud into which it was almost entirely converted by the havoc it was committing in its descent. Huge stones were continually rolling down, and some that we pushed in from the side disappeared along the cut with a rapidity which no eye could follow. It was really strange to see the water that came round the Rhymer's Hill gradually ebbing away as the new cut enlarged until, in half an hour, it was nowhere ankle deep, except in a few pools whither the startled trouts were struggling to save themselves. The banks of the cut, being undermined, rapidly gave way, falling in large masses at a time; so that, when we left the spot, as it grew dark, not quite an hour from the time it was opened, it had already produced an amazing change in its appearance. By eleven o'clock, the bottom of the cut was reduced to an inclined plane and, next

PLATE 17. NEW CUT OF THE DORBACK, TWENTY-FOUR HOURS AFTER THE RIVER WAS LET THROUGH

morning, about fifteen or sixteen hours after the opening was made, it was converted into a wide and complete river course; and, when I saw it at four o'clock in the afternoon, exactly twenty-four hours after the water was let through, it had worked its way back (Plate 17), quite up and across the old course, to the depth of eight feet below the level of its old, and now dry channel. Early on the morning of the 3rd of November, the Findhorn, below Forres, was polluted by the quantity of puddle brought down by the Dorback, and it continued in that state for many days. For some time after the evacuation of the old bed, a powerful and very disagreeable odour, like that of an animal oil, was sensibly experienced by every one. There was no mud, the bottom being pure gravel and sand. Could this odour have proceeded from the spawn of fish?

The facts attendant on this very interesting operation are very valuable, as illustrative of the force and action of water when confined to a channel too narrow for its quantity, and thrown over an unnatural height, as explanatory of many appearances of old river courses, which those unaccustomed to the attentive consideration of such things hesitate to believe ever were so; and they are highly useful, as affording practical information how to deal artificially with a river.*

In tracing the Dorback downwards, we are immediately arrested by a powerful proof of the effects of the deluge of the 3rd and 4th of August. This appears in a bank, about 100 feet high, immediately to the west of the new cut, which rose with slopes and terraces covered with a birch and alder wood. The soil, being naturally spongy, imbibed so much rain that it became overloaded, and a mass of about an acre in extent, with all its trees on it, gave way at once, threw itself headlong down, and bounded across the bed of the Dorback, blocking up the waters, flooded and wide as they were at the time. William Macdonald, the farmer of Easter Tillyglens, witnessed this phenomenon. He told me that it fell "wi' a sort o' a dumb sound" which, though somewhat of a contradiction in terms, will yet convey the true meaning better than any more correct expression. Astonished and confounded, Macdonald remained gazing. The bottom of the valley is here some 200 yards or more wide, and the flood nearly filled it. The stoppage was not so great, therefore, as altogether to arrest the progress of the stream. But this sudden obstacle created an accumulation of water behind it which went on increasing for nearly an hour till, becoming too powerful to be longer resisted, the enormous dam began to yield and was swept off at once, and hurled onwards like a floating island. But this was not

* *The Dorback has now (30th February, 1830) worked its new channel to the depth of 20 feet below the level of the old bed. It has also excavated it backwards, above 200 yards, and 50 yards forwards, in all 250 yards; and is still producing changes by every rise of the river.*

all; for while Macdonald was standing, lost in wonderment, to behold his farm thus sailing off to the ocean by acres at a time, better than half an acre more of it rent itself away from its native hill, and descended at once, with a whole grove of trees on it, to the river, where it rested most accurately on its natural base The flood immediately assailed this, and carried off the greater part of it piecemeal. Part of it yet remains, however, with the trees growing on it, in the upright position, after having travelled through a horizontal distance of 60 or 70 yards, with a perpendicular descent of not less than 60 feet (Plate 18).

PLATE 18. LANDSLIP AT TILLYGLENS

The meal-mill and carding-mill of Dunphail were recently erected on the right bank of the Dorback, immediately above a point where the glen narrows before joining the wider valley of the Divie, and within a few yards of the sloping, green, and birch-tufted bank on the eastern side; while the river, bending over quite to the western side of the glen, from a point some hundred yards above, seemed to leave them altogether beyond its reach. It is now about a year and a half since I visited these premises to inspect the machinery of the carding-mill, constructed by the ingenuity and enterprise of a most unexceptionable and meritorious young man, William Sutherland, the miller; and, on my report, a handsome premium was awarded him from the Board of Trustees for the encouragement of Scottish manufactures. I have seldom spent an hour with greater pleasure than I did that day in the contemplation of the ingenious, clean, and thriving establishment of this industrious lad. My next visit was to find it utterly ruined by the flood, and to learn the sad circumstances of its demolition.

It was in the afternoon of Monday the 3rd that the Dorback began to send so much flood-water down the mill-run as to occasion a stream to flow between the dwelling-house and the partially wooded bank in front of it. This soon became so deep and strong that, before the miller could get out his pony and his five cows, it was impossible to ford it; and the whole family, consisting of the miller, his brother the assistant-miller, a lad, and a servant girl, were thus surrounded by the flood. The partial subsidence noticed everywhere else took place here in the middle of the night, and the flood fell so considerably that the prisoners might have got out, but conceiving that all danger was over, they neglected to avail themselves of this opportunity. But, as they were engaged in religious worship, down came the river suddenly again upon them, and re-established with greater strength and depth than ever the stream in front that cut off their communication with the bank, and very soon afterwards it rose on the house, and poured into it both by the door and windows. "I ran", said the miller, "to the bed where my little brother lay, and snatching him up, I carried him out to the meal-mill, the floor of which was elevated and dry, and I kindled a fire on the bricks to keep him and the lass warm. By this time the cattle were up to their bellies in water in the byre, and I ran to throw straw bundles under them and the pigs, to raise them, to prevent their being drowned. I had hardly returned to the house, when the south gable, which had the current beating against it, fell inwards on the other room, and I was instantly obliged to knock out that window in the north gable to let the water escape, otherwise we must have perished where we were. About five o'clock, I observed my neighbours, John Grant and his wife, standing on the bank in front. The distance between us was not thirty yards, yet I could not make them hear for the fearsome roar of the water, which was now quite tremendous. Large trees were constantly coming down and striking against the carding-mill. The look up the water was awful. It seemed as if a sea was coming down upon us, with terrible waves, tossing themselves into the air, much higher than the houses.* I saw Grant's wife go up the bank, and she returned some time afterwards with four men. We watched them consulting together, and our hopes rose high; but when we saw them leave the place without making any attempt to save us, we thought that all hope for us in this world was gone. Willingly would I have given all I had, or might expect to possess, to have planted but the soles of my feet, and those of my companions, on yon bit

* *Macdonald, the farmer of Tillyglens, tells me that the waves were so high that he could not see the mills at all from his side of the river, till he climbed the bank.*

green sod then still untouched by the waters. Every moment we expected the crazed walls of the house to yield, and to bury us in their ruins, or that we and it together should be swept away. We began to prepare ourselves for the fate that seemed to await us. I thank Almighty God, that supported me in that hour of trial. I felt calm and collected, and my assistant was no less so. My little brother, too, said "he was na feared"; but the woman and the lad were frantic, and did nothing but shriek and wring their hands".

"While we were in this situation, we suddenly saw about sixty people coming down the bank, and our hopes revived. The four men had gone to raise the country, and they now appeared with ropes. All our attention was fixed on their motions. They drove a post into the ground, and threw the end of a thick rope across to me. This we fixed to a strong beam, and jammed it within the front window, whilst they on the bank made fast the other end of it to the post. A smaller rope was thrown over. This I fastened round the boy's waist, and he was dragged through the water to the bank, supporting himself all the way on the larger rope, that was stretched between the window and the post. The lass lost her hold, and was taken out half drowned; but, thank Providence! we were all saved. By six o'clock in the evening, the water had so fallen that I made my way in to give provender to the beasts. I then found that the whole Dorback had come over from the west side of the valley, and cut a new course close at the back of the mills. All the mill-leads were cut entirely away. A deep ravine was dug out between the houses and the bank - their foundations were undermined in that direction - the machinery destroyed; the gables next the river carried away; and all, even the very ground, so ruined, that it is quite impossible ever to have mills here again". (Plates 19 and 20)

PLATE 19. RUINED MILLS OF DUNPHAIL ON THE DORBACK

Such was the miller's own account of his disasters. Mr. Cumming Bruce said of the ravages committed here and in other parts of the valley, that they reminded him more of the devastation that took place at Martigny in 1818, than anything else. I was there two months after that awful calamity took place. There God's judgment came and passed away with the swiftness of the thunderbolt! There the mischief was concentrated too, and the food for destruction lay more abundantly in its way. The ruin was therefore on a greater scale, and the loss of human life most calamitous. But the ravages of the flood of the 3rd and 4th certainly approached much nearer to that of Martigny than those of any former domestic disaster of the same kind.

PLATE 20. RUINED MILLS OF DUNPHAIL ON THE DORBACK

Nothing could be more desolate than the whole scene about these mills when I looked down on them in the afternoon of the 4th, from the brow of the western bank. They were still isolated by a strong stream running between them and the eastern bank. But the mill-yard was clear of water, and whilst no human being was to be seen about the deserted premises, a litter of young pigs, having escaped from their sty, were gambolling about, glad of their liberty, and a parcel of young cockerel chickens were keenly sparring with each other, as if in derision of the surrounding ruin, provoking me to quote, in burlesque, Byron's sublime description of the battle of Thrasimene:-

And such the storm of battle in this day,
And such the phrensy, whose convulsion blinds
To all save carnage, that, beneath the fray,
An earthquake rolled unheededly away!
None felt stern Nature rocking at his feet.

It was then I saw that the destruction of the mills had been occasioned by the small burn of Wester Tillyglens, which, coming in from the left, at about 150 yards above, threw so much gravel and stones into the river as to force it over on the mills. And if it had not been for a rock that appeared where the water struck, not even a fragment of the buildings would have been left. I have noticed that this is invariably the effect of tributary streams, however small.

The beautiful Swiss bridge, a little lower down, that gave access to the mills, was not only carried off almost whole, but the road of approach and an immense mass of the western hill disappeared, whilst the rocky channel was filled in one place, and new rocks were brought into view at another; so that we might now safely bid defiance to the ablest engineer to erect another, with any certainty of its remaining entire for half a year.

CHAPTER 6

The River Divie through Dunphail

ABOUT 200 or 300 yards below the junction of the Divie and Dorback, a block of gneiss containing 1000 cubic feet and weighing about 100 tons, appears lying on a bare shelf of schistus (Plate 21). There is no rock of precisely the same kind either on the spot or for a considerable distance above. This was not moved a hair's-breadth by the flood of the 3rd and 4th. It is shaped with a remarkable projecting ledge near the base, which may have been thickly encrusted with a float of ice, and its specific gravity being thus so far overcome, its removal to its present position may be accounted for. Yet what must have been the power of that flood which brought it there?

PLATE 21. Large stone in the Divie, below its junction with the Dorback

Mr. Cumming Bruce's new house of Dunphail, already partly inhabited, and on the eve of being finished at the time of the floods, is admitted by all to be one of the happiest efforts of Mr. Playfair's classical taste. It stood on a wide lawn, retired about 50 feet from the verge of a bank in front, at the base of which was an old channel where there was little water except in floods, and as rock appeared all along its bottom it was conceived to be quite proof against encroachment. The proper and ordinary course of the river runs along the steep and wooded bank bounding the valley to the west, exactly 600 feet from the house, a fact which it is worth while to keep in view in forming an idea of what took place. The intermediate space was occupied by a broad, green, and partially wooded island, of some acres in extent.

About six o'clock in the evening of Monday the 3rd, the river rose so much as to carry away two handsome wooden bridges, one for carriages and the other for foot passengers, and an embankment at the upper end of the island having given way, a mighty torrent poured down towards the house. The flood continued, and became so alarming that the carriage was ordered, and Mr. Cumming Bruce prevailed on his lady to leave Dunphail with her daughter. Previous to quitting the place their anxiety had been extremely excited for the fate of a favourite old pony, then at pasture in the island. As the spot had never been flooded in the memory of man, no one thought of removing him until it was too late. When the embankment gave way and the patches of green gradually diminished, Dobbin, now in his twenty-seventh year and in shape something like a 74-gun ship cut down to a frigate, was seen galloping about in great alarm as the wreck of roots and trees floated past him. As the last spot of grass disappeared, he was given up for lost. At this moment he made a desperate effort to cross the stream under the house - was turned head over heels by its force - rose again, with his head up the river - made boldly up against it, but was again borne down and turned over. Everyone believed him gone, when, rising once more, and setting down the waste of water, he crossed both torrents and landed safely on the opposite bank.

After escorting the ladies to the house of a friend, Mr. Cumming Bruce returned to Dunphail at ten o'clock at night. He says there was something inexpressibly fearful and sublime in the roar of the torrent, which by this time filled the valley, the ceaseless plash of the rain, and the frequent and fitful gusts of the north wind that groaned among the woods. He found his people in great alarm. The river had now undermined the bank the house stood on, which had already been carried away to *within four paces of the foundation of the kitchen tower*, and as mass after mass fell with a thundering noise, some fine trees, which had stood for more than a century on the terrace above it, disappeared in the stream. The operations of the flood were only dimly discovered by throwing the faint light of their lanterns over its waters, and judged of by marking certain intervals of what remained of the terrace. One by one these fell in, and at about eleven o'clock they had the river still rising, and *only three yards space left to count on*.

The house was now considered as lost. The furniture was ordered to be removed and, by means of carts and lanterns, this was effected without any loss, even in the most delicate ornamental moveables of a drawing-room. About one o'clock on Tuesday morning, the partial subsidence of the flood, mentioned elsewhere, awakened a slight hope;

but it rose again in an hour, 2 feet higher than ever, came within 12 feet of the height of the bank, and must have been flowing 16 or 18 feet deep immediately below. The bank fell in *within one yard* of the foundation of the east tower! Mr. Cumming Bruce ordered every one to quit the building, and he and his people took their station at some distance to witness the fall of this beautiful structure. But it pleased Providence to spare him so great an additional calamity. About four o'clock the clouds appeared lighter, the river again began to subside, and by degrees a little sloping beach became visible towards the foot of the precipice. The flood ceased to undermine, and the house was saved.

PLATE 22. HOUSE OF DUNPHAIL

The ruin and devastation of the place was dreadful. The shrubbery all along the river side, with its little hill and mosshouse, had vanished; two stone and three wooden bridges were carried off; the beautiful fringe of wood on both sides of the river, with the ground it grew on, were washed to the ocean, together with all those sweet and pastoral projections of the fields which gave so peaceful and fertile a character to the valley. The once green island, robbed of its groups of trees and furrowed by a dozen channels, was covered with large stones, gravel, and torn-up roots. The rock in the old channel had been rendered unavailing by the great quantity of gravel brought down, which raised the water over it so that it acted against the superincumbent mass of mortary gravel that was incapable of resisting it. Thus the house was left in the midst of ruin, like a precious gem, the lustre and effect of which have been destroyed by its setting being injured, and the stone itself left in jeopardy (Plate 22). "Dreadful, indeed," says Mrs. Cumming Bruce, feelingly, in a billet written in reply to our inquiries, "is the devastation that a few hours have wrought. But we must be thankful that all around us are safe. God's will be done. I daresay we were all too proud of the beauty of our valley, a beauty which we had not given and could not take away, but which has vanished in an instant before His sweeping arm." Mr. Cumming Bruce's losses are given in at £5000.

The ruins of the castle of Dunphail crown a green and partially wooded conical hill on the right bank of the river. A deep, narrow, and extremely romantic glen surrounds two-thirds of it, opening to the valley at either end, and isolating it entirely from its eastern bounding banks. This wears every character of an old bed of the Divie, though, even at its lower end, it cannot be less than 50 feet above the present level of the river. Two courses, intermediate between the ancient and modern beds of the stream, are quite apparent. Here the recent cut in the Dorback at the Rhymer's Hill very much enlightens us, by proving how soon such a course as this may have been abandoned, by the river finding softer materials, to work out to a lower level in another direction. The same illustration will apply to the ravine of *Slochk-nan-cean*,* corrupted since the Gaelic language was lost in this parish, into Slaginnan, about half a mile farther down the river, on the right bank. This is one of the most Salvator Rosa looking chasms I ever beheld; precisely resembling the wildest and narrowest parts of the present bed of the Divie, though devoid of water. It has two entrances at the upper end, and the ancient courses which led the river into these successively are easily traceable. The lower extremity of the ravine terminates abruptly over a steep rock, about 40 feet high, above the Divie that flows at its base. This spot is extremely interesting to the geologist, and very much so to the botanist. Nor is it less attractive to those who, from idleness, or an ardent love of Nature, take pleasure in following her into her most secluded haunts where she most delights to luxuriate, for such could not fail to feel the enchantment of this wild and wizard spot.

But Slochk-nan-cean has another source of interest, capable of producing a yet more general excitement. Near the upper end of the ravine, there is a curious cavern formed of the huge masses of fallen crags that cover the bottom of the place. It enters downwards like a pit, and the mouth, which is no more than wide enough to admit a man, is not easily discovered. Here it was that the brave Allister Bane secreted himself after the battle of the lost standard.** At this time the Castle of Dunphail was besieged by Randolph, Earl of Moray; and Allister Bane, who could no longer make head against him in the open field, contented himself with harassing the enemy. Knowing that his father and his garrison were reduced to great want,

* *The hollow of the heads.*

** *See page 44.*

he and a few of his followers disguised themselves as country men, and driving a parcel of horses yoked in rude sledges, laden with sacks, they came to the edge of the glen where Randolph's beleaguering party lay, and pretending to be peasants carrying meal from the low country to the Highlands, they entreated their protection for the night from one Allister Bane, of whom they were afraid. Their prayer being granted, they unyoked their horses, and took care to leave their sledges at the brink of the precipice, so that, on a given signal agreed on with the garrison, they tumbled sledges, sacks and all, over into the glen below; and the garrison making a sally at the same time, each man bore off a sack on his back, whilst the pretended peasants sprang on their horses, and were out of sight before the astonished sentinels of the enemy had well given the alarm.

Randolph was so provoked, on learning who the author of this trick was, that he set a price upon his head. A certain private pique led a Cumin to betray his master's lurking place. His enemies hurried to the spot to make sure of their game but, when they saw the small uncouth-looking aperture, they paused in a circle around it. One only could descend at a time, and the death of him who should attempt it was certain; for the red glare of Cumin's eye in the obscurity within, and the flash of his dirk-blade, shewed that he had wound up his dauntless soul to die with the *'courage!'* of the lion on his crest. They called on him to surrender at discretion. He replied by hurling a deep note of defiance from the dark womb of the rocks, "Let me but come out, and, with my back to that craig, I will live or die like a Cumin!". "No," exclaimed the leader of his foes, "thou shalt die like a fox as thou art!". Brush-wood was quickly piled over the hole, but no word of entreaty for mercy ascended from below. Heap after heap was set fire to, and crammed blazing down upon him. His struggles to force a way upwards were easily repelled by those above and, after a sufficient quantity of burning matter had been thrust in to ensure his suffocation, they rolled stones over the mouth of the hole.

When the cruel deed was done, and the hole opened, Allister Bane was found reclining in one corner, his head muffled in his plaid and resting on the pommel of his sword, with two or three attendants around him, all dead. To make sure of them, their heads were cut off, and thrown, one after another, into the fortress, with this horrible taunt to the old man, "Your son has provided you with meal, and we now send you flesh to eat with it."* The veteran warrior recognised the fair head of his son. "It is a bitter morsel indeed," said he, as he took it up, kissed it, and wept over it; "but I will gnaw the last bone of it before I surrender!"

* *From this has arisen the Morayshire proverb, employed in designating any action of revenge, "Beef for your bannocks, like the Cumin's head."*

A green mound outside the garden at Dunphail existed after the middle of the last century, and was known to be the grave of the headless Cumins. The estate was then in the family of the Dunbars, who rose on the ruins of the Cumins. Mr. Dunbar, intending to enlarge the garden, opened the mound, when five or six rudely constructed stone coffins were found, each containing a skeleton complete, with the exception of the skull.

CHAPTER 7

THE RIVERS DIVIE AND FINDHORN, FROM RELUGAS TO THE CRAIG OF COULTERNOSE

ENTERING the Relugas property from the Dunphail march, a branch of the pleasure-walks led down the left bank of the Divie, for above two miles, quite to the point of its junction with the Findhorn. Having had some severe lessons from former floods, especial care had been taken to conduct the line at an elevation considered by everyone to be quite beyond all risk of injury. The rocks and recesses of the wooded banks and the little grassy slopes were covered in a wild way with many thousand shrubs, of all kinds, especially with laurels, rhododendrons, azaleas, lilacs, and a profusion of roses which were thriving vigorously, and beginning to bear blossoms, whilst the rocks were covered with the different saxifrages, hung with all sorts of creepers, and enamelled with a variety of garden flowers, all growing artlessly as if sown by the hand of Nature. The path was therefore considered to be not unworthy of the exquisite scenery through which it led. But the flood of the 3rd and 4th of

PLATE 23. THE GALLERY ON THE DIVIE - A LINE SHOWS THE FLOOD LEVEL 32 FEET PERPENDICULAR ABOVE THE USUAL LEVEL

August left not one fragment of it remaining, from one end to the other. Not a tree, or shrub, or flower, or piece of soil, nay, or of moss or lichen, is to be seen beneath that boldly and sublimely sketched line of flood that appears on either side, and from end to end, of these rocks like the awful handwriting of God upon the wall.

At one point the river is compelled to make a sudden turn to the right, and round a towering rock, by a narrow gorge called The Gallery, from the walk having been there cut along the crag in that form. This narrow pass was quite unable to receive the body of water brought down by the flood, great part of which breached over the neck of the isthmus to the left of the rock (right of the sketch, Plate 23) and, falling again into the main stream below, down an alluvial bank 32 feet high, cut it backwards for 30 or 40 horizontal feet; and, if the flood had lasted but a few hours longer, our experience of the cut of the Dorback tells us that the whole isthmus of 30 yards wide must have been opened up as a direct course for the river, and the gorge left as another Slaginnan. A number of trouts were left by the flood on the top of the neck of land.

PLATE 24. OPENING OF THE RAVINE BELOW THE MILL ON THE DIVIE, AT RELUGAS - A LINE SHOWS THE FLOOD LEVEL 50 FEET PERPENDICULAR ABOVE THE USUAL LEVEL

On Sunday the 2nd of August, I returned from church by the river-walk. The day was sultry and cloudy, and a gentle shower began to fall, which hardly penetrated the canopy of leaves overhead but added freshness to the surrounding natural objects, and especially to the roses and rhododendrons that were flowering among the rocks. The generally confined channel of the river is particularly narrow at the waterfall, about 400 yards above the house, but widens immediately below the mouth of the ravine at the place called Macrae's Loup.* (Plate 24). Below this, a part of the water was led off to the left as a mill-stream. This, which surrounded a large piece of ground called the Mill Island (see Sketch of the pleasure grounds, Plate 25), was retained, as a fine feature in the scene, at the time the mill itself was removed as a nuisance. It ran peacefully along the base of a superbly wooded bank, sloping down from the garden above, where the trees of all kinds grew 80 feet or more in height, and so thick as to produce an impenetrable shade. The side of the Mill Island next the river was defended by a spine of wooded rocks, rising abruptly, and terminating at the upper end in a picturesque castellated mass, called the Otter's Rock, 24 feet high above the surface of the water. On the Mill Island itself the greatest care was lavished, the peaceful mill-stream, the lawny grass glades, the winding walks, and the rocky ridges having been adorned with all that was most rare, till it was converted into a spot of delightful retirement. At its lower extremity the mill-stream returned into the river over a broken cascade, crossed by picturesque bridges, where a little rustic Doric temple, partly constructed of masonry, and partly of unpeeled spruce trees, occupied an isolated rock. Into this I was driven for shelter, by the shower increasing, and this was the beginning of the rain that continued, without intermission, all that night and for the next two days.

The chief part of the pleasure-grounds of Relugas occupies the peninsula, bounded to the east by the Divie and to the west by the Findhorn. The house stands on a terrace facing the west, in which direction the lawn stretches towards the Findhorn. The south front looks over the whole length of the garden below, extending up the glen of the Divie, and immediately above the wooded bank already mentioned, as sloping from it into the Mill Island. At the back of the house, a picturesque conical wooded hill, called the Doune, rises to the east. The Divie, coming from the south, strikes against the southern base of this hill, directly after skirting the whole length of the Mill Island, and then turns abruptly off to the eastward at a right

* *So called, from a gentlemen who, for his amusement, used to stand on the jutting rock on the right bank (left side of the Sketch), thirty-two feet above the surface of the river, jump into the deep and narrow abyss below, and swim down through the wild gorge below.*

angle; and, immediately above this point, the stables and other offices stand, 40 feet perpendicular, and 158 feet horizontal, from the water's edge, forming two sides of a square, corresponding to the angle of the river.

After leaving the offices, the Divie sweeps for a circuit of half a mile round the south, east, and north bases of the Doune, between lofty and rocky banks, luxuriantly wooded with stately timber trees and, passing under the bridge and along the mingled lawns and

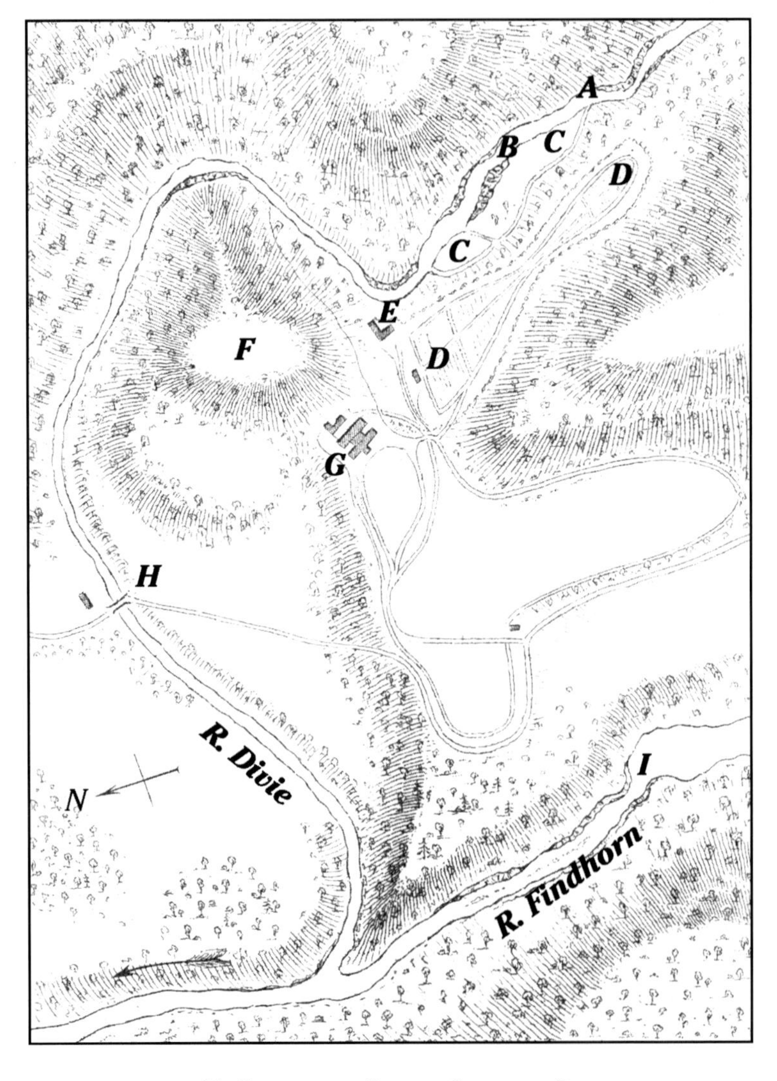

PLATE 25. SKETCH OF THE PLEASURE GROUNDS AT RELUGAS
A. *Macrae's Loup.* B. *Otter's Rock* C. C. *Mill Island* D. D. *Garden* E. *Stables*
F. *Doune* G. *The House* H. *The Bridge of Divie* I. *Randolph's Bridge*

wooded banks that slope towards its stream from the north front of the house, it pursues its course westward to join the Findhorn.

On the evening of Monday the 3rd August, we were roused, while at dinner, by the account the servants gave us of the swollen state of the rivers and, in defiance of the badness of the night, the whole party sallied forth. We took our way through the garden, towards our favourite Mill Island. "John", said I to the gardener as he was opening the gate that led to it, "I fear our temple may be in some danger if this goes on". "Ou, Sir, it's awa' else!" replied he, to my no small dismay; and the instant we had passed out at the gate, the Divie appalled us!

Looking up its course to where it burst from the rocks, it resembled the outlet to some great inland sea that had suddenly broken from its bounds. It was already 8 or 10 feet higher than any one had ever seen it, and setting directly down against the sloping terrace under the offices, where we were standing, it washed up over the shrubs and strawberry beds with a strange and alarming flux and reflux, dashing out over the ground 10 or 15 yards at a time, covering the knees of some of the party standing, as they thought, far beyond its reach, and retreating with a suction which it required great exertion to resist. The whirlpool produced by the turn of the river was in some places elevated 10 or 12 feet above other parts of it. The flood filled the whole space from the rocks of the right bank on the east to the base of the wooded slope forming the western boundary of the Mill Island, thus covering the whole of that beautiful spot except where two rocky wooded knolls, and the Otter's Rock beyond them, appeared from its eastern side. The temple was indeed gone, as well as its bridges, and four other rustic bridges in the island. Already its tall ornamental trees had begun to yield, one by one, to the pressure and undermining of the water, and to the shocks they received from the beams of the Dunphail wooden bridges. The noise was a distinct combination of two kinds of sound; one, a uniformly continued roar, the other like rapidly repeated discharges of many cannons at once. The first of these proceeded from the violence of the water; the other, which was heard through it and, as it were, muffled by it, came from the enormous stones which the stream was hurling over its uneven bed of rock. Above all this was heard the fiend-like shriek of the wind, yelling, as if the demon of desolation had been riding upon its blast. The leaves of the trees were stript off and whirled into the air, and their thick boughs and stems were bending and cracking beneath the tempest, and groaning like terrified creatures, impatient to escape from the coils of the watery serpent. There was something heart-sickening in the aspect of the atmosphere. The rain was descending in sheets, not in drops, and there was a peculiar and indescribable lurid, or rather bronze-like hue, that pervaded the whole face of nature, as if poison had been abroad in the air. The flood went on augmenting every moment, and it became difficult to resist the idea of the recurrence of a general deluge. We could not prevent ourselves from following it out, and we fancied the waters going on rising till first the houses and then the hills of the glen, where we had so long happily lived, should be covered; and all this in spite of our reason, which was continually prompting us to stifle such dreams. But, indeed, even reason was listened to with doubt, where we saw before our eyes what was so far beyond anything that experience had ever taught us to believe possible.

And now the magnificent trees in the Mill Island were overthrown faster and faster, offering no more resistance to their triumphant enemy than reeds before the mower's scythe. Numerous as they were, they were all individually well known friends. Each as it fell gave one enormous plash on the surface, then a plunge; the root appeared above water for a moment; again all was submerged; and then up rose the stem, disbranched and peeled; after which they either toiled round in the cauldron, or darted like arrows down the stream. A chill ran through our hearts as we beheld how rapidly the ruin of our favourite and long-cherished spot was going on. But we remembered that the calamity came from the hand of God; and, seeing that no human power could avail, we prepared ourselves to watch every circumstance of a spectacle, the like of which our fathers never saw, nor can generations who may come after us be expected to look upon its parallel.

At the bridge over the Divie, to the north of the house, the river, bounding out from the rocky glen behind the Doune, was fearful. The arch is 24 feet high, and its span from rock to rock is 60 feet. The flood filled more than two-thirds of its height, being above 16 feet up within it; and, throwing away the 6 feet of the ordinary depth there, as a balance for the curve of the arch, we have a column of water of 976 square feet, or nearly so, of transverse section, passing with a velocity apparently equal to that of a swift horse. As we stood on the bridge, we were distinctly sensible of a continued tremulous motion, besides which we felt as if its fabric received sudden blows at irregular intervals. It required nerve to stand in the centre and look over its upper parapet at the stream, struggling mightily against its wing-walls like some strong wrestler eager to overthrow a sturdy adversary. It appeared wonderful that the wide body of water which covered the Mill Island could pass through so narrow a space; but the escape from the arch was rapid, in consequence of the greater expansion of the banks below. Yet the fate of this most important bridge appeared extremely doubtful, and I sat up the greater part of the night with considerable anxiety, and only retired when a servant reported to me that partial subsidence of the flood so universally noticed elsewhere.

The first news I had in the morning was that the bridge was safe, but that the coachman, and the gardener and his men, all of whom live in the offices, had sat up the whole night in dread of the buildings being carried away. I hurried out but, prepared as my mind had been for a scene of devastation, how much did the reality exceed my worst anticipations! The Divie had apparently subsided, it is true, but it was more because it had widened and disencumbered its course, than from any actual diminution of its waters. The whole Mill Island was cleared completely of shrubs, trees, and soil, except the hard summit towards the Otter's Rock; and, instead of the space being filled with that wilderness of sweets into which the eye found difficulty in penetrating, one vast and powerful red-coloured river, dividing itself into two branches against the Otter's Rock, flowed in two large streams around it without one single obstacle to its action; with less turmoil than before indeed, but with the terrible majesty of a mighty conqueror sweeping sternly over the carnage of his recent victory. And well might the enemy triumph! For, besides the loss of the Mill Island, which I had looked for, the beautiful hanging bank, covered with majestic forest and ornamental trees of all kinds, and of growth so fresh and vigorous, had vanished like the scenery of a dream and, in its place, was the garden hedge, running for *between 200 and 300 yards, along the brink of a red alluvial perpendicular precipice 50 feet high*, with the broad remorseless flood rolling at its base, eating into its foundation and, every successive minute, bringing down masses of many cubic yards. And then, from time to time, some tall and graceful tree on the brink of the fractured portions of the bank at either end, would slowly and magnificently bend its head, and launch into the foaming waves below. The whole scene had an air of unreality about it that bewildered the senses. It was like some of those wild melodramatic exhibitions, where nature's operations are out-heroded* by the mechanist of a theatre, and where mountains are thrown down by artificial storms. Never did the unsubstantiality of all earthly things come so perfectly home to my conviction. The hand of God appeared to be at work, and I felt that He had only to pronounce dread fiat, and millions of such worlds as that we inhabit would cease to exist.

Descending from 'The Great First Cause' to the means by which He operates, I may mention that the ruin I have described was very much owing to the confinement of the Divie for a great way above the waterfall, and its bursting at once from the gorge below it, called Macrae's Loup, into the wider theatre of its havoc. The height of the flood at Macrae's Loup was no less than 40 feet above the ordinary

* *Publisher's Note: This expression, meaning 'to exceed in cruelty', was used, if not coined, by Shakespeare in 'Hamlet'.*

level.* The view from this spot, over the Mill Island, towards the house and offices, used to present one of the richest scenes imaginable (Plate 26). But how cruelly was it changed! (Plate 27). When the water had ebbed away, nothing was to be seen but a deep ravine of sand and gravel covered with huge rounded lumps of stone. The offices were within a yard of the crumbling precipice of earth, and a large and favourite old sycamore near them was standing half undermined. No such flood as this could have affected the Divie for many ages. The Mill of Relugas is marked, in the oldest map extant, as existing in the precise spot from whence I removed it; but if it had been still there, the water would have nearly gone over its roof, though of two storeys high; and it would not only have been swept away, but the very site of it was excavated 10 or 12 feet in depth, so that no mill could have been placed there again.

PLATE 26. VIEW OF RELUGAS BEFORE THE FLOOD

The quantity of gravel and stones brought down was great in all the rivers; but it was greater in the Divie than in any other. This river was remarkable for the depth of its pools; but the flood completely obliterated them and, for many weeks afterwards, a dog might have walked down its whole course from Edinkillie Church to the Findhorn, without having occasion to swim one yard. The swimming pool at Relugas, for example, was 16 feet deep. It has now 20 feet deep of gravel laid into it and is converted into a shallow, the bottom of which is 4 feet higher than the former surface of the water. This temporary raising of the river's bed added greatly to the mischievous

* *See Plate 24 again.*

influence of the flood, and I may attribute to this cause the ruin done me by the Divie below the bridge where, besides the entire removal of a considerable island covered with trees, it cut away a beautiful piece of lawn and some very fine timber.

PLATE 27. VIEW OF RELUGAS AFTER THE FLOOD

The next spot I visited on the morning of the 4th was the Findhorn, at Randolph's Bridge. I have already mentioned that the flood rose to the height of 50 feet there. I found it in its greatest grandeur, flooding over the whole Haugh of Rannoch, carrying large trees, with their roots and branches, triumphantly around it, and washing so far up the road leading down to it, as very nearly to run into a course which I have often been wondered at for calling an ancient channel of the river. The turmoil of the surges was so tremendous that the primitive rocks shook, as the Divie bridge had done the previous evening. Nothing can convey an idea of the violence and velocity of the water that shot away from the whirling sea above the cliffs. It was scarcely possible to follow with the eye the trees and wreck that floated like straws on its surface. The force was as much more than that of a raging ocean, as gun-powder ignited within the confined tube of a cannon is more terribly powerful than the same material when suffered to explode on the open ground. I was particularly struck here with an example of the fact that trees exposed to occasional struggles with torrents, instinctively prepare themselves to resist them. I observed one tall ash, growing a little way above Randolph's Bridge, covered to at least four-fifths of its height. It was broken over at last but, having been taught by experience to resist the action of water, it was not rent away, whilst all those which had never been visited by floods before, were torn up like weeds. Before I left this spot I saw one of the under gardeners wade into the water as it had begun to ebb on the haugh and, with his umbrella, drive ashore and capture *a fine salmon at an elevation of 50 feet above the ordinary level of the Findhorn*.

The point of junction between the Divie and the Findhorn was terminated by a picturesque rock, covered with trees, and rendered accessible by a rustic bridge. The waves at this meeting of the waters were terrific, tossing themselves 20 feet into the air, and throwing up the drift trees and other bodies to a great height. The bridge and the trees on the rock were swept away, and not even a blade of grass or a tuft of moss left.

The damage done to Relugas by the flood is perhaps not more, in actual value, than £1200; yet, when the rocky defences all along this very small property are considered, even this sum is great. But the beauties of nature cannot be estimated in money; and although Relugas has yet enough left to captivate strangers, and to make them wonder how there could have been any thing to regret; yet ten thousand points of locality are lost on which hung many long cherished associations with the memory of those who can never return to sanctify the new scenes resulting from the late catastrophe. The flood of the 27th did no injury here. Principal Baird, being on his way to Relugas from Forres on that day, called to the post-boy to stop as he was crossing the Divie bridge, that he might enjoy the view of the scenery. "Na, na, Sir!" roared the lad, smacking his whip, "these are ower kittle times to be stopping on brigs!"

The terraces on the sides of the hills bear evidence that the double valley of the Findhorn and Divie must have been at one time filled with a lake.

Besides the general loss of trees along the banks, nearly two acres of very fine full grown timber covering a triangular piece of ground below the orchard at Logie were carried off, soil and all. The mill at Logie stands about 72 horizontal feet from the brink of the rock over the river, and about 15 perpendicular feet above the level of its mid-channel. The flood filled the lower storey of the mill, rose into the upper storey 3 feet deep, and ran in a strong stream between the upper mill-door and the bank. The height of the water on the mill-walls being 13½ feet, the whole height of the flood here, above ordinary level, was 28½ feet, with a breadth of about 80 yards. The mill was protected by a row of large ash trees, firmly rooted between it and the river. But the soil was scarified around them, and a very little longer continuance of the flood would have torn them away. This mill was saved, because the lower storey was filled by the flood quite solidly up to the ceiling with sand, which prevented the water working within it. The flood of the 27th was only 2 feet up in the lower mill; therefore it was 11½ feet lower than that of the 3rd and 4th.

The character of the scenery, stretching from Relugas to Sluie inclusive, is the wild, the grand, and the picturesque; everywhere tempered with a peculiar beauty arising from the luxuriance and the extent of the wooding. The rocks are lofty and often finely formed. The narrowest and most perpendicular part of the craggy pass through which the river rushes is at the Esses, a series of falls, rapids, and salmon leaps, about a mile above Sluie. I measured, with the greatest care, the height of the flood on an overhanging cliff on the right bank, about 100 yards above the pool called Craigock, and found it to be precisely the same as at Randolph's Bridge, *that is to say, 50 feet above the ordinary level*. From accurate observation, I am enabled to say that it nowhere rose to a greater height than this.

Before leaving the parish of Edinkillie, I avail myself of the returns made by the parochial committee to the central committee at Elgin, appointed to distribute the subscription fund for sufferers by the flood in the county of Moray, to state that there were 26 cases of families rendered destitute by this calamity, locally residing in this parish.

From Sluie, downwards to the Craig of Coulternose, the rocks are of the flœtz series, the character of wildness disappears with the rugged primitive crags, and those of grandeur, beauty, and richness continue. At the Heronry, the sandstone cliffs are of great height.* Sir William Cumming lost a quarter of an acre of timber trees, of magnificent growth, from a beautiful spot near the fishing-pool called the Roane; and a wooded island, 160 yards long by 20 broad, was swept entirely away from opposite the north-west corner of the Ramflat Haugh. The beautiful vale of St. John, vying with the richest park scenes of the Thames, has suffered severely on both sides the river. From Lord Moray's Haugh of Logie, on the left bank, some of the largest oaks in Scotland have been rent away, and seven acres of very valuable land were carried off, to the depth of many feet. Sir William Cumming, too, lost some fine trees from the right bank, but his greatest misfortune hereabouts was the annihilation of his Cothall Mills. These consisted of an extensive group of buildings, three storeys high, containing flour, meal, and barley mills, with all manner of appurtenances. They were placed at the distance of 80 yards from the river but, on Tuesday morning, the 3rd, the flood covered the whole lower haugh where they stood, and stretched far over that on Tarnawa side. About eleven o'clock the water made its way into the door of the barley-mill loft and soon drove out the lower gable. Having thus opened a passage through the upper storey, it poured in picturesque cascade over the north and fractured end of it, until the

* *This part of the river is annually animated by a numerous assemblage of herons, for the purpose of incubation. These add highly to the effect and interest of the grand and picturesque scenery.*

building gradually gave way altogether. The destruction of the meal and flour-mills went rapidly on soon afterwards and, when the flood subsided, all that remained was a portion of the walls of the flour-mill, about 14 feet long. Even that fell a few days afterwards, and the flood of the 27th completely finished the work. Never was there a more perfect destruction. Not a vestige of mills, mill-runs, sluices, or any thing of or belonging to a mill is to be seen, and the whole force of the river now runs through the spot where they stood. *I myself saw one of the freestone lintels, 3½ feet long by 1 foot one way, and 9 inches the other, lying two miles below the site of the mills*. The whole of the miller's land, amounting to five acres, was cut away to a great depth.

The medium width of the channel at the limestone crag of Coulternose is 185 feet. The mean depth of a number of soundings, taken across the river in its ordinary state, is about 3 feet 4 inches, above which the flood rose 14 feet 8 inches, making the total depth 18 feet; so that a transverse section of the column of water passing through here must have had a superficial face of 3330 square feet, moving with force and velocity perfectly inconceivable. It is proposed to build the new bridge here, of a single arch of 160 feet span, which will unquestionably form the grandest feature of one of the finest possible landscapes.

Sir William Cumming's magnificent drive, which ran under the bluff Craig of Coulternose, superbly finished, and beautifully planted with ornamental trees and shrubs, was completely destroyed, and 16 acres of land were cut off entirely from his farm of Mundole.

CHAPTER 8

THE LEFT BANK OF THE RIVER FINDHORN, BELOW COULTERNOSE, WITH THE INCIDENTS OF THE FLOOD IN THE PLAIN OF FORRES, TO THE CONCLUSION OF OLD KERR'S STORY

THE discharge of water, wreck, and stones that burst from the pass at the Craig of Coulternose, over the extensive plain of Forres, spreading devastation abroad on that rich and beautifully hedge-rowed country, was quite terrific. In treating of this important part of my subject, I shall first discuss the incidents on the left bank.

On Monday the 3rd of August, Dr. Brands of Forres was called professionally to the western side of the river. He forded on horseback and, ere he had crossed the second branch of the stream, he saw the flood coming thundering down. His horse was caught by it; he was compelled to swim; and he had not long touched dry land, ere the river had risen 6 feet. Whilst at dinner at Moy, he observed it branching out into numerous streams, and a lady present emphatically repeated the remarkable old prophecy

"Says Divie to Dorback whar shall we sweep,
Through the middle o' Moy when a' men sleep."

After dinner Mr. Suter accompanied Dr. Brands to visit a cottage on the embankment, tenanted by James Findlay, a boatman, better known by his *nom de guerre* of 'Old Rodney'. From the back of his house, they beheld the Findhorn rolling along in awful grandeur, the effect being greatly heightened by the contrary direction of the northerly wind, then blowing a gale. Mr. Suter earnestly urged the old man, and his wife Janet, to abandon their dwelling, and go up to the house of Moy. "Thank ye, Sir", replied Rodney, "we'll gang up to the Black Barn, at the Square, whar I'm thinkin' we'll hae plenty company ere lang". The gentlemen then went to a row of cottages, called Stripeside, which they likewise urged the inhabitants to quit. Their advice was taken by all but the family of one Kerr, who, trusting to their great distance from the river, refused to move.

After their return to Moy, the door of the apartment where the gentlemen were sitting was suddenly burst open, about ten o'clock, by a servant boy breathless with haste and alarm. "The Findhorn's rolling by the Square, Sir! There's a heap o' houses down at the Broom o' Moy, and four or five fouk drooned, and a' the rest o' them in the kitchen, Sir!" Actuated by one impulse to fly to the aid of their fellow creatures, both sprang up and hurried down stairs. Entering the kitchen to gather further intelligence, they found a number of dripping and shivering women and children crowding round a blazing fire. A knocking at the door was heard, and without further preface, in stalked one Andrew Smith, with a child in his arms, inquiring, "Is Maister Suter here? Ou aye, I see he is. Come awa ben then, lassie", said he, looking over his shoulder to his wife who followed him, "this is no a time for ceremony", and Mrs. Smith immediately appeared with six or seven children hanging about her. "The water's a' in aboot the hooses o' the Broom o' Moy, an' some o' them hae fa'en else. Thank Providence that we hae escapit. I ken ye'll no grudge us quarters, Mr. Suter. But troth I fear", added he, shaking his head portentously, "there's mony a ane will no hae siccan luck. There's twa families yonder wholly surrounded, and as for poor Sandy Smith! Poor *Funns*! Naebody can ever houp till see him or his family again". The general anxiety was greatly excited by this alarming account of the situation of Sandy Smith, an active boatman, commonly called 'Whins', or, in the provincial pronunciation, '*Funns*', from his residence on a piece of furzy pasture, at no great distance from the river. The site of his dwelling was the most critical of all; and, by the united opinion of those who were present, he was already given up for lost. But, on going out, they were cheered by observing the far distant gleam of light that issued from his window. "I have often heard of a ray of hope", said Mr. Suter, "but this is the first time I have ever experienced it in a literal sense."

Hurrying away to a field in the vicinity of the offices, they found a number of people stretching their eyes through the gloom of night, athwart the inundation, anxious for the fate of the Kerrs whose escape from Stripeside had been arrested by the flood surrounding the houses. But further consideration for them was extinguished for a time by the loud screams that proceeded from the gardener's wife and children near the offices at Moy. They hastened thither, and found the flood rushing strongly about the house. It was not yet too deep to wade, but the river was making rapid advances whilst the people were debating what was best to be done. "I will go myself and save them!" cried Mr. Suter. "God forbid that ye should risk yoursel' alane, Sir!" said an elderly woman standing by. "I'll gang wi' ye." "Come along then, madam," said he, offering his arm to the old lady whom he now recognised to be Widow Ross, his washer-woman, who had only a short time before escaped with her children from her house at Stripeside, with the loss of everything she had in this world. "Come along! we shall try it, at all events." They entered the water, and, after three or four paces, it became deep. They had to pass through a gate, where the current was strong. "No fear, Widow!" said Mr. Suter, "lean more on my arm." By this time they were up to the middle in water. "Haud mair to that side, Sir," cried the widow, "there's a deep well here, and we may fa' intil't." They reached the cottage door. "What's the meaning of this delay?" demanded Mr. Suter. "Come, young fellow," said he, addressing himself to the gardener's youngest son, and bending his body to receive him, "leap upon my back." The little urchin joyfully obeyed and, in ten minutes, the whole family were saved.

By this time the lawn was covered with cattle and sheep, and the stables filled with horses from the adjacent farms; and, on visiting the Black Barn, Old Rodney's bulky form, and the tall erect figure of his wife Janet, were seen rising over such a group as might have furnished Wilkie with materials to fill a canvas. Mr. Suter gave orders for everything necessary for their comfort, and most of the women and children were sent up to the house for better accommodation.

The gentlemen returned drenched to Moy. "Have the gardener's people been taken care of?" demanded Mr. Suter. "I was in the servants' hall this moment," replied Mrs. Suter, "where I saw no less than thirteen children round an immense bicker* of brose, using their spoons to the best possible purpose." "Let candles be placed in all the windows of the house," said Mr. Suter, "that poor Whins, if yet in existence, may know that he is not forgotten amidst the horrors of this awful night. But, alas! his light no longer burns!" Seeing that, in the midst of tempest and darkness, any attempt to assist those who were in distress must be utterly vain, Mr. Suter proposed to retire to rest. "Why are you not in bed?" demanded Mrs. Suter, of an old and privileged woman-servant, whom she met in her way. "Me in bed!" was the reply; "Hoo could I gang till my bed, and five or sax weans in't?"

At day-break Dr. Brands hurried down to the offices, and ascended the tower to look out from the top. The prospect was awful. The wide waste of waters was only bounded by the rising grounds about Forres, skirting the flooded plain to the south, and by those about Dalvey to the west. Towards the north and east, the watery world swept off uninterruptedly into the expanding Firth and the German Ocean. He looked anxiously for the houses of Stripeside. They were still standing, but the powerful and agitated stream that rolled around them, and between them and the offices, seemed to threaten their speedy destruction. The embankments appeared to have everywhere given way; and the water that covered the fields, lately so beautiful with yellow wheat, green turnips and other crops, rushed with so great impetuosity in certain directions as to form numerous currents setting furiously through the quieter parts of the inundation, and elevated several feet above it. As far as the eye could reach, the brownish-yellow moving mass of water was covered with trees and wreck of every description, whirled along with a force that shivered many of them against unseen obstacles. Even in the immediate vicinity of the offices, the Doctor saw one of those streams, created by a hollow in a turnip field, root up two large spreading elms and sweep them into the abyss. There was a sublimity in the mighty

* *Wooden dish, made with staves and hoops like a tub, but shallow and broad.*

power and deafening roar of the waters, heightened by the livid hue of the clouds, the sheeting rain, the howling of the wind, the lowing of the cattle, and the screaming and wailing of the assembled people, that rivetted Dr. Brands for some time to this elevated spot. As he stretched his eyes anxiously over the watery plain, he could dimly descry the far-off dwelling of poor 'Funns', its roof rising like a speck above the flood that had evidently made a breach in one of its ends. The southern gable of the row of houses at Stripeside, too, was broken, and they appeared to be in the greatest jeopardy.

Anxious for the fate of the Kerrs, Mr. Suter went to the offices, about seven o'clock in the morning, and there he found their son, his servant, Alexander Kerr, who, since last night, had never left the spot. He was still gazing towards Stripeside, in an agony of mind, and weeping for the apparently inevitable destruction of his parents, their rescue appearing utterly impossible. Mr. Suter tried to comfort him but, even whilst he spoke, the whole gable of Kerr's dwelling, which was the uppermost of the three houses composing the row, gave way and fell into the raging current. Dr. Brands, who was looking on intently at the time with a telescope, observed a hand thrust through the thatch of the central house. It worked busily, as if in despair of life; a head soon appeared; and at last Kerr's whole frame emerged on the roof and he began to exert himself in drawing out his wife and niece. Clinging to one another, they crawled along the roof towards the northern chimney. The sight was torturing. Kerr, a little ahead of the others, was seen tearing off the thatch, as if trying to force an entrance through the roof, whilst the miserable women clung to the house-top, the blankets which they had used to shelter them almost torn from them by the violence of the hurricane (Plate 28); and the roof they had left yielding and tottering, fell into the sweeping flood. The thatch resisted all Kerr's efforts; and he was

PLATE 28. HOUSES OF STRIPESIDE DURING THE FLOOD

now seen to let himself drop from the eaves on a small speck of ground higher than the rest, close to the foundation of the back wall of the buildings, which was next the spectators. There he finally succeeded in bringing down the women, and there he and they stood without even room to move. "Good God, friends!" exclaimed Alexander Shaw, nephew to old Kerr, and brother to the girl who was in danger so imminent, "will you allow human beings to perish before your eyes, and do nothing to give them help? If I had but a boat I would try to save them. Will nobody give me a horse to go in search of one?" "Take mine!" said Mr. Suter, whose horse was standing by, "Take mine, and ride where you will." "And I will go with you," said Dr. Brands, throwing himself into his saddle.

All direct communication with the country northward of Moy was cut off by the flood of the burn meeting that of the river, and floating entirely over the bridge; they therefore took their way by the avenue on the south side of the house. At the gate, about 100 yards in front of it, they found the water very deep but, though their horses were frequently swimming, they managed to get on by keeping the line of the road. At the distance of a mile from Moy, the water became so deep and strong that they were compelled to make for the rising grounds. The lad now left Dr. Brands, with the intention of going round by Dalvey, towards Earnhill and Kincorth, whilst the Doctor proceeded towards the Bridge of Findhorn, with the hope of getting one of the fishermen's cobles. As he was approaching the bridge, he learned that the last of the three arches, that on the west, had fallen the instant before; and, when he got to the brink the waters were sweeping on, as if it had never been, making the rocks and houses vibrate with a distant and tremulous motion. At the Turnpike House, at the end of the bridge, he was told that all the boats had been swept away.

From the brow of the bank to the north-east of the toll-house, Dr. Brands commanded a full view of the flooded country from one extremity to the other. The mightiness of the inundation baffled all description. The waters, breaking out from the pass at Coulternose, covered Mundole and swept furiously through the estate of Balnagieth, carrying corn, trees, hedges, and everything along with them, and rolling over the strong embankment lately constructed along the turnpike road by Mr. Leslie. Meanwhile the chief current was playing furiously against the southern approach of the bridge. Whilst Dr. Brands was looking at it, the usually dry arch, at its farther end, burst with a loud report, its fragments, mixed with water, being blown into the air as if by gunpowder. Sweeping past the ruins, and striking against the rock on the left bank, it rushed onwards till it encountered the current from Balnagieth. The strife of their contention was terrible. The left flank of the flood was forced over a young plantation on the estate of Dalvey and the farm of Waterside, while the main body rushed directly down on the Greeshop embankments, sweeping them, and the wood behind them, clear before it with resistless force, rolling over the whole of that estate and over the flat land on both sides of the turnpike road, straight onwards to Forres. The row of fishermen's houses, on the right bank, a little below the bridge, were already in one mass of ruin, and the scene of devastation was complete. The centre of the main stream was hurried on at an elevation many feet higher than the rest of the surrounding sea of waters, the mighty rush of which exhibited a power and velocity altogether indescribable. Magnificent trees, with all their branches, were dashing and rending against the rock, and the roaring and crashing sound that prevailed was absolutely deafening.

Looking down to the houses of Waterside, the hamlet of Broom of Moy and others, the Doctor could see nothing but a few roofs peeping from the midst of the inundation; and, as there was now no chance of getting a boat, he returned towards Moy. In his way thither, his mare was compelled to swim for a great way, and she afterwards stuck in the mud where she touched the ground, and was nearly drowned.

PLATE 29. FUNNS AND HIS FAMILY IN THE MIDDLE OF THE FLOOD

When the Doctor reached the house, about ten o'clock, he found Mr. Suter looking through a telescope at poor Funns and his family. The glass was a good one, and brought them so close that the eye could detect every movement they made. They were huddled together on a spot of ground a few feet square, some 49 or 50 yards below their inundated dwelling (Plate 29). He was sometimes standing and sometimes sitting on a small cask and, as the beholders fancied, watching with intense anxiety the progress of the flood, and trembling for every large tree that it brought sweeping past them. His wife, covered with a blanket, sat shivering on a bit of a log, one child in her lap, and a girl of about 17, and a boy of about 12 years of age, leaning against her side. A bottle and a glass on the ground, near the man, gave the spectators, as it had doubtless given him, some degree of comfort. Above a score of sheep were standing around, or wading or swimming in the shallows. Three cows and a small horse, picking at a broken rick of straw that seemed to be half afloat, were also grouped with the family. Dreading that they must all be swept off if not soon relieved, the gentlemen hastened to the offices and looked anxiously out from the top of the tower for a boat. At last they had the satisfaction to see one launched from the garden at Earnhill, about a mile below. The young man who had gone earlier in the direction of Kincorth, found that Mrs. Grant had already ordered out a pair of horses to convey the boat to the spot where it was committed to the waves; and it was immediately manned by Donald Munro, overseer to Mr. London at Earnhill; William Smith, salmon-fisher, and Tom Fraser, floater, who nobly volunteered to proceed, in the first place, to the rescue of the family of a man named John Smith, who were in the most perilous situation imaginable in the island opposite to Earnhill. The gentlemen on the tower watched the motions of this boat with the liveliest interest. They saw it tugging up till an intervening wood hid it from their view. Again it was seen beyond, making as it were for Rodney's cottage, as they hoped with the intention of reaching Stripeside. But in an instant it dashed into the main stream, and disappeared behind the wood with a velocity so fearful that they concluded its destruction certain. But in a moment it again showed itself, and the brave fellows were seen plying their oars across the submerged Island of Earnhill, making for John Smith's cottage; the thatch, and a small part of the side-walls of which only were visible above the water. By the means of the telescope, the gentlemen saw the poor inmates actually dragged out of the windows, from under the water, having been obliged to duck within, ere they could effect their escape. The boat then swept down the stream towards a place called The Lakes, where John Smith, his wife and her mother were safely landed.

The boat was now again brought up by the Kincorth horses to a point near the bridge over the Moy Burn. There Donald Munro again sprang forward, and Sergeant John Grant, an old pensioner from Findhorn, with David Reat from Kinteasock, and Robert Dallas, claimed the honour of the Stripeside adventure. After bringing the boat across the flooded bridge, they, with great difficulty, crossed the stream on the Moy side of it, and pulled along the road till the current became so strong that the people who waded breast deep to meet them were compelled to haul them up by means of ropes. There was one individual in the boat whose exertions Mr. Suter says he can never forget. The others were sufficiently active, but he was both physically and morally more energetic than they, and his conduct was so conspicuous as to call forth the frequent and united plaudits of all present. This was Donald Munro, who, from certain remarkable parts of his dress, was that day called 'Straw Hat' and 'Yellow Waistcoat' - titles under which he gained so much honour that he may well be proud of them for the rest of his life. He was now at the prow, now at the stern, now in the water to the neck, and again he was tugging hard at the oar; in short, he seemed to be the chief instrument of deliverance.

Having pulled up as far as they could in the still water, they approached the desperate current formerly noticed as having swept away the two elms, and fearlessly dashed into its tumultuous waves. For a moment the spectators were in the most anxious doubt as to the result for, though none could pull a stronger oar, yet the boat, in crossing a distance equal to its own length, was swept down 200 yards. Ten yards more would have dashed them to atoms on the lower stone-wall. But they were now in comparatively quiet water and, availing themselves of this, they pulled up again to the park, in the space between two currents, and passed with a little less difficulty, though in the same manner, the second and third streams, and at length reached the houses. The spectators gave them three hearty cheers. By this time the Kerrs had been left scarcely three feet of ground to stand on, under the back wall of the houses. A pleasing sight it was to see the boat touch that tiny strand, and the despairing family taken on board. After they were safely stowed, 'Yellow Waistcoat' was observed wading, and sounding his way with a pole, till he reached the west end of the building, where he pounced upon an enormous hog which he lugged down to the boat, and threw in as easily as if it had been a rabbit. "My indignation was stirred up against the Kerrs," said Mr. Suter, "thinking that, at such a time, they could have thought of risking Munro's life for such a purpose." But I was afterwards pleased to learn that it was to preserve "poor Widda Ross's soo, which was a' that was noo left till her."

How anxiously did the spectators watch every motion of the little boat that was now so crowded as very much to impede the rowers. They crossed the two first streams, and finally drew up for the last and dreadful trial. There the frail bark was again whirled down and, notwithstanding all their exertions, the stern just touched the wall. The prow, however, was in stiller water; one desperate pull; she sprang forward in safety, and a few more strokes of the oar landed the poor people amongst 50 or 60 of their assembled friends. Then was there a meeting between parents and son! What gratulations! What greetings and embracings! What grappling of hearts and moisture of eyes ensued! All crowded round them to obtain one squeeze of their hands. "Hoot toot, nonsense!" cried the weather-beaten Rodney, dashing his rough hand across his eyes, "What's this o't? Toots! I canna stand this mair than you, bairns. Od, I maun just greet it oot."

Old Kerr's account interested them all. Seeing their retreat cut off by the flood, they attempted to wade ashore. But the nearer the shore the deeper and more powerful was the current. The moment was awful. The torrent increased on all sides and night, dark night, was spread over them. The stream began to be too deep for the niece, a girl of twelve years of age. She lost heart, and began to sink. At this alarming crisis, Kerr seems to have been gifted with preternatural strength and presence of mind. He seized the trembling girl and placed her on his back and, shoulder to shoulder with his wife, he providentially, but with the greatest difficulty, regained his own house. Between eight and nine o'clock, he groped his way, and led his wife and niece up into the garret. He could not tell how long they remained there, but supposed it might be till about two o'clock next morning, when the roof began to fall. To avoid being crushed to death, he worked anxiously till he drove down the partition separating them from the adjoining house. Fortunately for him, it was composed of wood and clay, and a partial failure he found in it very much facilitated his operations. Having made their way good, they remained there till about eight o'clock in the morning, when the strength of the water without became so great that it bent inwards the bolt of the lock of the house door, till it had no greater hold of the staple than the eighth part of an inch. Aware that if the door should give way, the back wall of the house would be swept down by the rush of the water inwards and that they would be crushed to atoms, he rummaged the garret and fortunately found a bit of board and a few nails. Standing on the stair, he placed one end of it against the door, and the other on the hatch forming the entrance to the garret, and so nailed it firmly down. At last the roof of the second house began to crack over their heads, and Kerr forced a way for himself and his companions through the thatch, as has been already told.

"We syne crawled out ower the tap o' the neist hoose," said Kerr, in telling his own story, "and, on our way, Jean's leg gaed throw an awfu' gap atween the lumm and the roof. I then thocht to try Meggy Ross's winda in the front, but Jean wudna lat me, for fear I might fa' i' the water, an' syne she thocht a' wad be lost. I then gid to the back, and tried to get into Hugh's but I wusna' fit to break the kebbers o't; an' it was as weel, for a pairt o't soon fell. I then teuk for the grun', and drappit doon on a wee bit spat, where I fand an auld cupple log, which Hugh had bocht for fire. I heezed it up. There was a hunnin pin in't, and that was like a stap, and sae I gat them doon, praised be the Lord!" Here the poor man gave a heartfelt sigh of gratitude. "I then brak Hugh's back winda, and we gat in. Hugh's twa kists war soomin' through the room like onything. There was a cauf bed and some claes there, and that keepit huz some warm; and, as soon as it was some clear, Jean wadna' bide in, for fear o' the hoose fa'in'. Whan we saw the boat first, we thocht it was for huz; but what was our thocht when we saw it whurlin' awa doon the water again!" "Did you pray at all?" demanded Mr. Suter. "Deed, Sir, I dinna ken fit we did, but fan we heard the hooses fa'in' aboot huz, and it sae dark, troth we couldna think o' onythin' but death."

CHAPTER 9

CONTINUATION OF THE OCCURRENCES ON THE LEFT BANK OF THE RIVER FINDHORN, BELOW THE COULTERNOSE

AGAIN Yellow-waistcoat and his gallant fellows plied the oar, the boat darted down the stream, and then, labouring against the counter current of the Burn of Moy, it with difficulty reached its destination, a lonely cottage among the alders, a little way above the bridge (Plate 30). There three helpless old women, one of them for years bed-rid, were confined in their flooded dwelling, part of the back wall of which had already given way. No sooner had the boat touched the front, than Yellow-waistcoat sprang out, knocked in the window, and entered with Grant. They found the inmates sitting on chairs which, though placed in a wooden roofed bed, were still immersed in water, which was 4 feet deep in the house. They were already nearly dead with cold, and certainly could not have existed many hours longer. Yellow-waistcoat and Grant lifted them, one by

PLATE 30. HOUSES OF THE THREE OLD WOMEN AT THE BURN OF MOY

one, through the window, and they were soon landed where Mr. Suter was ready to administer to them from a bottle and glass. Being conveyed to the house in a cart, some warm broth was given them from the plentiful provision of it made for the people by Mrs. Suter's orders, and they were put to bed. As Mr. Suter dealt whisky to the brave fellows who had risked their lives, he offered Sergeant Grant a second dram. "Na, I thank ye, Sir," said the Sergeant, eyeing it askance, and retreating beyond the influences of its temptation, "I like it ower weel, an' if I tak' it I may forget mysel', an' God kens we need to hae a' oor wits aboot us the day. But an we get a' the poor fouk safe, I'se no' say but I'se get fou."

John Smith, who had been rescued from the Earnhill Island, William Smith and Tam Fraser now manned the boat; but Yellow-waistcoat was still at the post of danger in the cause of humanity. They were eager to attempt to save poor Funns, who still remained with his family in the critical situation discovered by Mr. Suter's telescope. But a consultation being held as to the state of the boat, it was declared by all to be too small and fragile for so desperate a voyage. It was accordingly determined that they should row across to the Moy embankment, near Rodney's house, where a larger boat was moored. To effect this, they were compelled to act precisely as they had done in going to Stripeside. But, unfortunately, on entering the third stream, they permitted the boat to glide down with it, in the hope that it would carry them in safety through the gate of the field, and across the road into that beyond it. In this, however, they were mistaken, and the boat was swamped. Fortunately for them, however, they were carried into smooth water and, by wading shoulder deep, they reached the large boat. Having brought her up, they soon righted the first boat, which they tied to a pillar of the gate that appeared above water. Getting on the top of a wall, they attempted to drag the large boat through the gateway, against the stream; but it was filled with water, swamped and, notwithstanding all their exertions, they found it impossible to get it up. The anxiety of those on shore was great. The brave fellows were seen wading with their heads only above water, till they made their way to the smaller boat which was now all they had to trust to. Finding it impossible to get the boat over the wall, they rowed along the road till they were hid by a plantation. The fears of the spectators became excessive, being aware that they were proceeding to a place where the strong stream broke into a cataract over the wall. Their apprehensions were but too well founded. The boat was overwhelmed; and, had not the men most providentially caught and clung like bees to a haycock that happened to be floating past at the moment, they must have been lost. They were carried along with it till it stuck in some young alder trees, where each of them grasped a bough, and the haycock sailed away, leaving them, where those on shore could just see them, at times endeavouring to support themselves among the weak and brittle branches. "Send for a boat!" was the first sentence that came from them. "What has become of your own?" shouted some one in return. "A boat! a boat! - send for a bo-o-oat," was the only response. Some thoughtless creature among the crowd bellowed out, "Why don't you use your own bo-o-oat?" There was a degree of mimicry in the tone of his voice that excited a momentary smile; but the next instant a hoarse murmur of disapprobation went round, and the abashed caitiff slunk away behind backs, to shun the general indignation he had excited. For two hours these brave men hung there and a thousand schemes were proposed for their rescue, and all successively rejected. Towards five o'clock, Dr. Brands and Sergeant Grant had already got ropes, and were preparing to make the hazardous attempt of swimming to their aid, when, to the astonishment and joy of all assembled, they beheld Yellow-waistcoat baling out the water from the boat with his straw-hat. Soon afterwards they were seen pulling along the road, and making for the bridge of Moy. On their way thither, they were the means of saving Betty Findlay, the celebrated biscuit-baker, who, in endeavouring to wade across the bridge, was swept off her feet and was floating down, supported by the buoyancy of her outspread drapery, when they fortunately caught and rescued her.

The circumstances attending the recovery of the boat are fully equal to most of those conveniently marvellous coincidences so serviceable to novelists. William Smith, being unable to hold on longer by the boughs, let himself gently down into the water with the hope of finding bottom. "I feel the boat!" shouted he to his companions; and, strange as it may seem, the small boat, which had last swamped with them, had actually drifted to the root of the very tree whither fortune had carried them! But this was not all. Some salmon nets and ropes had also, by the strangest accident, been lodged there. One of these Smith contrived to pull up with his foot and, making a noose, and slipping it on his great toe, he descended once more and managed to fix the rope round the stern of the boat. Having passed the rope over a high branch of a tree, he threw the end of it to his companions. "Now, haul upon that, my lads!" cried he with great glee, and joining with them in chorus, they, with much trouble, succeeded in righting the boat. The oars, being fixed to the side with iron pins, were all safe. Mr. Suter ordered the men up to the house for warmth and refreshment.

It was now that an alarm arose in the house of Moy, where the water began bursting up in columns through the floor of the lower storey, to the horror of the maids who lost all heart, and began weeping and wailing, believing that the universal deluge was about to be forthwith re-enacted. "For whan the very yearth begins to spew out water," argued they, philosophically, "fit can be expeckit but we'll be a' drooned?" The phenomenon was merely the result of the covered drains being surcharged, and their running level destroyed by the flood in the river and burn.

The boat being transported to the spot most convenient for embarking for the Broom of Moy, it was manned by Sergeant Grant; Andrew Smith, Broom of Moy; John Fraser, of the same place; John Smith of Earnhill; and Dr. Brands. The first house they made for was that occupied by a family of the name of Cumin, consisting of a poor invalid old man, father-in-law to Funns; his wife, nearly as infirm; their daughter, an elderly woman; and her son, a boy (Plate 31). By the time they reached the cottage, its western side was entirely gone, and the boat was pushed in at the gap. Not a sound was heard within, and they suspected that all were drowned; but, on looking through a hole in a partition, they discovered the unhappy inmates, roosted like fowls on the beams of the roof. They were, one by one, at last transferred safely to the boat, half dead with cold; and, melancholy to relate, the old man's mind, being too much enfeebled to withstand the agonizing apprehensions he had suffered, was now utterly deranged.

PLATE 31. COTTAGE OF OLD CUMIN'S FAMILY DURING THE FLOOD

After landing the Cumins, the next house of the hamlet the boat went to was that of Widow Speediman, an old bed-rid woman, with whom resided her niece, Isabella Morrison, an elderly person. One of the walls of this house was gone, and the roof was only kept up by resting on a wooden boarded bed. Here those in the boat beheld a most harrowing spectacle. Up to the neck in water sat the niece, scarcely sensible, and supporting what was now the dead body of her aunt, with the livid and distorted countenance of the old woman raised up before her. The story will be best told in her own words, though at the risk of some prolixity.

"It was aboot eight o'clock, an' my aunty in her bed, fan I says till her, Aunty, the waters are cumin' aboot's; an' I had hardly spoken fan they waur at my back. 'Ging tae my kist,' says she to me, 'an' tak oot some things that are to be pit aboot me fan I'm deid.' I had hardly takken oot the claes fan the kist was floated bodalie through the hoos. 'Gie me a haud o' your hand, Bell,' says my aunty, 'an' I'll try an help ye into the bed.' 'Ye're nae fit to help me,' says I, 'I'll tak a haud o' the stoop o' the bed.' And sae I gat in. I think we waur strugglin' i' the bed for aboot twa hoors; and the water floatit up the cauf-bed, and she lyin' on't. Syne I tried tae keep her up, an' I took a haud o' her shift to try to keep her life in. But the waters waur aye growin'. At last I got her up wi' ane haun' to my breest, and hed a haud o' the post o' the bed wi' the ither. An' there wuz ane jaw o' the water that cam' up tae my breest, an' anither jaw cam' an' fuppit my aunty oot o' my airms. 'Oh! Bell, I'm gane!' says she; and the waters just chokit her. It wuz a dreadfu' sicht to see her! That wuz the ficht an' struggle she had for life! Willin' wuz she to save that! An' her haun', your honour! hoo she focht wi' that haun'! It wad hae drawn tears o' pity fae a heathen! An' then I had a dreedfu' spekalation for my ain life, an' I canna tell the conseederable moments I was doon in the water, an' my aunty abeen me. The strength o' the waters at last brak the bed, an' I got to the tap o't; an' a dreedfu' jaw knockit my head to the bed-post; an' I wuz for some time oot o' my senses. It was surely the death-grip I had o' the post; an' surely it wuz the Lord that waukened me, for the dead sleep had cum'd on me, an' I wud hae faun, and been droon't in the waters! After I cam' to mysel' a wee, I feelt something at my fit, an' I says tae mysel', this is my aunty's head that the waters hae torn aff! I feelt wi' my haun', an' tuk haud o't wi' fear an' trumlin'; an' thankfu' was I fan I faund it to be naething but a droon't hen! Aweel, I climbed up, an' got a haud o' the cupple, an' my fit on the tap o' the wa', an' susteened mysel' that way fae maybe aboot hauf-past ten that night till three next aifterneen. I suppose it wuz twelve o'clock o' the day before I saw my aunty again, after we had gane doon thegither, an' the dreadfu' ocean aboot huz, just like a roarin' sea. She was left on a bank o' san', leanin' on her side, and her moo was fou o' san'. Fouk wondered I didna dee o' cauld an' hunger; but baith cauld an' hunger waur unkent by me, wi' the terrification I wus in wi' the roarin' o' the waters aboot me. Lord save me."*

The corpse of the poor old woman Speediman was put into a cart, together with her niece Bell, whose state of exhaustion was so great that it was difficult to tell which was the living, and which the dead, body.

The boat next rescued three old women, of the name of Macdonald, one of whom afterwards died in Elgin Hospital, from dropsy brought on by cold and wet. They then pushed for Mr. Munro's house, which was surrounded by the water, and had a considerable stream running past it that undermined a part of the offices. The horrors of that dreadful day affected Mrs. Munro's mental, as well as her bodily, health, and it was most fortunate that a large straw stack was floated from the west end of the buildings and deposited in such a position at the east end of them as to cut off from Mrs. Munro's sight the distant view of the perilous situation of Funns and his family. The Munros were relieved, and safely landed.

Every thought was now turned towards poor Funns, seen far over in the midst of the inundation, with his family, and cattle, clustered like flies on their little speck of land. It was between six and seven o'clock, the weather was clearer, and the waters were subsiding. Yet was the enterprise the most hazardous of any, and

* *This poor woman has since become a perfect cripple from rheumatism.*

none but the most skilful rowers were allowed to undertake it. These were Sergeant Grant; Peter Macintyre, overseer to Mr. Grant of Kincorth; and Andrew Smith, of the Broom of Moy. But a fourth was wanting. "What are ye blubberin' there for, ye splay-fittit gouk?" cried Smith to a certain James Fraser, who was standing on the top of a wall, rubbing his eyes and looking anxiously over the water in great distress; "are ye blubberin' because ye canna see yer hoos, that's a' sweept awa? What need a single man like ye care for that?" "It's no ma hoos, man," replied the other; "it's no ma hoos, but ma trunk - ma blue kist. A' the bit penny that I hae earned for thirty years by-past was in't. But, as ye say, it's wrang to repine. I hae yet life an' health; sae tak' me into the boat, for Funns, poor man, and his family, are even waur aff than me, an' may tyne life itsel' an' we dinna succour them. I've twa hands left still: she hasna ta'en them fae me, thank God!" and, so saying, he leaped into the boat; and, being peculiarly adroit, he had one of the larboard oars assigned him, that being the lower side of the boat.

One wide inundation stretched from Munro's house to the tiny spot where Funns and his family were; and five tremendously tumultous streams raged through it with elevated waves. The moment they dashed into the first of these, they were whirled down for a great way; but, having once got through it, they pulled up in the quieter water beyond to prepare for the next; and, in doing so, Sergeant Grant stood in the prow, with a long rope, the end of which was fixed to the boat, and wherever he thought he had footing, he sprang out and dragged them up. The rest followed his example, and in this way they were enabled to start afresh with a sufficient advantage, and they crossed all the other streams in the same manner. The last they encountered, being towards the middle of the flood, was fearful and carried them very far down. But Funns himself, overjoyed to behold them, waded towards them and gave them his best help to drag up the boat again. Glad was he to see his wife and children safely set in the boat. The perils of their return were not few, but they were at length happily landed opposite Moy House, where the same hospitality greeted them that had already cheered so many before them. The women had suffered so much from cold that the youngest daughter fainted on being brought near the fire. Dr. Brands suggested that she should be put to bed with some of the maids, to restore the animal temperature. "Put her in amang my bairns," cried a woman who was standing by; "there are five o' them in ane o' Mrs. Suter's beds." The proposal was adopted; and warm wine, warm broth, and a good night's sleep, perfectly restored her.

Funns and his family having been driven from their dwelling at about eight o'clock on Monday evening, waded to the only place they could fly to. They had just time to throw blankets over them, and he fortunately had the precaution to carry out a small bag of meal. His cows, pony and sheep being let out, had the instinct to take to the same spot where there was, fortunately for them, a rick of straw. The area of this fragment of yet uncovered ground was rapidly diminished as the flood rose; and the poor quadrupeds, being chilled by standing so long in the water, were continually pressing inwards on them. Seizing a passing log, Funns contrived to make a kind of seat for his companions with it, and an old box. A little meal and whisky was all the nourishment they had. The wind and rain beat on them so fiercely that it seemed as if the spark of life itself must be extinguished within them. "It was an awfu' thing," as Funns himself said, "to be expectin' every minute to be swept into yeternity in sic an unprepared state, and our lugs driven deaf wi' the roarin' o' the waters, an' the crashin' o' the great trees that cam' bommin' past us ilka minute; an' a'thing dark aboot us, an' naething to be seen but the far distant glimmer o' Maister Suter's caunils. But their licht was some little comfort. It seemed as if the Lord hadna just a'thegither forsaken us." Upon being asked if he had prayed, "Aye, Sir, lang and strang," replied he earnestly, "an' mair fervently than I ever did in my life afore; and thankful to Providence was I when I kent my prayers waur heard. Fan the grey o' the mornin' cam', I began to notice twa white things standin' oot o' the roughest part o' the water below me. I couldna mak' oot fit they waur, an' troth, sometimes I couldna help thinkin' it might be the ghaists o' some o' my friends that war drooned, tarrying till we should come, an I was gey an' fleid. But as the licht made a'thin' mair clear, I ventured to gie them anither glour, an' syne I saw they war the twa white stumps o' a stranded tree; yonder they're stickin' up yet. But, on lookin' round me, I saw naething but waters on ilka side o' me, an' Stripeside in ruins, an' the hooses o' the Broom an' a', an' the awfu' gap in the brig far aboon me. I thocht my wife, poor body, wad faunt gin she saw 't, an' sae I happit up her heid in the blanket, by ways o' keepin' her warm. I lookit round me again, and then it was that I saw the Lord had heard my prayers, for the Greeshop embankments war broken; an' fit wad hae become o' us, an' they hadna gi'en way. I feelt a warm glow come o'er my hairt; an' at nine o'clock, fan the waters begood to fa' a wee thing, I bad' my wife look roun' an' see what had happened, an' praise the Lord for a' His mercies, for that noo we had houps. It was a great mercy the brakin' o' thae banks. I'se be gratefu' to God a' my days. It's muckle comfort till a poor man to feel that the Lord is his friend." These poor people had everything in their house carried off, but what most distressed the wife was the loss of a tubful of clothes. "It just sailed oot at the door," said she, "an' was whamled afore my vera twa een."

Amidst so many perils, it is certainly very wonderful that so few fatal results took place. I have only one to add here to that of the poor woman Speediman, and it is a case less to be attributed to the flood, than to carelessness and mismanagement. The son of Duncan Spence, residing at the north end of what was the bridge of Findhorn, had got a boat up on Wednesday the 5th, with the intention of turning a penny by ferrying people across at the bridge pool. He had no oars; and he and his companions, in poling the boat over with their first fare, allowed the stream to carry it so far down, that they found it necessary to drag it up again. While the two assistants got out, and began to haul by the rope, Spence remained in the boat to guide it with the pole but, at length, the current became so strong that it pulled the rope out of the men's hands. Seeing the boat at the mercy of the stream, Spence attempted to leap ashore but fell into the water and sank. His hand appeared again for a moment, and he was seen no more till his body was found, an hour and a half afterwards, a little below the Broom of Moy.

PLATE 32. WATERSIDE, AFTER THE FLOOD

It is pleasing to turn from a distressing subject, such as this, to the anecdote I am about to tell. Soon after the subsidence of the flood, Mr. Alexander, the artist, then at Moy, happening to take a walk about the grounds, observed some one at the edge of a field, working up to the knees in the mud of a ditch. Curiosity led him to approach, when, to his surprise, he discovered old Rodney. "What are you doing there, my good friend?" demanded Mr. Alexander. "Od, Sir, I'm howkin' oot something like a kist here." "Do you think you have found a treasure, Rodney?" asked Mr. Alexander. "Troth, Sir, I'm no sure," replied the veteran; "I'm thinkin', for ane thing, that it's fu' o' water; but, an' I'm no mista'en in the colour o't, I'm jalousin' it may be the poor chield Fraser's blue kist, wi' a' he had i' the warld in 't. But it's lockit fast, an' I'm glad that you're here to see that it's a' safe for me; Troth, it's just the vera kist," added Rodney, as he at last succeeded in bringing it to the surface. "Weel, I'm rail glad o't, for the poor chield's sake!" People talk of the poetical justice of fiction, but the plain matter-of-fact of everyday human life sometimes proves to us that the Great Governor of the

Universe occasionally condescends, for His own good purposes, to mould the most insignificant matters into moral lessons for our improvement. Let us not therefore refuse to turn by the way-side to read them.

PLATE 33. JAMES NICOL'S HOUSE, AFTER THE FLOOD

To catalogue or estimate the damage done by the flood in the plain of Forres, on the left bank of the Findhorn, would be a vain attempt. Besides the houses I have particularised as carried off or destroyed, there are the Waterside houses very much ruined (Plate 32); the houses on James Nicol's farm reduced to a perfect skeleton (Plate 33), and in the hamlet of Broom of Moy (Plate 34), nine or ten houses were so completely demolished that even the vestiges of

PLATE 34. HOUSES AT BROOM OF MOY, AFTER THE FLOOD

many of them have disappeared. The house that Funns occupied, now a ruin, is equally cut off from both banks of the river. He was very desirous to show it to me, and volunteered to carry me across two rapid streams, which have permanently established themselves to the northward of it. "Ye should see it yersel', Sir," said he, "for seein's believin'." I cheerfully acceded to his proposal and, aided by a pole to grope his way with, he succeeded in transporting me on his back. He gave me the whole story on the spot; and there, as if it had never been visited since, lay the old box, the log, and some other little matters. "Here stood I," said Funns, placing himself in attitude; "Here stood I, tryin' to keep the great muckle trees - Sir Thomas's trees," interjected he, *sotto voce*, glancing knowingly at the same time to a gentleman who was with me, "Here I stood, to keep them fae bommin' against us, an' sweepin' us a' to yeternity." We saw enough, even then, to satisfy us of the danger he ran from this cause, for the whole ruined plain, for many acres around us, was so covered with enormous trees that it resembled an uprooted forest. Indeed, if they could have been set up, and all their branches restored to them, they would have formed a forest of great grandeur. Among others, I at once recognised the magnificent three-limbed ash that grew above the Bridge of Ferness. The matted mass of its roots still measured 15 feet in diameter, and portions of the gravel bank in which it grew, still adhered to them. The houses of Stripeside, when viewed in front, with the far-stretched flat country towards Findhorn behind them, all of which was ruined by the flood, have a strangely wild and desolate appearance (Plate 35).

PLATE 35. HOUSES OF STRIPESIDE FROM THE SOUTH, WITH FINDHORN IN THE DISTANCE

Mr. Macleod of Dalvey's loss in land, plantations, and embankments, cannot be much under £1000. I am convinced, from all I have seen, that Mr. Grant of Glenmoriston's damage, on his estate of Moy, in embankments and land swept away, could not be estimated at much less than £8000. Mr. Grant of Kincorth has not suffered to a great extent, owing to the river running with less violence over his property, which is farther from the point where the flood burst from the upper country. I even conceive that he must often gain in such cases by the deposition of mud, which naturally floats farther than the heavier matters. Wherever the waters reached, the crops were ruined; and nothing could be more deplorable than to see the richest wheat, and other grains, which had been buried many feet in the sand, exposed again in certain places by the cutting of water-runs. The losses of the poor hereabouts were very great, seventy-five cases of families reduced to misery having been reported from the parish of Dyke.

A great deal of damage was done along the whole course of the Burn, called the Lethen, Earlsmill, Brodie, Dyke, Dalvey, and Moy Burn, as it passes each of these places respectively, but my limits forbid me to detail it. One circumstance that happened, in consequence of the appendix flood of the 27th, however, I must notice. A poor, old, frail, and both bodily and mentally infirm couple, were in bed in a cottage near the Burn of Earlsmill. In rushed the water, and filled the house four feet deep, and the miserable creatures were compelled to remain in this situation till it subsided. But what will the reader say when he is told that they were the very individual unfortunate Cumins, who were rescued by a boat from the Broom of Moy on the 4th!

A lady, who felt a charitable interest in these poor people, visited them at the Broom of Moy after the subsidence of the flood. She found the old man lying on a damp bed, under a defenceless roof, exposed to wind and rain. His moans were unceasing, save when his wandering mind led him to talk wildly of drowning, and of the water being at his feet. His wife, scarcely less imbecile, sat rocking herself to and fro on a low seat, called a *sunkie*, before a fire which she in vain tried to make burn, complaining to herself of a hurt in one of her legs, received at the time the flood filled the house, when the daughter, by an almost miraculous exertion of strength, raised her parents and her son up to the place whence they were rescued. Unconscious whence the blessing came, the poor creatures eagerly drank the wine the lady had brought them; and when, a little afterwards, she looked for the bottle that she might give a glass to their daughter, she found that with the selfishness dotage sometimes brings with it, the old woman had contrived to hide it in a corner of her bed.

Their daughter, who is quite deaf, was employed in digging various articles out of the sand. Her hand had been severely cut by an adze, while in the act of dragging up her parents from danger. "It will be o' nae use," said she, refusing to have it bound up, "for I maun aye be dabbling." It was the lady I allude to who made them comfortable in the cottage, where they were disturbed by the flood of the 27th. But the succession of miseries to which they have been exposed have not been without their good result, since they have but widened that field for benevolent exertion in which a truly angelic mind delights to occupy itself.

CHAPTER 10

The Plain of Forres on the right bank of the Findhorn, to the seaport of that name, and the Altyre Burn

THE view of the inundated plain of Forres from the Castle-hill of the Borough, on the morning of the 4th, though truly magnificent, was such as to overwhelm the mind of the spectator with dismay. From Mundole, about two miles to the west of Forres, and from Forres to Findhorn, about five miles to the north, the whole plain was under water. The river and the burn met under the Castle-hill, and the inundation spread over the rich and variously cropped fields, and over hedges, gardens, orchards, and plantations. In this 'world of waters', the mansions of proprietors, the farm-houses and offices, the trees, and especially the hedge-rows, giving its peculiarly English appearance to the environs of Forres, the ricks of hay, and here and there a few patches of corn standing on situations more elevated than the rest, presented a truly wonderful scene. Terror was painted on the countenances of some, and amazement on those of everyone.

One-half of the bridge of Forres over the burn, immediately under the Castle-hill, had disappeared during the night, having parted longitudinally; and, over the part that yet remained, the people on the west side of the burn were hastily removing their families, cattle and furniture to the hill on which Forres stands, after having waded to the middle to rescue them from the flood. It was pleasing to witness the efforts of all to save their neighbours' persons and property. One poor aged and sick woman was got into a cart, and dragged through the water by a number of respectable men, whilst one held an umbrella over her as she lay, to shelter her from the rain. A man, who had been saving the furniture of a poor neighbour, fell over the bridge and was swept under the broken arch, carried down by the stream, and then most wonderfully cast on the bank by the mere force of the torrent. "Fit did ye think o' when ye was in the water?" demanded a by-stander. "Think o'?" replied the other; "feggs, I was thinkin' hoo I could get oot, and hoo I could catch my bonnet."

A figure was observed from the Castle-hill, struggling through the distant waters on the Pilmuir road. It was a man breast-deep in water, and manifestly in great danger, and great anxiety for his safety arose among the spectators. But, as he drew nearer, the crowd, forgetting his peril, burst into a loud laugh; and truly there was some cause, for this apparently drowning man was exerting all his strength of arm to support an umbrella, as if determined to keep his hat and head dry, whatever should become of the rest of his person.

Mr. Gordon, chief-magistrate of Forres, had, on the preceding night, brought his lady and family into the town, and had returned to his house at Edgefield with the intention of having his servants and cattle removed. On reaching the approach leading from the turnpike-road to his house, he met the river marching knee-deep. He found it was too late to leave Edgefield that night as the water, covering the whole estate of Greeshop, surrounded the house, three feet deep, whilst a strong current roared along through the still water in front. He therefore ordered the cattle to be turned loose to shift for themselves; and, as the water inundated the ground-floor, he and the servants ascended to the upper storey where they spent the night, with the main body of the flood thundering along behind them, and the currents raging in front. Anxious to get to Forres on the morning of Tuesday the 4th, he got a ladder applied to a window of the upper storey, by which he descended to the back of a stout horse and, with a servant sitting before him, he set out on his precarious journey. He got easily through the still water, passed the current with very great difficulty, and at last reached Forres. As the fires at Edgefield were drowned out, and the store-rooms flooded, Mr. Gordon was desirous of sending some bread to his people. One of the most daring men in Forres was, therefore, dispatched with it, mounted on a powerful horse, but by the time he reached the current it was impassable, and he was compelled to abandon the attempt.

The Reverend Duncan Grant, minister of the parish, who went to the top of the tower of the tollbooth to see if he could descry any boats coming, declares the view from that elevated position to have been the most awful and magnificent he ever beheld. "Never," said he, "did I before see so great a manifestation of the might and majesty of God, in the dispensations of His Providence; nor evidence so convincing of the weakness, the utter helplessness, of man, when his Maker 'pleads with him by His great power;' nor of the blessedness and safety possessed by those who are shielded by the arm which controls 'the balancings of the clouds,' and the roarings of the deep; and Who, dwelling on high, is mightier than the noise of many waters; nor of the misery that must result from opposition to a Being with Whom there is majesty so terrible." Whilst looking out from the bartizan of the tower, towards the house of Tannachy* that rose from a dry speck of green afar off in the midst of the waters, Mr. Grant descried a boat. His eyes followed it, during its long voyage, while it scudded across fields and tilted over hedges and banks, and on going down afterwards to the Castle-hill, he saw it threading between the hedges of Edgefield and, after tossing on the current that arrested the horse, it sailed down the turnpike road towards Forres, and landed at the Little-bridge-end, amidst the cheers of the multitude. This was the '*Nancy*' of Findhorn; and as I think an extract from her log-book will form a curious item in this eventful history, I shall here give it as received from Donald Munro, or, as more

* *Publisher's Note: Tannachy is today known as Invererne.*

commonly called, *Young Whisky,** fisherman of that port, who was aboard of her. The rest of her crew were William Smith, Alexander Masson, John Bremner, James Masson, with James Thompson and Alexander Roy, salmon-fishers, who were volunteers.

"*Tuesday, August 4, 1829.* - Sailed from Findhorn at half-past ten A.M.; wind blowing hard from N.N.E.; tide high, but considerably against us; sea in the bay rough, so that we shipped much water. In danger of foundering from trees and other land wreck running foul of us. Breakers ahead on the sea embankment of Netherton. Tried to run up the channel of the Forres Burn, but the strength of the current drove us on a bank, and nearly capsized us. Hauled our wind, sailed west, and coasted along the north side of the embankment, till we came abreast of the farm steading, where the water ran very nearly over the top of it, and there, with some difficulty, we dragged the boat across. Set all sail, scudded, with a fair wind, over Mr. Davidson's farm, and steered for a small house on the north side of the estate of Tannachy. Fell in with a very strong current there, but, by the great efforts of all hands, fetched the house, garrisoned by Rory Fraser, shoemaker, his daughter and two children, who were sitting aloft on twa or three deals, placed on the kebbers of the house, wi' the water up at their feet, and without a morsel to eat. Brought the stern of the boat to the door to receive the inmates, and sung out to Rory. His daughter and her twa laddies, terribly fleggit, and makin' muckle din, came down a wild trap kind o' a stair, and were handed aboard. Rory himsel' was unca scared like. The house had been shaking violently for the greater part of the night. Made sail for Mr. Williamson's, Westertown of Tannachy, sounding all the way over the fields, with three or four feet water, her bottom grazing the tops of the wheat and other grain. About noon got to the house, which had upwards of three feet of water in its hold. Mrs. Williamson and three bairns, wi' a feck o' her braws, and best gear, were safely dry-docked in chairs in a bed. The servants, and one of the daughters, were paddling about the room, *skellachin'* at a sad rate. The other Miss was up stairs, and had gane to bed. Stowed them all away in the boat, and the bed, chest of drawers, chairs, and other such craft, being lightened of their cargoes, began to float through the room. We also took in a maid-servant, twa bit lassies, and twa men. Mr. Williamson and his grieve, thinking that the waters were ebbing, remained to look after the sheep and other live stock, wha were in a woeful state. We now hauled up for the house of Tannachy, and landed our passengers on a dry spot at the back of the house where they were received by Major Grant. Sailed from Tannachy, and

* *All our northern fishermen have what they call 'to-names', which are rendered necessary where frequent intermarriages create a repetition of the same family and Christian names among different individuals.*

steered by the west side of the square of offices to the grieve's house, but found that his people had already got out on horseback. Bore up, and steered in a S.W. course, and passing over dykes and corn fields, made Mr. Smyth's of Waterford. House deserted, and some of his bestial in a pitiful condition. Crossed the road, and made for John Macdonald's on the estate of Greeshop. Current between his house and Waterford very strong, and had nearly swamped us. Neared the house and hailed, and at last heard voices within. One of the crew jumped out, but found no bottom and was like to be drowned. He caught an oar, pushed nearer to the door, and found bottom, with five feet water on the walls. Found John, his wife, and two other women. Got them on board safe, but sair drucket. We then stood up for Edgefield, and saw, on the starboard hand, a strange witch-looking woman, far across in the middle o' the water, a little below Funns' house. She had on a white sort o' dress, wi' a black bonnet on her head, and looked like something by common. We thought she waved to us, but there were currents running about her that nae boat, biggit by human hands, could ha' lived in and, unless she was Davy Jones' wife, it is a raial mystery how she could wather it.* Came alongside the front of Edgefield; hailed a man, who was climbing up a ladder on the outside; answered, "All's well!" and asked if Mr. Gordon had sent us. Told him "No," on which he said they did not want our assistance, and that we might sheer off. Made sail for the turnpike and, as we got into the road, saw a man catch a fine salmon in one of the fields a-starboard. Making way along the turnpike road, came up with a man who had got his grog aboard, and who would have been drowned if we had not hauled him into the boat. Coming abreast of Mr. Tulloch's, he gave us all a dram; but, when we landed our passengers at the old tanyard, I suppose the people thought we were all in the same state as the drunk man for, though they gave us plenty of cheek-music and cheering, no one ever said, "Colley, will ye taste?" Having taken in Mr. Smyth of Waterford's grieve, and two men-servants, we sailed down the market green, and by the end of the Leebrig, and out the road to Waterford. Mr. Smyth's servants waded in to look to their cattle, after which we sailed to John Macdonald's stable, abreast of which there was a strong and deep stream. Opened the doors, got ropes made fast to the halters of the two horses, and sailed across the stream with the ropes. The two men held them while we forced the horses into the stream. They swam across, and the men mounted them, and made the best of their way to Forres through the water. By this time the water had fallen eighteen inches on the side of the house; and it ebbed so fast as we sailed towards Tannachy, that we should not have been able to get the boat along, if we had not followed

* *This the reader will at once perceive was Funns himself.*

a ditch which led us to the sea-dike, over which we had great difficulty in hauling the boat. Got to our moorings at Findhorn about seven o'clock P.M." "Was it nae hard," said Munro, when delivering the above, "that, after a' that we had done, thay idle, weel-held-up loons, the Preventives, gat a' the praise i' the newspapers, while we poor fisher bodies were never mentioned at a', although the lazy lubbers never pat their noses oot ower the door the hale day."

Four other fishing-boats sailed from Findhorn, on the same charitable voyage. The second was the *Bounty*; crew - Robert Storm, Alexander Munro, James Masson, and William Munro. This boat went to Moy Carse, found the house deserted, and in danger of being swept down. Mr. and Mrs. Watson and family, to the number of 16 souls, were found in the stable-loft, sitting round a pot half filled with a peat fire. They were taken into the boat, and carried to Findhorn. The third boat, called the *Lovey*, was manned by Alexander Bremner, John Munro, Alexander Wright, Alexander Kelly, and George Munro. She sailed to Mr. Davidson's farm of Netherton, found 5 feet water in the house, and the people in a corn loft, starving of hunger; sailed back to Findhorn, and brought them provisions. The horses were forced to mount a stair to a temporary loft. The fourth boat was the *Findhorn*; Thomas Macdonald, officer of the fishery, skipper; crew - James Storm, John Munro, Hugh Wright, William Wright, John Masson, James Smith, John Elder. This boat was nearly carried into a strong current and swamped irrecoverably, but was saved by three of the crew jumping in up to their necks, and dragging her into stiller water. Having got among the corn, one of them spied a large salmon by the root of a tree and seized it by the tail, but the creature escaped; and, in the struggle, the man was laid on his back in the water. They touched at Tannachy and, some time afterwards, saw a man, near a corn-yard, holding up a hat on a long pole. Made towards him and discovered it to be Mr. Williamson* of Westertown, and his men servants, who were in great distress about 200 sheep that were drowning in a clover field. The boat went to the rescue of the beasts, and carried them, by twenty-five or thirty at a time, to a place of safety. On their way home they killed some hares with their sticks on the sea embankment, and picked up a large hog which had swam all the way from Edgefield, above three miles. The water between Tannachy and Findhorn was literally covered with wreck, furniture, cradles, saddles, cattle and sheep, and four inches of fine black mould was left on the beach. None of the sand banks of the bay were seen, as usual, at low tide; and, at full tide, not one drop of salt water was admitted within the bar! All the mussel-scalps were swept away, and the crops of bait destroyed for two or three years

* *Whose family was relieved by the first boat.*

to come. The fifth boat, called the *Star* - crewed by George Masson, William Wright, Robert Allan, John Masson, and William Wright, - visited Mr. Williamson's, Tannachy, and the farm of Netherton, but found no employment.

Before parting with these gallant men, who so readily launched their boats, in defiance of danger, to save the lives and property of their fellow creatures, I must earnestly call public attention to their high deservings, that they may not go without that honourable reward which they have so well merited. That there were different degrees of peril and usefulness I do not question; and, if so, it were well to ascertain, by strict inquiry, how these gradations may stand, and to mark them accordingly. Yellow-waistcoat and his brave companions, in their small boat, perhaps encountered the greatest risk. But no one who nobly volunteered in such a service, should be without some memorial to hand down to his children, in token of the good and glorious actions performed by their father, in the great floods of August, 1829.*

The harvest of firewood at Findhorn was immense. One mysterious character, called 'Muckle Jamie', carried home about 50 cargoes in his coble. This man is now a great-great-grandfather, yet he was never known to fail in crossing the bay with his coble, be the weather what it might, except once, when another man rowed the opposite oar. They were then indeed driven back, but Jamie instantly disembarked the man, and alone succeeded, in spite of wind and tide, whether by his own physical strength, or by some unseen aid, is still matter of speculation with some.

Though the ground immediately around the house of Tannachy was dry, yet the family were alarmed by the flooding of the sunk storey, from the drains, exactly as it happened at Moy. As Moy was the place of refuge on the left bank, so Tannachy, from being a central point of the inundation on the right bank, was similarly besieged, and displayed similar hospitality. Nothing could be more strange than to behold a sea of water from whatever window of the house one looked; to see the boats landing, and the sailors carrying the people on shore. Sweeping the eye round from Moy to Kincorth, Binsness, Findhorn, Kinloss, to Forres and the Cluny Hills, the space within that circle was one entire sheet of water, with here and there a trifling patch of green or yellow ground whither all the cattle in the vicinity had crowded; whilst the boats were seen sailing in various directions among the hedge-rows (Plate 36). *The inundation covered a space of something more than 20 square miles in the Plain of Forres.* Within this space, I may say the whole crop was destroyed. No one who has not seen this great theatre of the main action of this

* *I am happy to say that measures are now being taken to forward a subscription for a medal, to be bestowed on these gallant individuals.*

PLATE 36. TANNACHY HOUSE AND THE COUNTRY BELOW FORRES, FLOODED

disaster can form any conception of the desolation, both temporary and permanent, that was produced. As my friend the Reverend Duncan Grant remarks, "Before these floods was the Garden of Eden, and behind them a desolate wilderness." To particularise the damage would take a volume of itself. Of the beautiful Bridge of Findhorn, consisting of one arch of 95 feet, and two others of 75 feet span each, nothing now remains but a fragment of the northern landbreast, and part of the inclined approach from the south. To this, the ruins of the row of fishermen's houses that ran along the turnpike road, form a most appropriate foreground (Plate 37). A mile of the turnpike road between the bridge and Forres was ruined, and left in deep holes, full of salmon. After the flood the salmon were killed in great numbers in corn and potato fields, in bushes, and in hedges. A boy was seen with a rabbit in one hand and a salmon in the other, which he said "he had catched wi' his ain twa hands." Where there were no trees the rabbits were drowned in great numbers; but where there were plantations, and especially where there were spruces and larches, the creatures climbed them, and were saved. The damage done on the estate of Balnagieth has been given in at £416, but I conceive it to be greatly underrated. I also think that the loss on Mr. Peterkin's estate of Greeshop, &c., has been understated at £4150; the farms of Buchtily and Edgefield, belonging to that property, being in a manner completely ruined. Mr. Smyth's loss at Waterford is not more than £350, but the farm of Moy Carse, belonging to Mr. Grant of Glenmorriston, which paid £136 of rent, is now not worth 5 shillings, and a new cut of the river runs directly through it, and close by the house. These are a few samples only; but the Reverend Duncan Grant thinks that the loss of property of all kinds hereabouts cannot be much less than £20,000; and I confess that from all I have seen I am much inclined to be of the same opinion. The flood has produced 188 cases of utter destitution in the parish of Forres.

PLATE 37. BRIDGE OF THE FINDHORN AND FISHERMEN'S HOUSES, RUINED

The appendix flood of the 27th was only injurious because the other had preceded it, and left the whole country exposed. It was observed to break over above Edgefield about twelve o'clock, and soon afterwards it was seen marching, in what in military language is called double quick time, after two women who were coming along the turnpike road to Forres with great burdens of dry wood on their backs. One of them looking round, and seeing the water about to overtake her, threw down her load and ran. The other, unwilling to lose that she carried, quickened her speed, but seeing that she could not trot fast enough with so great a weight, she also let her burden go, and scudded after her companion. The river rolled on, overtook them, and before they could effect their escape, they were wading up to the knees.

And still the country lies at the mercy of the Findhorn, and frequently has it visited Forres since. It is easy to accuse the proprietors of supineness. But men are seldom supine where their own worldly concerns are at stake. The fact is, the matter is by no means easy where so many complicated interests are involved. No permanent security can be given to so great an extent of country, but by the whole proprietors joining in the execution of one great plan. This

Mr. Jardine, the celebrated engineer, has sketched out for them, in one bold straight line, slightly curved at the two extremities, and running from the Craig of Coulternose to the point called The Lakes, to be excavated to the dimensions of a sufficient channel for the river. A stream naturally labours to make its course as straight as possible. Were such an artificial cut made for the Findhorn here, its sides well defended, and its channel kept clear, there might be some hope that the proprietors on either bank might sleep in security as to the safety of their property. But the great obstacle to their repose would arise from the fact that nature can seldom be regulated or controlled in one way, without running riot in some other. A river breaking from the higher to the lower country, if left to itself, covers the plain with the debris of its floods, and thus gives a gradual and somewhat equable rise to its whole surface. But the moment the agriculturist begins to hem it in by embankments which prevent it from spreading over the plain, its deposits become confined to its bed. This is soon raised to a level with the plain and, as it goes on to rise, the elevation of the embankments requires to be increased, so that, by the alternate raising of the river's bed on the part of nature, and the heightening of the bulwarks on that of art, the channel is gradually converted into an artificial canal, running high above the level of the country through which it flows. Any one who may have noticed the tributary streams of the Val d'Arno, which are precisely so circumstanced, must be satisfied that a river so artificially treated, cannot fail, in a long course of years, to become a magazine of destruction, liable at any time to burst suddenly and awfully over the adjacent regions.

The devastations of the Burn of Forres were identified with those of the Findhorn; but, higher up, it did much damage both at Altyre and Sanquhar. Sir William Cumming had for years been lavishing his money and his good taste in the adornment of Altyre. The house was surrounded, and the greatest alarm excited. The splendid groups of rare evergreen, and other shrubs of magnificent growth that decorate the lawn, were in the greatest danger of being torn up. The havoc on the dressed banks, and among the extensive walks and shrubberies, was ruinous; and, in the lower or kitchen garden, over which the flood spread entirely, the current was running furiously among the hot-houses and pineries, and actually carried off the gardener on one of his melon frames, to take an aquatic excursion among his gooseberry bushes and cauliflowers. The ruin here forms one large item in Sir William's account of loss; and I am now about to proceed to another scene, where he has also been a severe sufferer.

CHAPTER 11

The River Lossie

THE River Lossie rises among the hills dividing the Findhorn from the Spey. Its course cannot be much more than 20 or 25 miles, through a direct line of country. It is nowhere very rapid, and the lower part of its run, from Birnie downwards, is winding and rather sluggish.

The damage done by the flood to Sir William Cumming's estate, above the Church of Dallas, is very great - so much so as to defy enumeration within the limits I must prescribe myself. At the haugh of Bethlem, the river came so furiously down, about four o'clock of the evening of the 3rd, that the house, situated at a great distance from the usual channel, was instantly flooded three or four feet deep, and the man's wife had no more than time to snatch up her child, and run for her life. The fine farm of Craig Roy, attached to the Mill of Dallas, was utterly ruined as to crop and soil, and the river opened an entirely new channel through the finest part of the land. The mill itself made a narrow escape. Much of the land of the opposite farm, on the right bank, was carried off; and farther down it swept away a wood of alder, and utterly ruined an arable haugh of several acres belonging to the glebe. At the manse it was 9½ feet above the usual level, where the breadth was about 430 feet. It came nearly up to the house, swept down the walls of the garden, and passed right through it.

About four o'clock in the afternoon, the river burst its left embankment, immediately below the narrow pass where it enters the open vale, and the whole force of the stream poured down over the inclined plain towards the village which, consisting of one street of thirty-two houses, running at right angles to it, lay at the distance of one-fifth of a mile from it. Entering broadside into the middle of the street, which is rather higher than the rest of its level, it established two furious currents running towards its two extremities. At about five o'clock on the morning of the 4th, the rush became so great that it rose three feet in the houses, and a boat might have sailed on the street. Alarm and confusion now prevailed, and people of both sexes, and of all ages, were seen struggling in the torrent. Some were taking their wives and children out of windows; others were carrying the young or the infirm away on their backs. Carts and horses were pressed into the service, and all were leaving their property to the mercy of the deluge. At length, by the strenuous exertions of the more vigorous, one hundred and twenty people with a number of children, and many cattle, were placed on dry and elevated ground. There was a certain John Grigor, better known by the name of 'Quarry Jock', a man of uncommon strength and active spirit, disposed to signalise himself in all cases of extremity, who was particularly useful. The greater part of the people were kindly received at the school-house and manse. "Our parson," said one of his parishioners to me, "had a great many more wives that morning than the Grand Sultan." Even so late as the evening of the 4th, Kenneth Maclean, a blacksmith, was nearly drowned in the street, but was fortunately saved by James Edwards, a shoemaker, who caught him by the clothes after he was under water. Maclean had remained to attend to a favourite sow that was about to have an accouchement; and this, strange to say, she had to the letter of the phrase; for the flood so inundated his premises that he was compelled to carry her up stairs to his own bed where, in due time, she presented him with a beautiful litter of promising young pigs. These, with the mother, being likely to do well, were speedily conveyed up into the garret, to remain there till her recovery should be perfected. The water continued to flow through the village, till a temporary bulwark was erected on the 5th. The poor people had their houses and furniture much injured, and their whole stock of winter fuel swept away.

PLATE 38. LAKE-BED OF KELLAS

Their crops were completely destroyed. Even such parts of them as were not buried in sand had their fructifying process completely arrested by the chill of the water. "Sir," said Mr. Cumming, mine host of the Altyre Arms, "It's no worth naething; it's just a' as an 'twere boiled at the roots, and has never filled onything to speak o'," and of this he showed me ocular demonstration by rubbing out some of the ears in his hand. This has been universally the case where the flood prevailed. About 210 acres of arable land, and 400 acres of pasture, were flooded. The height of the water above the usual level was 8½ feet at the Dorral Bridge, though it covered all the lands between the Hill of Melundy and the Knowes of Turacastle. In this parish there are 17 cases of families rendered destitute by the flood. Sir William Cumming's total loss here, and at Altyre, and elsewhere, cannot be less than £8000.

In passing down through the district called Kellas, belonging to Lord Fife, I was particularly struck with the appearances indicative of a large ancient lake-bed (Plate 38). Three others of smaller size succeed to it. I regret that my limits forbid me attempting to describe what would be unintelligible without a very minute detail. As usual in such cases, they have ravines connected with them, through which the river now escapes. The scenery of one of these is extremely romantic, the river boiling through it in a succession of rapids (Plate 39). I measured the flood-mark here, and found it 18 or 20 feet above

PLATE 39. ESS OF LOSSIE

the ordinary level. At the pass called The Dun-Coo's-Loup, a little farther down, where the width from rock to rock is 120 feet, the flood seemed to have been about 10 feet above the ordinary level. At a place called Fosse, immediately above the Hill of Birnie, there is an ancient course of the Lossie, by which it must have once run down through a totally different line of country from that which it now waters. Its modern level is considerably below the mouth of this. But, in the fourteenth century, Alexander Barr, Bishop of Moray, had a plan for restoring it to this channel, in order to relieve the valuable lands of the church from its troublesome inroads. Birnie was the first Episcopal seat of the Bishopric of Moray. The sanctity of the old church is still so great that it is common to send from great distances to ask the prayers of its congregation for people in extremity. The popular saying is, "If a man be ill, let him be prayed for in the Kirk of Birnie, which will either end him or mend him." There is a

PLATE 40. RONNELL BELL OF BIRNIE

beautiful Saxon arch in the interior, and a very ancient stone font. But the most curious piece of antiquity is the Ronnell bell of Birnie (Plate 40), said to have been brought from Rome by the first Bishop. It is about 18 inches high by 6 inches one way, and 4 inches the other, at the mouth. Its shape is angular, and joined at the sides with nails. It has a handle at the top, and no tongue remaining. Its metal seems to be bronze, but the popular tradition is that there is a great deal of silver in it. I think I have seen bells resembling it used in religious processions in Italy. Opposite to Birnie, part of the river broke away into an old channel, and did not join the main body of the stream for two miles.

The extensive plain below Birnie was, unquestionably, a vast lake in ancient times. Mr. Isaac Forsyth, of Elgin, tells me that, having occasion to dig a well in his farm-yard here, the workmen went down through 10 feet of rich alluvial earth, below which they penetrated through 10 feet of peat moss, filled with fragments of trees lying horizontally, and under that they came to coarse gravel and sand, with a plentiful supply of water. The Lossie and the Blackburn, meeting in this plain, spread over an extent of about 400 acres, flooding the farms of Allerburn, Pittendreich, Shooting Acres, Oldrachty, Mosstowie, Inverlochty, and Lochinver.

At Lochinver, the river, breaking into the Loch of Inverlochty, flooded from 150 to 200 acres of the country to the westward. Mr. Duff, of Elgin, who leases Lochinver, rode out in that direction on the forenoon of the 4th, but his progress was arrested before he reached Palmers-cross. Gaining the high ground, his anxiety was excited by observing the house of Whinnyhall standing in the midst of the waters; and, dreading that the inhabitants might perish, he galloped back towards Elgin, got a boat from Oldmills, where it had been employed in rescuing the live stock, and had it conveyed in a cart to the spot where it was launched, and steered directly for the premises, then rising from a small spot of earth, wearing all the appearance of an island. He found the place deserted, the people, and even the animals, having been removed early, all save a pig and a calf with which he despatched the boat to the shore; and, resolving to go to Lochinver by water, he remained till the boat should return to pick him up. His description of the silence and desolation of the scene that surrounded him, whilst thus left alone in this circumscribed space, the limits of which the flood was every moment diminishing, is very striking. All was still as the grave; no inmate of the house appeared; no herd was in the stall; no living thing was to be seen; and the rising lake was slowly filling the little court in front of the cottage. The crop around showed only its bearded ears above the water. It seemed like some enchanted dwelling. If he had not been aware of the sudden nature of the calamity, the composure that dwelt on every object his eye rested on might have almost persuaded him that this state of things had existed for centuries. Anon a partridge, or other wild bird, started from the small remnant of dry ground around the house; but the whirring sound of its wings could not disturb the dream which the solitariness of the spot had thrown him into, but rather heightened the illusion: for, seeing that the wildlings of nature had thus nestled here, it almost required an effort to convince himself that so few hours only had elapsed since the good man's hearth had been made cold, his house desolate, and the verdant knoll, the scene of his daily action, rendered inanimate and soundless. It was the return of the boat alone that brought back the full conviction of recent events.

The mills and farm-offices of Oldmills were filled with water, to within a foot of the door lintels in most of them, and up to the roofs in some of the houses. The old Bow Brig stands on this farm. Its single arch, of great antiquity, withstood the force of the flood but was partly relieved by the water breaking out over the low land. All the flat lying to the north of Elgin, with its gardens and nurseries, presented one unbroken expanse of water, but the width being great, and the fall trifling, the current was comparatively gentle, and the damage was less than might have been expected, though some walls, hedges, and embankments were broken. The house of Mr. Grigor, the nurseryman, was so flooded that the family were compelled to take refuge in the upper rooms, until they were relieved and removed into Elgin. The Bridge of Bishopmill, of two arches, was swept away by the accumulated pressure on it. The flood was 2 feet 4 inches higher on the wall of the house, beside the bridge, than the mark placed there to record the height of that of 1825, an excess very wonderful when considered as extending over so great a width of surface. All the houses in the low line of the suburb of Bishopmill, running eastward by the base of the hill on the left bank, were filled 6 or 8 feet deep with water. Those who had houses of one storey were obliged to flee for their lives, whilst others, who had little attics, or small garrets, roosted in them till the flood subsided. The farms of Deanshaugh, Newmills, Woodside, and St. Andrew's, on the left, and the Panns, Reikitlane, Braemuckity, and Sheriffston, on the right bank, comprising the low ground to the eastward of Elgin, were submerged to the extent of greatly above 200 acres. The loss of crop was immense; but, from the naturally sluggish run of the Lossie, from Birnie downwards, and its great expansion, the permanent damage to the soil was comparatively inconsiderable.

One immense stream ran up the road from the Pann's Port, past the large beech tree, to the turnpike road and along its line for a mile, as far as the Stonecross Hill. Part of it broke over the road, and flooded the lands of the Maison Dieu, as far as Ashgrove. Elgin was thus almost surrounded and, when viewed from the Castle Hill, it presented the strange appearance of a city built on an elevated island in the midst of an inland sea. The family of Mr. Forbes, the nurseryman at Pinefield, were in the greatest peril, and escaped with the utmost difficulty. One of the sons, confined to bed in consumption, was taken out in a carriage when the water had almost reached him where he lay. Mr. Brown of Dunkinty's young horses were seen in a part of the lands of Panns, gathered into a group on a dry hillock in the field. They were in great danger; but the paling being got at, and broken down, by means of a boat, they were enabled to escape. The hillock was found covered with the dead and mutilated bodies of an immense number of moles, mice, rabbits, partridges and hares which, having been driven there for safety, like the colts, had been trodden under foot by the hoofs of the affrighted and restless animals.

It was curious to notice how accurately the Lossie indicated its old channels, in the lowlands of the Panns, and elsewhere to the eastward of Elgin, by sending streams through them. One, in particular, ran through the pool called *The Order Pot*, which unquestionably owes its origin to the workings of Lossie, though at a period of immense antiquity. When the river was seen spreading out to so great an extent, the fulfilment of Thomas-a-Rhymer's prophecy seemed impending:-

The Order Pot and Lossie gray
Shall sweep the Chan'ry Kirk away.

But the Cathedral, unrivalled as a Gothic ruin, still rears its venerable towers. A certain fulfilment of part of the prophecy has already taken place; for, when the Cathedral ruins were recently cleared out, many hundred cart loads of the debris were thrown into the Order Pot, without materially lessening it. Tradition says it is unfathomable, and no one has taken the trouble to prove its falsehood. It was the place where witches and other unfortunate criminals underwent the water ordeal, whence its vulgar and corrupted name. Whether it may have been also used for cleansing lepers may be matter of conjecture, from the land beside it being called the Leperland.

Nine cases of destitute families were produced by the flood in the suburb of Bishopmill, by the loss to mechanics of wood, tools, dye stuffs, and bleaching materials. Even the iron, and the large bellows of a smith's forge, were carried off. A great quantity of grocery goods were also destroyed.

The small brook that passes through the village of Lhanbryd, tributary to the Lossie, was so swollen about sunset on the 3rd of August that it flooded the dwelling-house and offices of Widow Milne, and the men in the neighbourhood ran to the poor woman's assistance. John Proctor, the miller, was among the foremost of these. Rashly trusting to the rotten remains of a very old bridge, he sprang upon it, and down it went with him. He was plunged into the stream which, though not more than 4 feet deep and 12 feet broad, was so impetuous that nothing could resist it. One feeble little old woman, standing at her door, saw the accident and ran screaming to the bank; and her cries brought others to the spot. They saw him catch at a ragweed as he was swept past it, but the plant was no more effectual in its help than was the wretched creature who first beheld his fall. It failed him. He uttered one piteous shriek, sank with it in his grasp, and was seen no more. The body was found next day, at some distance below, half buried in the sand, his hat still on his head, and one of his shoes gone.

The Loch of Spynie was anciently an arm of the sea, and was probably cut off from its connection with its parent ocean by the operations of the Lossie. Previous to 1810, it presented the appearance of a dull, uninteresting sheet of shallow water, three miles long by one mile broad, claiming attention only as it reflected the stern image of the ruins of the Bishop of Moray's ancient fortified palace of Spynie, or as being the winter quarters of large flocks of wild swans, which were seen floating on its bosom, or wheeling their graceful flights in midway air, circle within circle, as if in contemplation of the beautiful forms that seemed to animate the mimic sky below them.* It was drained in 1810 by the contiguous proprietor, who drove a canal from Lossiemouth into it, at the expense of £7000. The late flood produced a complete, though temporary, restoration of it. This was occasioned by two irruptions of water from the Lossie; one that burst out at Wester Calcots, through the left bank of the river, and ran across the fields for about a mile and a half, in a line between Spynie and Pitgaveny House, and entered the drained bed of the loch at a point a little to the eastward of the palace; and another, that flooded over at the farm of Brigsies and, after traversing a distance of about a quarter of a mile, entered the alveus of the lake at its north-eastern angle. The house of Pitgaveny, and a great part of the grounds around it, were thus converted into a large island. The re-filling of the loch went on with amazing rapidity. The inundation first covered all the eastern end, the turnpike road from Elgin to Lossiemouth that passes across the dry lake-bed having for some time acted as a dam to prevent its farther progress. But, surmounting this by degrees, and breaking down the bridge there, it pushed its waters entirely over the country to the westward, inundating several farms in the parish of Duffus. The quantity of

* *The mildness of the climate here insured them from being blocked up with ice for any length of time but, on one occasion, a frost of unusual severity and duration occurred. A neighbouring farmer having risen early, observed a small horse-pond near his house literally filled with them. The ice had been removed from it the previous evening, for the purpose of watering the cattle; and the loch being completely sealed up, they had flocked to this little open place, and kept it free of ice during the night by their natural warmth. The farmer snatched up a large mouthed wall-piece-looking gun, loaded it largely, and ran down to the pond. The heads of the birds were then down but, alarmed by his footsteps, they were all suddenly erected at one moment. He put his portable cannon to his shoulder, and gave fire among them. The result was his prostration on his back, and when he scrambled to his legs and ran to the pool, he found that he had killed no less than fourteen of them.*

rich soil which the water carried on its surface, gave to certain parts of the restored loch so much the appearance of ploughed clay land, that it actually deceived many experienced eyes who beheld it. The water continued to flow from the breaches in the embankments of the Lossie, through the fine farms of Sheriffston, Fosterseat, Calcots, Bogs of Leuchars, Gordonsward, Milton, Blackleas, Carse, and Inchbroom; and Mr. Barclay of Calcots, the ingenious author of the Sequel to the Diversions of Purley, calculates that the inundation in this neighbourhood, between the bridge and the sea, and on both sides of the river, *could not have covered less than 3500 acres*. The damage done to the crops over so large an extent of flooded ground, of very valuable quality, was very great, but it was rather a general injury done to the quality of the grain, by its being "boiled at the roots," as the Dallas landlord expressed it, than any very serious total loss. The injury done hereabouts to land by the Lossie was trifling; that on the Fife estate being calculated at about £600 only; on Milton Duff £150; Bilbohall, £100; Sir Archibald Dunbar, Bart., £100; and Pitgaveny, £500.

Very remarkable depositions of rounded stones and gravel extend from Drainie all along the coast to the eastward and about the mouth of the Spey. To these I have referred in the 57th page of a paper on the Parallel Roads of Lochaber, in the ninth volume of the Transactions of the Royal Society of Edinburgh, in the belief that they throw light on the hypothesis that, previous to the evacuation of the Lochaber lakes, the waters now emptying themselves into the West Sea at Fort William formed a part of the River Spey. To assert to persons unaccustomed to pursue geological inquiries step by step, that the Spey at one time very probably ran towards the Plain of Elgin, through the Glen of Rothes, would be to fill them with astonishment and incredulity. But this, I confess, I am much disposed to believe and, if there be any truth in the supposition, so large a river as the Spey then was, being combined in operation with the Lossie, and perhaps with the Findhorn, might have easily produced these immense deposits. Then the sea, by throwing them back again into a high ridge, by the mere power of its tide might, in after ages, have occasioned its own exclusion from the Loch of Spynie. It certainly had a communication with it in 1383, for Bishop Alexander Barr, in his protest, preserved in the Chartulary of Moray, speaks of "the Port of Spynie," and "the inhabitants of Spynie sailing as fishers from Spynie to the sea." A personal examination of the subject, would, I think, convince most practical geologists of the rationality of this theory, and I am much mistaken if the recent operations of our floods have not opened many less inquiring minds to the ready admission of such speculations.

CHAPTER 12

THE RIVER SPEY TO ABERNETHY

THE River Spey holds the third place among Scottish rivers. It rises about 16 miles south from Fort Augustus, has a run of about 96 miles, and drains not less than 1300 square miles of country.

The Spey, and its tributaries above Kingussie, were but little affected by the flood of the 3rd and 4th of August. The western boundary of the fall of rain seems to have been about the line of the River Calder, which enters the Spey from the left bank, a little to the westward of the village. The deluge was tremendous, accompanied by a violent north-east wind, and frequent flashes of lightning without thunder. The barometer sank very little, but this was attributed to the direction of the wind.

About Belleville, and on the Invereshie estate, the meadows were covered *to the extent of 5 miles long by 1 mile broad*, and both the land and embankments of those belonging to Mr. Macpherson Grant, on the right, were much destroyed. The proprietor's damage is estimated at £500. Mr. Macpherson of Belleville's losses are to the extent of £820, though they chiefly result from the action of a small rivulet. Having filled its channel with stones and gravel, it burst over its banks, spread devastation around, rushed into the square of offices, and carried away the end of a strong stone and lime house. The beatiful Loch Inch, 3 miles long by 1 mile broad, was raised between 7 and 8 feet, an astonishing accumulation for so wide an expanse of water.

The River Feshie, a tributary from the right bank immediately below Invereshie, was subjected to the full influence of the deluge. It swept vast stones and heavy trees along with it, roaring tremendously. Mr. Macpherson Grant's losses on this river, chiefly in wood, have been very considerable. Those of Mr. Mackintosh of Mackintosh are calculated at £480, though he possesses but a small portion of one side of the glen. John Grant the saw-miller's house, at Feshieside, on this property, was surrounded by 4 feet of water, about eight o'clock in the morning of the 4th. The people on the top of a neighbouring hill fortunately observed the critical situation of the family, and some men, in defiance of the tremendous rush of the water, then 200 yards in breadth, gallantly entered, as Highlanders are wont to do in trying circumstances, shoulder to shoulder, and rescued the inmates of the house one by one from a peril proved to be sufficiently imminent by the sudden disappearance of a large portion of the saw-mill. But, great as was the danger in this case, the lonely and deserted situation of Donald Macpherson, shepherd in Glenfeshie, with his wife and six little children, was still more frightful, and required all the firmness and resolute presence of mind characterizing the hardy mountaineer.

His house stood on an eminence at a considerable distance from the river. Believing, therefore, that whatever might come he and his would be in perfect safety, he retired with his family to bed at the usual hour on the evening of the 3rd. At midnight he was roused by the more than ordinary thunder of the river and, getting up to see the cause, he plunged up to the middle in water. Not a moment was to be lost. He sprang into his little dwelling and lifted, one after the other, his children from their beds, and carried them almost naked, half asleep, and but half conscious of their danger, to the top of a hill. There, amidst the wild contention of the elements and the utter darkness of the night, the family remained shivering, and in suspense, till day-break, partially illuminating the wildness of the scenery of the narrow glen around them, informed them that the flood had made them prisoners in the spot where they were; the Feshie filling the whole space below, and cataracts falling from the rocks on all sides. Nor did they escape from their cliff of penance till the evening of the following day.

The crops in Glenfeshie were annihilated. The romantic old bridge at Invereshie is of two arches, of 34 and 12 feet span. The larger of these is 22 feet above the river in its ordinary state, *yet the flood was 3 feet above the keystone*, which would make its height here above the ordinary level about 25 feet. The force pressing on this bridge must have been immense; and if we had not already contemplated the case of the Ferness Bridge, we should consider the escape of that of Feshie to be a miracle. Masses of the micaceous rock below the bridge, of several tons weight, were rent away, carried down, and buried under heaps of gravel at the lower end of the pool, 50 or 60 yards from the spot whence they were taken.

The Feshie carried off a strong stone bulwark a little farther down, overflowed and destroyed the whole low ground of Dalnavert, excavated a new channel for itself, and left an island between it and the Spey of at least 200 acres. The loss of crop and stock by the farmers hereabouts is quite enormous, and the ruin to the land very great.

The burn of Dalraddy, which runs into Loch Alvie, on the left bank, did much mischief. A rather whimsical result followed the flood at the farm of Dalraddy. The tenant's wife, Mrs. Cumming, on going out after the flood had subsided on Tuesday afternoon, found at the back of the house, and all lying in a heap, a handsome dish of trout, a pike, a hare, a partridge and a turkey, with a dish of potatoes, and a dish of turnips, all brought down by the burn and deposited there for the good of the house, except the turkey which, alas! was one of her own favourite flock. The poor hare had been surprised on a piece of ground insulated by the flood, and had been seen alive the previous evening exhibiting signs of consternation and alarm. The stream rising yet higher during the night, swept over the spot, and consummated its destruction.

The Manse of Alvie is beautifully situated on a swelling knoll, almost surrounded by the peaceful lake of that name. On Tuesday morning, Loch Alvie rose to an unprecedented height, covering one half of the minister's garden. The whole road leading to the church was inundated to a depth that made it impossible for a horse or carriage to pass, and Mr. Macdonald and the clergymen who had assisted him at his Sacrament were confined prisoners at the manse till the flood subsided on Wednesday forenoon.

The Duke of Gordon's delightful retreat, Kinrara, fortunately escaped with little injury. But at the Doune of Rothiemurchus the whole flat part of the lawn was inundated, and the house stood on an island. The fine farm there suffered considerably, and the damage to the property is valued above £600. The scenery hereabouts is well known to be of the grandest character. I speak not of the minutiæ of Nature, of her cabinet pictures. I speak of her as reigning over wide valleys, mighty pine forests, rocky hills, and giant mountains. To have beheld such a region whilst it was the theatre of the elemental war of the beginning of August last, must have been to look on something that poets have dreamed of, rather than historians recorded. The weather here, up to the evening of Saturday the 1st, was temperate and natural, but a north-easterly wind then sprang up, bringing a thick haze with it. On the morning of the 2nd, the air became very cold, and the wind increased in strength. Threatening clouds began to collect and, before night, the sky presented one unbroken vault of pitchy black. The rain commenced that night, and did not cease till three o'clock P.M. of the 4th. Nothing could equal the sublimity of the scene on Tuesday morning. The clouds ever and anon seemed to be gathering all their stores to pour upon the hills, as a last effort; and yet they never forsook their post, notwithstanding their incessant discharge, and the struggles of the hurricane against them. An entire river poured itself over the rugged and precipitous brow of the hill of Upper Craigellachie,* converting its furrowed front into one vast and diversified waterfall. Every object around was veiled in a sort of half obscurity, save when occasional glimpses of the lofty Cairngorum burst forth amidst the fury of the tempest, and he reared his proud head, as if in mockery, above it.

The Druie, entering from the right bank, swept away a house at Upper Dell, and the inhabitants were nearly lost in their ineffectual attempts to save their furniture. The river broke away from its channel and, running in a parallel at the distance of 200 yards, it bore down every object, natural or artificial, that presented itself, and surrounded the house of the Dell of Rothiemurchus with an immense body of water, though its site was 500 yards from its bed.

** The two crags, Upper and Lower Craigellachie, mark the western and eastern limits of the Grant country. The watch-word of the clan is, "Stand Fast, Craigellachie."*

The family were thrown into the greatest consternation, and Mr. Mackintosh, who was in bad health, was carried out in a cart, with the greatest difficulty and danger, and was set down on dry ground at a distance of 400 yards from his house. The whole place was cut up and ruined, and the sawmills, which were much damaged, escaped utter destruction only by the breaking of the embankment higher up.

The garden of the inn at Aviemore was flooded as high as the upper wall. Mr. Mackenzie, the innkeeper, lost two oxen and several sheep. One sheep was seen to cross the Spey to the south side on the 4th and, on the 5th, it was again feeding about the house on the north bank. Several others were found alive on the tops of the trees at the foot of the garden, having scrambled into them when they were bent down by the pressure of the water. Lachlan Grant, the tenant of Dellifaber, below Aviemore, had a large copper kettle carried off. He immediately got on a rude kind of raft with the gallant intention of giving chase to it. But he was soon glad to abandon the enterprise and, if he had not been a very powerful man, he would have been lost in the current. The great damage on this part of the Spey is in the agricultural produce destroyed.

One of the most extraordinary circumstances attending the flood took place in Loch-na-mhoon, a little lake near Avielochan, about two and a half miles to the eastward of Aviemore, a mile from the Druidical circle on the plain, and within sight of the great road. It lies in a hollow, and has a fir wood beyond it to the south. The loch is about ninety yards long from north to south, and about fifty yards across. The centre of it was filled with a swampy island, which was now and then seen to rise and fall a little with the surface of the loch. During the flood, one of the cross drains of the road sent a stream directly down a hollow, and into the loch with so great a force that it actually undermined and tore up the island. The surface of the water being thus raised fifteen or twenty feet, and the wind blowing furiously from the north-east, the huge mass was floated and, drifting to the southern shore, was stranded on the steep bank where it now lies like a great carpet, the upper half of it reclining on the slope of the bank, and the lower half resting on the more level ground close to tbe water's edge. The island is composed chiefly of *Eriophori*, *Junci*, and other aquatic plants, with strongly matted roots to a depth of about 18 inches, and having 18 inches of soil attached to them, making the whole thickness of the solid part of it about 3 feet. In form it approaches the circular, and it is 30 yards in diameter. One of the most curious facts regarding this strange phenomenon is that it is perforated by one large hole, 5 or 6 yards square, and two of a smaller size, which exactly correspond in magnitude, form, and position, to the three hillocks of earth adhering to the bottom of the loch, and appearing above water, which are, in reality, nothing more than three of the roots of the wrecked island (Plate 41).

PLATE 41. LOCH-NA-MHOON, OR THE PEAT LOCH, FROM WHICH THE ISLAND WAS DRIFTED AND STRANDED ON THE SHORE

On the right bank of the river, the beautiful loch of Pityoulish, in the district of Kincardine, lying to the east of that pretty wooded hill in Rothiemurchus called the Calart, rose above 5 feet, and the small rill that issues from it into the Spey, strange to say, ran from the Spey into the loch, flooding the road, and standing in some places 10 feet deep. It was in the pass close to the loch that Shaw *Cor-fhi-a-cailach*, or Bucktooth, waylaid and murdered the last of the Cumins of Rothiemurchus. Tradition reports that Shaw placed an old woman on the top of the Calart, apparently engaged in *rocking the tow*, or rolling the flax on the distaff, but really for the purpose of giving him notice on which side of the loch the Cumin party would advance. The watchword for the north was, '*Tha na gobhar 's'a Chalart*,' 'The goats are in the Calart;' and for the south, '*Tha na gobhar 's'a chal*,' 'The goats are in the kail.' The graves of these Cumins are still pointed out, in a hollow on the north side of the Calart, called *Lag-na'n-Cuimineach*. It is unnecessary to mention that the Shaws fell into immediate possession of Rothiemurchus, and continued to hold it till they, in their turn, were expelled by the Grants of Muckrach, in Strathspey. Young Dallas of Cantray married the widow of Shaw of Rothiemurchus, and took up his abode there with her. As young Shaw, the widow's son by her former marriage, grew up, he began to regard Dallas with a jealous eye, avoiding his society, and spending his time in hunting and fishing. Returning one day from the pursuit of the deer, and passing by the smithy which was then, as now, the great place of resort in every district, a favourite dog that had entered it was driven out yelping, from a kick bestowed by some one within. Fired by the supposed insult, young Shaw hastily entered the smithy, and discovering, on inquiry, that his stepfather was the aggressor, he waylaid Dallas as he came home that night, and murdered him. Returning to Rothiemurchus, he rushed into his mother's presence, his hands red with the blood of her husband, and told her what he had done. To avoid his immediate fury, she so commanded her feelings as to appear to be little moved by the intelligence but, early next morning, she gathered together all the title-deeds of the estate, and other papers of importance, and fled to Castle Grant, where she delivered over the property to the laird. Unwilling to bring trouble on himself by this affair, he surrendered the rights to his son, Peter of Muckrach, a brave but turbulent man, who soon took means to secure possession of the gift. There is still a large stone, forming the lintel of a door at the Dell, said to have been brought from Muckrach when the Grants moved from thence. It bears the Rothiemurchus arms, and the motto is, '*In God is al my traist*,' with the initials P. G. engraven on it, and the date 1598.

At Cullachie of Gartenmore, a hamlet of sod houses, standing about a quarter of a mile from the Spey, on the right bank, my attention was arrested by the vast extent of the flood-mark. The cottages stand on a green hillock rising out of the cultivated plain, some 6 or 8 feet above its level. The flat stretches from the Spey in their rear, and sweeps towards the moor in front of them. The Abernethy Road runs across the edge of this sweep of the flat. I was struck by the failure of one of its conduit bridges, and seeing the remains of river-wreck on the edge of the moor, and being incredulous that the inundation could have spread so far, I turned aside to the house of Widow Cameron, who gave me the history of her disasters. "Ou, Sir," said she, "ye see, Spey was just in one sea a' the way fae Tullochgorum yonder, on tither side o' the strath, to thay muiry hillocks out by there, ayont the King's road fornent us; and, or e'er we kent far we waur, the watter was a' in aboot huz, and up 4 or 5 feet in oor hooses, an' it destroyed a' oor meal, an' floated aff oor peat-stacks. See till some o' the peats lyin' oot on yon hillock-side yonder, twa hunner yairds fae whaur we're stannin'. I was feart oot o' my judgment for my bairns, and sae I but to be oot o' this wi' them." "And how did you escape?" demanded I, with the greatest anxiety. "Ou, troth, just upon a brander," replied Mrs. Cameron. "A brander!" exclaimed I with astonishment arising from ignorance that the word was applied to anything than a Scotch gridiron, and thinking that the riding to the moon on a broom, or the sailing in a sieve to Norway, were nothing to this. "A brander! what do you mean by a brander?" "Ou, just a bit float," replied the widow; "a bit raft I made o' thay bit palins an' bits o' moss-fir that waur lyin' aboot. "What! and your children too?" exclaimed I. "Ou, what else!" replied she, amused at my surprise; "what could I hae done wi' them else? nae horse could hae come near huz. It was deep aneuch to droon twa horses." "And how did you feather yourself over?"

inquired I. "Troth, sir, I hae nae feathers," replied Mrs. Cameron very simply; "I'm no a dewk to soom. But, ye see, I sat on my hunkers on the middle o' the brander, wi' my bairns a' aboot me, in a knot; and the wund, that was blawin' strong aneuch fae the north, just teuk us safe oot to the land." "And how did your neighbours get out?" asked I. "Ou, fit way wad they get oot, but a' thegither upon branders," replied Mrs. Cameron. Let the reader fancy to himself this fleet of branders, with their crews of women and children, floating gallantly *vent en poupe*, towards the land, and he will have before his mind's eye a scene fully as remarkable as any which this eventful flood produced.

CHAPTER 13

THE RIVER NETHY

THE damage done by the river Nethy, tributary to the Spey, on the right bank is enormous. Mr. Forsyth, of the Dell of Abernethy, was on his way down from Rothiemurchus, in his gig, on the morning of the 4th. On reaching the summit above Gartenmore, he was astonished to see the public road in front of the cottages of Cuillachie flooded, as I have described it in the previous chapter. Aware of the difficulties he would have to encounter, two of his people came to meet him on horseback, easily passing round the impediment by riding over the rough muir to the south. These lads entered the water before Mr. Forsyth, and piloted him along the road till, being ignorant of the broken cross drain, the horse of one of them plunged over head and ears into it, and he and his rider narrowly escaped drowning. Having turned the vehicle, and got out with great difficulty, Mr. Forsyth proceeded by the old road.

The river here assumed the appearance of a lake of several miles in extent, having its margin skirted by the houses of Tullochgorum,* Curr, Ballintomb, Belliefurth, Ballimore, Coulnakyle, Rothiemoon, Tomdhu, Gartenmore, and Boat of Garten, variegated with little islands consisting of hillocks, elevated specks of corn fields, and the farm houses of Cuillachie, Tomchrochar, Tombae, and Lord Seafield's wood establishment at Broomhill. As Mr. Forsyth approached the Bridge of Nethy, the first sight he saw was a house on the left bank bowing its roof towards the river, and disappearing headlong into it. The work of destruction went on with fearful rapidity. In fifteen minutes the road leading up the left bank towards the house of Dell was swept away, and a large breach made in the field beyond it. Unable to proceed in the gig, Mr. Forsyth walked up the riverside, large masses of the bank tumbling every now and then into the torrent. After getting near the corner of his garden, where a rill 2 feet wide and 2 inches deep, was wont to run, he found his further progress arrested, and his house surrounded, by a broad and powerful current of so great depth as to be quite unfordable. He saw the back of his house, about 60 or 70 yards before him. In it were his children, and he had no means of knowing what might be the extent of the operations of the river beyond. A half rotten paling, that had as yet resisted this sudden foreign flood, appeared dipping from either bank into the stream before him. What it might be in the middle he did not know, for there it was already submerged. The hazard was tremendous but, goaded on by his anxiety, he took his determination. Poising a long ladder on the quivering poles, he made

* *Famous for giving name to the spirited Strathspey so called.*

a desperate adventure. By God's providence he achieved it, and found all safe in the house though the water was a foot deep in it. This alarming state of things was caused by a tributary called the Dorback, rushing into the Nethy from its right bank; and, with the usual influence of such lateral streams, driving the Nethy over towards its left bank, which it cut through, and bursting over Mr. Forsyth's luxuriant field of turnips, ruined his farm and sent that newly created river down the hollow that interrupted his return home. This stream continued till the breach was repaired, but Mr. Forsyth's simple mode of embanking is speedily executed. Three rows of strong piles are driven down, sloping slightly to the river, and are left above ground of the height of the intended embankment. Two feet intervenes between the rows of piles, as well as between the piles of each row, and the piles of the different rows cover each other individually, as rear rank men do those in the front rank. Young fir trees, with all their branches on, are then laid diagonally across between the piles, but differing from Colonel Mackintosh of Farr's plan so far that, instead of the points of the brush being turned down the stream, they are laid so as to oppose it, by which means they arrest the sand and mud brought down by the river, and each successive stratum of them is covered by it in its turn. Six inches of gravel is laid over each layer of brush, between the piles, and whole fir tree logs are placed along, between the rows, over the gravel. These layers are repeated till the work is of sufficient height, and large stones are thrown in at top, to give solidity to the mass, which speedily assumes all the appearance of a natural bank by the daily accession it receives from the river. I saw this embankment, which in a few days excluded the water and perfectly withstood the appendix flood of the 27th of August.

The Nethy carried off a barn and cowhouse at Inchtomack, and did great damage to the fields there as well as to all the land along its course. As it is the great medium of transport to the Spey of the timber from the magnificent native pine forest that covers this district, it is of the highest importance to have the stream clear for floating. To facilitate this, a new cut was made for the river in 1813, at great expense, through the moss of Cluihaig. The banks are from 10 to 15 feet deep, and six or eight strata of roots of trees are to be seen in its sides, in the natural position, all the growth of successive ages. The trunks of some lie horizontally embedded in the moss; others have evidently been burnt to the surface. In one part of the bank, the lowest stratum is of birch roots, about two feet above the gravel the moss rests on. Then come three successive strata of fir roots, 18 inches apart, another stratum of birch roots, and above that one or two more of fir, that do not seem to have attained any great size. Lastly, there are firs now rooted and growing on the surface, but these are small and stunted, and are called, in the language of the country, *darrachs*. In the evening of the 3rd of August, the Nethy burst its bulwarks, demolished this work, and returned to its former and natural channel.

In casting a drain on the farm of Dell, in 1825, and at a depth of five feet below the surface, half a wooden platter was found, together with the knot of a birchen rope, called in Scotland a *woodie*, as also several other curious cuttings of small sticks. The soil consisted of two feet of mould next the surface, and three feet of moss below. Mr. Forsyth was kind enough to send me the platter. It has much the appearance of having been made by a knife, and is so cut as to imitate those concentric circles frequently put on such vessels by the rustic turner.

The Dorback, which joins the Nethy at Dell, did serious injury along its banks. Alexander Fraser, the fox-hunter, at the Drum of Dorback, a place in an out-of-the-way corner far up its stream, had his house situated some twelve feet above the level of the water. "I thought nothing," said he, when telling the story himself, "of the height o' the water on the Monday night, until about the gloamin', when down she cam', in a few minutes space, fearfully upon us. First she struck the gable o' the byre, and it went. Syne the gable o' the firehoose* partly fell, an' the water began to come in on us at sic a rate, that I made haste to get oot the wife and the sax bairns, the auldest o' them nae mair than twal' year auld. Wi' some ado I carried them to the bare braeside. I then steekit the door o' the hoose, to haud oot as muckle o' the water as possible, and made a hole through the back o't, to lat oot what was in. Syne, wi' the help o' some neebours, I got oot a muckle kist o' drawers, and twa cloth kists. By this time the furniture was going fast, and we tied a strong rope to a new bed, but we had hardly done that when the water cam' and carried off bed, and hoose, and a' thegither. Syne the barn, fu' o' corn, and a' kind o' fairmin' tools and gear, gaed aff too. For lang the wife and bairns clang to the bank, seein' a'thing ta'en awa', cauld and weet as wund and watter could mak' them, ill wullin' to leave it till the last. But, when the last houp, the hoose, was gane, I got them carried aff to a neebour's barn. It wis a' we could do to get to the bank aifter the hoose was gane, staundin' as it did on a wee bit plain by the waterside. But that, and my gairden, field, and corn-yard, are a' gane to the sea, and the place is noo a bare *claddoch*** wi'oot a vestige o' onythin' that might gar ye believe it had ever been the bield o' ony human creature." I understand that this poor fellow's house and farm were furnished in a very superior manner to those of most of his condition.

At some distance below the Dell of Abernethy, and on the right

* *Dwelling-house.*

** *A barren spot covered with stones.*

bank of the river, lay the *Iron Mill Croft*, the history of which is so curious as to demand a very particular detail. We are informed by the Reverend John Grant, in his statistical account of this parish, that those immense tracts of pine still covering the country at the roots of the Cairngorum Mountains, the relics of the great central forest of Scotland, were, down to the beginning of the eighteenth century, of little or no value to the proprietors. At that period, the Laird of Grant got a merk, or twenty pence, a year, for whatever one man chose to cut and manufacture with his axe and saw. Then the Laird of Rothiemurchus, commonly called MacAlpin, brought it to five shillings a year, and a pound of tobacco. Some time previous to the year 1730, however, a branch of the York Buildings Company purchased a portion of the forest of Abernethy for £7000, and continued to work it till 1737 "the most profuse and profligate set," says Mr. Grant, "that ever were heard of in this corner. Their extravagancies of every kind ruined themselves and corrupted others. Their beginning was great indeed, with 120 working horses, sawmills, iron mills, and every kind of implement, and apparatus of the best and most expensive sorts. They used to display their vanity by bonfires, tar barrels, and opening hogsheads of brandy to the country people, by which five of them died in one night. They had a commissary for provisions and forage, at a handsome salary, and, in the end, went off in debt to the proprietors and the country." Mr. Grant, however, allows them the credit of having made roads, introduced sawmills, and taught the inhabitants how to conduct the manufacture and transportation of wood. They also cut a passage through a rock in the Spey, that greatly impeded the process of floating. And, as the floats formerly made up were extremely clumsy and very ill put together, so they were conducted in a very hazardous manner by a man, sitting in what was called a currach, "made of a hide, in the shape, and about the size of a small brewing kettle, broader above than below, with ribs, or hoops of wood, in the inside, and a cross stick for the man to sit on, who, with a paddle in his hand, went before the raft to which his currach was tied by a rope. These currachs were so light, that the men carried them on their backs home from Speymouth. There is one of them now (1794) in the parish of Cromdale, below this. The York Buildings Company had eighteen of these currachs in their employment at first, with which they made little progress, till Mr. Aaron Hill, one of their number, constructed the large raft, as it is at present, consisting of two or three branders of spars in the bottom, joined end to end with iron or other loops, and a rope through them, and conducted by two men, one at each end, who have each a seat and oar, with which they keep the raft in the proper direction."

It is wonderful how little is now known about this company at Abernethy. Some large cast iron pillars, two of which have been used by Mr. Forsyth to prop the roof of a cart shed, and two iron beams with the date 1730, are among the few vestiges that remain of them. It was believed that the company had had an iron-mill somewhere about the croft called by that name; and it was known that they carried iron-ore from the hills of Lecht, at the source of the Burn of Conglass, near Tomintoul, to Abernethy, and smelted it there. A hammerhead, 21 inches high, by 11 and 12 at the base, which must have been moved by machinery for pounding the ore, still lies on the top of a high bank on the right side of the Nethy, immediately over the Iron Mill Croft. But the croft itself bore no traces of any such work having been there, and was all cultivated,

PLATE 42. FOUNDATIONS OF THE OLD IRON MILL ON THE NETHY

except a part of it at the lower end, covered by a grove of tall alders, standing between the arable ground and the river running to the west. Such was the state of things, when the flood of the 3rd and 4th of August scooped out a new and very broad channel for the river, right through the arable croft, and a part of the alder grove, excavating it to the depth of 6 or 8 feet. Under this, and in the middle of its new channel, to the astonishment of every one who has seen it, appear the lying beams or frame-work of a gangway across the water (Plate 42). A platform on the left of the sketch, which is nicely jointed and morticed together, seems to have been the foundation of the mill-house. There seem to have been upright posts in some of the beams, probably to support a platform above; the sluices for conveying water to the works, and for the escape of flow-water, appear to have been between these upright posts. The whole timber is perfectly fresh, and the mortice ends of the beams are all carefully numbered with the axe. The haugh above must have formed a reservoir for supplying the machinery with water. On the brow of the high right bank of the Nethy, the flood has exposed a bed of charcoal 18 inches thick, probably deposited there for the use of the smelting works. A fine spring of water, issuing from the left bank of the river, immediately opposite to the site of the iron-mill, is known to this day by the name of Crowley's Well, from a certain John Crowley, one of the workmen who constructed it, and that with much trouble and care in its formation and embellishment, as has been made more apparent by the operation of the flood. This has brought into view a wooden spout, laid along the base of the bank, some two feet below the surface, with an inclination downwards towards the well, thereby collecting all the springs within its range to one point. There is a flagstone laid endwise in front, with a bore of two inches diameter through which the water flows; and, not many years ago, an iron spout inserted in this bore allowed vessels to be filled with ease, without disturbing the well. The lower haugh is said to have been wholly occupied by the company's gardens and houses. People say that a considerable quantity of silver plate was found in a cellar there, together with several other heavy articles of value, which they could not carry away with them in the hasty moonlight retreat they were compelled to make.

The excavations of the River Nethy, on the Iron Mill Croft, are extremely interesting to the geologist. We have here the history of the operations of a river for exactly a century. At this time, 100 years ago, the English company were pounding iron-ore with their ponderous hammers, moved by active machinery, in the bed of the River Nethy. These actors move off the stage, bonfires, tar-barrels and all, and the river, in some of its floods, soon obliterates all traces of them or of their works by filling up its bed with rounded masses of stone, mingled with gravel, and so, by shutting itself out of one channel, compelling its stream to seek another, considerably to the westward. But floods succeed floods; and the quieter portions of each successive inundation spread over the ground where, by degrees, they deposit a deep and fertile soil, forming a rich haugh of land, the surface of which is six or eight feet above the level of the ground the works stood on. The greater part of this beautiful flat is subjected to tillage, whilst the seeds of some neighbouring alder trees find their way into a portion of it, and spring up into a grove. The trees grow till they become tall and majestic; and agricultural labour goes on, till the iron-mill is as much forgotten as the face and figure of John Crowley, who worked in it; when comes the flood of the 3rd and 4th of August last, tears off the shroud that covered it, and brings all back again to light, save the busy human beings, who once animated the scene.

The whole of the Iron Mill Croft has disappeared, and is now a waste of sand, gravel, and stones. The sawmill immediately below was demolished, and two houses carried away. The river, previous to the flood, had a meandering course down towards the Bridge of Nethy; but, after making its burst on the 4th of August, it cut out a new bed for itself, in one broad straight line of destruction, annihilating the haughs on both sides. Terror and confusion spread fast among the inhabitants at Bridge of Nethy. Some were stupified; and others, more collected, removed their effects. The river filled the smithy and extinguished the smith's fire. One beautiful cottage, surrounded by a blooming and luxuriant garden, occupied the ground at the west end of the handsome bridge, and immediately above the approach to it. It was inhabited by Alexander Mitchell, an industrious tailor, who had made it particularly nice. About six o'clock in the morning, the river set its stream to work against its left bank, and soon swept away cottage, garden and road, scooping the ground and gravel out to an immense depth, and cutting off all communication with the

PLATE 43. BRIDGE OF NETHY, AFTER THE FLOOD

west end of the bridge. About eight o'clock, a number of people were standing on the middle of it, wondering at the immensity and the roaring of the river, that was carrying down large trees, and tossing them up perpendicularly, when all at once the enormous mass of timber building composing the saw-mill of Straanbeg, about 500 yards above, moved bodily off, steadily and magnificently, like some three-decker leaving dock. On it came grandly, without a plank being dislodged. It was tremendous - it was awful - to see it advancing on the bridge. The people shuddered. Some moved quickly away; and others, spell-bound, instinctively grasped the parapet to prepare for the shock. Its speed was accelerated, it was already within 100 yards, and the increased velocity of the current must bring it instantaneously upon them. Destruction seemed inevitable, when all at once it struck upon a bulwark, went to pieces with a fearful crash and, spreading itself abroad all over the surface of the waters, it rushed down to the Spey in one sea of wreck. The bridge was of grey granite, its central arch thirty-six feet, and its two side arches twenty-four feet span, and of a solidity that promised an endurance for ages. But the river having once breached through beyond its western land-breast, undermined it on the flank, swept away the western arch, and gravelled the others up eighteen inches above the spring (Plate 43). The height of the flood above ordinary level, at the bridge, was 15 feet, where it was spread out to a width of about 200 yards. Of four saw-mills that were in full operation here, one only could be restored, the very sites of the others having been so ruined as to render it impossible to re-establish them. The works formed all along the river for facilitating the process of floating, have so completely disappeared that, to replace them, and to clear the channel of the immense quantities of large stones left in it, must be the work of years. The cottages on the right bank of the river were considered safe; but a clump of alders, at some distance below the bridge, divided the stream and threw a strong current against them, that very speedily carried away three of them, with their furniture and gardens.

Captain Grant of Birchfield lost eight acres of very fine haugh land, and forty bolls of grain, together with the hay, turnips, and potatoes, and this on a farm of twenty-five acres. The adjacent farm of Rothiemoon lost above three acres of land, and the whole crops and grass were covered with gravel. A very curious relic of antiquity was discovered on this farm, by the flood having swept away about twenty yards of a green bank, opposite the house of Coulnakyle. This was a square stone building, about six feet wide and five feet high, having nine feet of bank over it. I had not the good fortune to see it, but Captain Grant thinks it must have been a place of concealment, as that which is now the bed of the Nethy was covered with growing timber about a century ago. The farm of Tombea lost four acres of land, and the greater part of the rest of it was covered with sand and rubbish.

Captain Macdonald of Coulnakyle, whose place is situated in the angle between the right bank of the Nethy and the right bank of the Spey, seeing his people tired with their day's work of carrying hay, on the evening of the 1st August, desired them to leave off. "You had better continue as long as you can, sir," said his overseer to him, "for ye'll lead nae mair these twa or three days to come." "Phoo!" said Captain Macdonald, "the mercury promises good weather." "That may be," said the man; "but dinna ye see twa suns i' the sky? Wha ever saw gude wather come aifter sic a fearsome sign as yon?" Next day the mountains forming the horizon far up the strath appeared as if they were only a few miles off; and Captain Macdonald fancied he should have to laugh at his weather-wise overseer. But at nine o'clock the wind shifted to the north, the barometer fell from 29 to 28½, at which point it continued whilst it rained for 42 hours, without intermission, the thermometer being all the while at 50°. At seven o'clock in the morning of the 4th, the house was surrounded. Captain Macdonald, who, as a sailor, has weathered many a rough gale, saw some of the floaters attempt to come with a boat over part of the inundation, when the wind blew so strong as "to put him in mind of Spithead in a fresh gale," so that it instantly filled the boat with water. The weather on the 5th was more calm and clear, and Strathspey was one vast sea, the water not having had time to run off below. "I am satisfied," said Captain Macdonald, "that I might have sailed a fifty-gun ship from the Boat of Bellifurth to the Boat of Garten, a distance of seven or eight miles." At the Broomhill, the extreme height of the flood above ordinary level was twenty feet, where it was about a mile broad, but the water comparatively dead. Of Captain Macdonald's farm of 200 acres, 150 were completely ruined by depositions of gravel and sand, to the depth of three feet, and covered with large trees.

Before leaving the district of Abernethy, I have to notice a wonderful ravine formed in the side of *Bein-a-chavirin*, near the Dhu-Lochan, above the bridle-road from Strathspey to Braemar, and about a quarter of a mile from the march of that country. It extends a mile in length down the steep slope of the mountain, is from forty to fifty yards wide, and of proportionable depth. Its former contents are now spread all over the base of the hill, covering an immense surface. The mountain side was formerly an entire and beautiful green sward, and there was no stream or spring there; but the new channel is now occupied by a rill, the remains of the tremendous burst of subterranean water that occasioned it. Soon after it took place, a man passing on horseback, who was not aware of the water-charged and unstable nature of the debris that had fallen from it, got so entangled in it that his horse broke its leg, and soon afterwards died.

At Bellifurth, a considerable lake, the remains of the flood, still covers the muckle meadow, and must continue to do so till removed by drainage or evaporation.

CHAPTER 14

The River Dulnain, The Spey, The Tilchen etc

LET us now give our attention to the river Dulnain, a large tributary to the Spey from its left bank. In a lonely spot among the hills, this stream, and a small burn that runs into it, surrounded Mr. Gordon of Lynevuilg's shepherd, and a boy who was with him, and kept them there, with no other food than meal and water, for two days, in the most dreadful state of suspense. And, at *Eilan Dorch*,* an infirm woman of 90, with her widowed daughter and grand-daughter, were so environed by the flood, and the island so cut away, that they expected every moment to be swept off with their houses, cattle, and all they possessed. But it pleased Providence to subdue the deluge when nothing but a mere fragment of the isle remained. The saw-mill of Dalnahatnich was nearly carried off, and the miller's house was so inundated that he was compelled to flee from it.

The Bridge of Sluggan, 32 feet span, was swept away; and, opposite to that place, the small farm of Inchluin was completely inundated. The occupants, a poor old man of 90 years of age, much gone, both in body and mind; his wife, an old woman; and a younger son, a cripple, with his wife and children, were all carried out from their inundated home by the elder son, who was the only efficient member of the family. It was truly afflicting to see the old man poised upon his son's shoulders, utterly unconscious of his danger, in the state of idiocy to which he was reduced, shouting out with childish joy at his strange and novel situation.

At the well-known stage, the Bridge of Carr, the old bridge, long since disused, was always a picturesque object, but the flood has rendered it still more so by entirely removing the remains of its wing-walls, and leaving its tall, round-shaped, skeleton arch, standing thin and meagre-like, opposed to the plump, well conditioned body of the more substantial modern erection (Plate 44). The inn stables on the left, though on the top of the rock and 10 or 12 yards back from its brink, would have been carried away but for the failure of the old wing-walls, and the south gable of the inn itself was very nearly going. A bridge over the Burn of Aultnacarnoch, on the Inverness road, was demolished. Immediately below the Bridge of Carr, the river swept away a fine bank of alders and, cutting back for more than 10 yards in breadth, and for several hundred yards in length, carried away Captain Cruickshank's dairy, and very nearly his dairymaid along with it, leaving his house of Dalrachney standing within a few yards of the mouldering brink of a gravel precipice 40 or 50 feet high. On the opposite side, it

* *The Dark Island, so called from the sun being excluded from it during some of the winter months by the deep pine forest in which it is embosomed.*

PLATE 44. BRIDGES OF CARR

swept off three ridge-breadths of land for an extent of 300 yards.

Near the Hamlet of Carr, on the right bank, a slate rock has been laid bare which, if properly wrought, might turn out to some account. About 150 yards to the westward of the houses, there is a small patch of land surrounded by a few stunted birches, called *Croft-na-croich*, or the Gallows Croft, having the following story attached to it:

Near the end of the 17th century, there lived a certain notorious freebooter, a native of Lochaber, of the name of Cameron, but who was better known by his cognomen of *Padrig Mac-an-Ts'agairt*, Peter the Priest's son. Numerous were the *creachs* or robberies of cattle on the great scale, driven by him from Strathspey. But he did not confine his depredations to that country; for, some time between the years 1690 and 1695, he made a clean sweep of the cattle from the rich pastures of The Aird, the territory of the Frasers. That he might put his pursuers on a wrong scent, he did not go directly towards Lochaber but, crossing the River Ness at Lochend, he struck over the mountains of Strathnairn and Strathdearn, and ultimately encamped behind a hill above Duthil called, from a copious spring on its summit, *Cairn-an-Sh'uaran*, or The Well Hill. But notwithstanding all his precautions, the celebrated Simon, Lord Lovat,* then chief of the Frasers, discovered his track and dispatched a special messenger to his father-in-law, Sir Ludovick Grant of Grant, begging his aid in apprehending *Mac-an-Ts'agairt*, and recovering the cattle.

It so happened that there lived, at this time, on the laird of Grant's ground, a man also called Cameron, surnamed Mugachmore,

* *Born at Beaufort 1668 and executed on Towerhill 9th April, 1747, in the 80th year of his age.*

of great strength and undaunted courage. He had six sons and a stepson, whom his wife, formerly a woman of light character, had before her marriage with Mugach; and as they were all brave, Sir Ludovick applied to them to undertake the recapture of the cattle. Sir Ludovick was not mistaken in his man. The Mugach no sooner received his orders, than he armed himself and his little band, and went in quest of the freebooter, whom he found in the act of cooking a dinner from part of the spoil. Mugach called on Padrig and his men to surrender, and they, though numerous, dreading the well-known prowess of their adversary, fled to the opposite hills, their chief threatening bloody vengeance as he went. The Mugach drove the cattle to a place of safety, and watched them there till their owners came to recover them.

Padrig Mac-an-Ts'agairt did not utter his threats without the fullest intention of carrying them into effect. In the latter end of the following spring, he visited Strathspey with a strong party, and way-laid the Mugach as he and his sons were returning from working at a small patch of land he had on the brow of a hill, about half-a-mile above his house. *Mac-an-Ts'agairt* and his party concealed themselves in a thick covert of underwood, through which they knew that the Mugach and his sons must pass; but seeing their intended victims well armed, the cowardly assassins lay still in their hiding-place and allowed them to pass, with the intention of taking a more favourable opportunity for their purpose. That very night they surprised and murdered two of the sons who, being married, lived in separate houses at some distance from their father's, and having thus executed so much of their diabolical purpose, they surrounded the Mugach's cottage.

No sooner was his dwelling attacked, than the brave Mugach, immediately guessing who the assailants were, made the best arrangements for defence that time and circumstances permitted. The door was the first point attempted, but it was strong, and he and his four sons placed themselves behind it, determined to do bloody execution the moment it should be forced. Whilst thus engaged, the Mugach was startled by a noise above the rafters, and looking up, he perceived, in the obscurity, the figure of a man half through a hole in the wattled roof. Eager to despatch his foe as he entered, he sprang upon a table, plunged his sword into his body, and down fell his stepson! whom he had ever loved and cherished as one of his own children. The youth had been cutting his way through the roof, with the intention of attacking Padrig from above, and so creating a diversion in favour of those who were defending the door. The brave young man lived no longer than to say, with a faint voice, "Dear father, I fear you have killed me!" For a moment the Mugach stood petrified with horror and grief, but rage soon usurped the place of both. "Let me open the door!" he cried, "and revenge his death, by drenching my sword in the blood of the villain!" His sons clung around him, to prevent what they conceived to be madness, and a strong struggle ensued between desperate bravery and filial duty; whilst the Mugach's wife stood gazing on the corpse of her first-born son, in an agony of contending passions, being ignorant, from all she had witnessed, but that the young man's death had been wilfully wrought by her husband. "Hast thou forgotten our former days of dalliance?" cried the wily Padrig, who saw the whole scene through a crevice in the door; "How often hast thou undone thy door to me, when I came on an errand of love, and wilt thou not open it now to give me way to punish him, who has, but this moment, so foully slain thy beloved son?" Ancient recollections, and present affliction, conspired to twist her to his purpose. The struggle and altercation between the Mugach and his sons still continued. A frenzy seized on the unhappy woman. She flew to the door, undid the bolt, and Padrig and his assassins rushed in. The infuriated Mugach no sooner beheld his enemy enter, than he sprang at him like a tiger, grasped him by the throat, and dashed him to the ground. Already was his vigorous sword-arm drawn back, and his broad claymore was about to find a passage to the traitor's heart, when his faithless wife, coming behind him, threw over it a large canvas winnowing sheet and, before he could extricate the blade from the numerous folds, Padrig's weapon was reeking in the best heart's blood of the bravest Highlander that Strathspey could boast of. His four sons, who witnessed their mother's treachery, were paralyzed. The unfortunate woman herself, too, stood stupified and appalled; but she was quickly recalled to her senses by the active clash of the swords of Padrig and his men. "Oh, my sons! my sons!" she cried, "spare my boys!" But the tempter needed her services no longer; she had done his work. She was spurned to the ground, and trampled under foot by those who soon strewed the bloody floor around her with the lifeless corpses of her brave sons.

Exulting in the full success of this expedition of vengeance, *Mac-an-Ts'agairt* beheaded the bodies, and piled the heads in a heap on an oblong hill, that runs parallel to the road, on the east side of Carr Bridge, from which it is called *Tom-nan-Cean*, The Hill of the Heads. Scarcely was he beyond the reach of danger, than his butchery was known at Castle Grant, and Sir Ludovick immediately offered a great reward for his apprehension, but Padrig, who had anticipated some such thing, fled to Ireland, where he remained for seven years. But the restlessness of the murderer is well known, and Padrig felt it in all its horrors. Leaving his Irish retreat, he returned to Lochaber. By a strange accident, a certain Mungo Grant of Muckrach, having had his cattle and horses carried away by some thieves from that quarter, pursued them hot foot and recovered them. He was on his way returning with them when, to his astonishment, he met *Padrig Mac-*

an-Ts'agairt, quite alone, in a narrow pass, on the borders of his native country. Mungo instantly seized and made a prisoner of him. But his progress with his beasts was tedious; and, as he was entering Strathspey at *Lag-na-caillich*,* about a mile to the westward of Aviemore, he espied 12 desperate men who, taking advantage of his slow march, had crossed the hills to gain the pass before him, for the purpose of rescuing Padrig. But Mungo was not to be daunted. Seeing them occupying the road in his front, he grasped his prisoner with one hand and, brandishing his dirk with the other, he advanced in the midst of his people and animals, swearing potently that the first motion at an attempt at rescue by any one of them, should be the signal for his dirk to drink the life's blood of *Padrig Mac-an-Ts'agairt*. They were so intimidated by his boldness, that they allowed him to pass without assault, and left their friend to his fate. Padrig was forthwith carried to Castle Grant, but the remembrance of the Mugach's murder had been by this time much obliterated, by many events little less strange, and the laird, unwilling to be troubled with the matter, ordered Mungo and his prisoner away.

Disappointed and mortified, Mungo and his party were returning with their felon captive, discussing, as they went, what they had best do with him. "A fine reward we have had for all our trouble!" said one. "The laird may catch the next thief his anesel'!" said another. "Let's turn him loose!" said a third. "Aye, aye," said a fourth, "what for wud we be plaguing oursel's more wi' him!" "Yes, yes! brave, generous men!" said *Padrig Mac-an-Ts'agairt*, roused by a sudden hope of life from the moody dream of the gallows-tree, in which he had been plunged, whilst he was courting his mournful muse to compose his own lament, that he might die with an effect striking, as all the events of his life had been. "Yes, brave men! free me from these bonds! it is unworthy of Strathspey men; it is unworthy of Grants to triumph over a fallen foe! Those whom I killed were no clansmen of thine, but recreant Camerons, who betrayed a Cameron! Let me go free, and that reward of which you have been disappointed shall be quadrupled for sparing my life!" Such words as these, operating on minds so much prepared to receive them favourably, had well nigh worked their purpose. But, "No!" said Muckrach sternly, "it shall never be said that a murderer escaped from my hands. Besides, it was just so that he fairly spake to the Mugach's false wife. But did he spare her sons on that account? If ye let him go, my men, the fate of the Mugach may be ours; for what bravery can stand against treachery and assassination?" This opened an entirely new view of the question to Padrig's rude guards, and the result of the conference was, that they resolved to take him to Inverness, and to deliver him up to the Sheriff.

* *The Old Woman's Hollow.*

As they were pursuing their way up the south side of the river Dulnain, the hill of *Tom-nan-Cean* appeared on that opposite to them. At sight of it, the whole circumstances of Padrig's atrocious deed came fresh into their minds. It seemed to cry on them for justice and, with one impulse, they shouted out, "Let him die on the spot where he did the bloody act!" Without a moment's further delay, they resolved to execute their new resolution. But on their way across the plain, they happened to observe a large fir tree, with a thick horizontal branch growing at right angles from the trunk, and of a sufficient height from the ground to suit their purpose. Doubting if they might find so convenient a gallows where they were going, they at once determined that here Padrig should finish his mortal career. The neighbouring birch thicket supplied them with materials for making a withe and, whilst they were twisting it, Padrig burst forth in a flood of Gaelic verse, which his mind had been accumulating by the way.* His song, and the twig rope that was to terminate his existence, were spun out and finished at the same moment, and he was instantly elevated to a height equally beyond his ambition and his hopes. No one would touch his body, so it hung swinging in the wind for some twelve months or more after his execution; and, much as he had been feared when alive, he was infinitely more a cause of terror now that he was a lifeless corpse. None dared to approach that part of the heath after it was dark, but in daylight people were bolder.

The schoolboys of Duthil who, like the frogs in the fable, gradually began to have less and less apprehension for him, actually bragged one another on so far one day, that they ventured to pelt him with stones. A son of Delrachney, who happened to aim better than the rest, struck the birchen withe, by this time become rotten, severed it, and down came the wasted body with a terrible crash. As the cause of its descent was hardly perceptible to any of them, the terrified boys ran off, filled with the horrible belief that the much-dreaded Padrig was pursuing them. So impressed was poor young Delrachney with this idea that, through terror and haste, he burst a blood-vessel, and died in two hours afterwards. Padrig's bones were buried about 100 yards to the north of the Bridge of Carr but, as if they were doomed never to have rest, the grave was cut through about thirty-five years ago, when the present Highland road was made, and they were re-interred immediately behind the inn garden. Should any idler, who may wander after dusk along the road leading by the base of the *Tom-nan-Cean*, see strange sights cross his path, let him recall the story I have narrated, and it may furnish him with some explanation of what he beholds.

* *This lament can still be said or sung by many in the vicinity of the spot, but the story has been already too long to admit of my giving it here.*

From hence to the Spey, the course of the Dulnain is about 7½ miles, along the whole of which the crops were annihilated, and great destruction was done to the land, many acres having been swept away. At the junction of the Burn of Duthil with the Dulnain, the House of Donald Mackintosh, a weaver, was carried off; and the poor man himself remained for some time, in great alarm, on a small spot surrounded by the river and the burn. Below Lynelish, a dyer lost half his dye-house, and all his dye-stuffs. The Bridge of Curr,* of a single arch of 65 feet span, had its southern abutment undermined by the water. An eye-witness informs me that the moment the support gave way, the force of the immense body of water was so great *that it made the arch spring 15 feet into the air.* While in the act of ascending, it maintained its perfect semicircular form, but as it descended, its ends came together. So tremendous was the impetus, that the arch seemed to be carried in a body to some distance on the surface, like that of the Divie above Dunphail. When it sank, the current received a sudden check. But the waters, boiling up as if indignant at the temporary restraint, again raged along with redoubled vehemence. A stone, 30 yards below the bridge, of fully 50 tons weight, was made to perform a circumvolution. Eleven cases of destitute families have been produced by the flood in the parish of Duthil.

The Burn of Craggan, or Kirkton, tributary to the Spey, from the left bank about a mile above Grantown, carried away its bridge, destroyed a great deal of ground and crop, and utterly demolished a house. But, as some small compensation, it brought a bed of primitive limestone into view, about 200 yards above the bridge. Mr. Houston's house of Kirkton was surrounded by the burn, and all access or egress cut off. Immediately below Kirkton is the beautiful old Churchyard of Inverallen, in which are the ruins of the church. This is the cemetery for the population of Grantown, and it is of great size. It is surrounded by wood, and stands about 12 feet above the level of the Spey, its south wall being about 15 yards from the river, and 4 feet high. Its area is thickly set with gravestones and, what was remarkable, the flood rose 15 feet or more here, inundating its whole surface and leaving visible only a few inches of one tombstone taller than the rest. There was something peculiarly striking in the circumstance, that not even the sacred mansions of the dead should have been left unvisited by the furious waters, but that their turbulent waves should have rolled, in angry contention, over the very dust of those with whom all worldly strife had for ever ceased.

The run of the Spey is quicker here; but the flat country, for miles above having been converted into a temporary lake, acted as a compensation-pond, and saved the banks for many miles below.

* *Not to be confounded with the Bridge of Carr.*

No damage was done, except the demolition of the smallest of the three arches of 86, 40, and 20 feet span of the old military Bridge of Spey, below Grantown. This bridge rose with a steep ascent, from the low left to the high right bank, and had its roadway and northern wing-walls heightened, which occasioned a concentration of the power of the stream that produced the injury. Three feet of the arch fortunately remained, and supported the spandrel and parapet walls on the lower side. But the other parts of the bridge are much shaken, though everything that the activity of Mr. Mitchell, the Inspector for the Parliamentary Commissioners, could accomplish has been done to save this highly useful bridge.

On Wednesday the 5th of August, Mr. Peter Forbes, farmer at Urlarmore, on the south side of Livet, despatched his servant, Donald Cameron, a tall, handsome, athletic man, about twenty-five years of age, to carry a message to Mrs. Forbes, then at Aitnoch, near the banks of the Findhorn. On arriving at the Bridge of Spey, and seeing its state, he quietly mounted the extremely narrow parapet. The river was still raging in all the fury of flood, and loud were the cries and expostulations of the spectators. Disregarding these, however, but without saying one word, Donald coolly and steadily walked onwards, with an air of perfect complacency, till he came to that part where there was a gap in the masonry of 40 feet, save in the single parapet alone. The increased cries of the beholders were luckily drowned by the roaring of the surges. Donald stayed but one moment, to cast his plaid more tightly about him, and again continued his dangerous path to the farther end of the parapet where, leaping lightly down, he pursued his way without once looking over his shoulder for applause, or showing the slightest symptom of being conscious that he had achieved anything extraordinary. A certain shopkeeper in Grantown, too, nicknamed Dear Peter, pressed by the urgency of some favourable chance of sale, did also essay the adventure of the perilous parapet. But, having a large pack on his back, he took the good mercantile precaution of doubling his security, by planting four legs, instead of two, under him. Squatted on hands and knees, Peter pursued his path, whilst his pack kept vibrating to and fro, like the pendulum of a clock; his features being, all the while, twisted in an opposite direction to that of his load. The spectators, notwithstanding their anxiety for their Dear Peter, were convulsed with laughter, till their shouts, mingled with the thunders of the Spey, had nearly made him lose his balance. But, with all his terror, he stuck to his pack, resolving that, if he did go, he should carry his goods with him. At last, however, he succeeded in carrying all safe to the opposite side, amidst the cheers of the multitude.

Immediately below the Haughs of Cromdale, where the well-known battle was fought, the road to Ballindalloch winds round the northern base of the isolated hill of *Tomanurd*, which appears as an advanced guard of the great mass of the Cromdale mountains. At a point about seventy yards above the road, a phenomenon, similar to that of *Bein-a-chavirin*, took place; and, although it was on a much smaller scale, yet we are fortunate in having the evidence of eye-witnesses to this, which may enable us to judge how very grand the larger burst of water must have been when in full operation. Mr. Grant of Culquoich happened to be passing, on Tuesday the 4th of August, at the time this prodigy took place. It commenced with a quaking of the earth for sixty or seventy yards around the spot, which continued for some time. At length an immense column of water forced itself through the face of the hill, spouting into the air, and tossing around large stones and great quantities of gravel. Sometimes it ceased altogether, and nothing was heard but the rush as of a considerable river. Again it would burst forth, like a geyser, with renewed energy tearing up whole banks of earth, and projecting them to the distance of 300 yards. Mr. Grant compares the magnitude of the body of water to that of the River Dulnain. It was quite transparent, and had so much the appearance of boiling, that Mr. Grant at first really imagined that it must be warm. Mr. Gordon of Ballintomb also reached the spot about fifteen minutes after the first appearance of the water. He compares the noise it made to the rush of a cataract down a steep rock. Some account for it from the circumstance that there is a large boggy flat on the summit, which they suppose may have been filled by the rain; and that, having no outlet, it forced its way downwards through the body of the hill. But this is manifestly absurd, for if the weight of so lofty a column of water as that from the summit of this high hill had been brought into operation, the effects would have been enormous. I can speak to the fact of the side of the hill being particularly dry previously. I am rather disposed to think that it must contain some subterranean reservoir, which produced tbe effect by becoming surcharged. My friend, Mr. Jardine, civil engineer, and I, saw it some weeks after it had appeared. We measured the ravine it had opened, and found that the quantity of solid matter thrown out by it amounted to about 7000 cubic yards. A tiny rill of water then ran from it, but it was pure and cool. I have since learned that a neighbouring spring has gone dry, a circumstance that highly corroborates my theory of it.

At some distance below Tomanurd, the Mill of Dalvey, on the right bank, was destroyed by its burn. Some miles lower down the Tilchen, tributary to the Spey from the left, completely cleared away the whole arable and pasture land that gave richness to its confined and picturesque glen. The meal-mill at its mouth is miraculously left perfectly entire, although the whole soil surrounding it disappeared to a great depth. So suddenly did the swollen stream come upon the people here that, at Wester Straan, the first announcement of the flood given to the tenant, Henry Grant, was the falling outwards of the gable of his house which, like the drawing of the curtain of a theatre, let the whole of his terrors burst on his eyes at once. Wild with alarm, he flew to the door, where he found a wide cascade eight feet high, pouring over between him and his farm offices. Though left in this perilous situation, he escaped destruction. Above 20 acres have been scarified and ruined at the mouth of the Tilchen. But why do I attempt to particularise, where the destruction of crop and of land has been so extensive? It is sufficient for me to state the sweeping fact that, after a careful examination, the soil and timber carried off, and other damage falling on the proprietor, is estimated at no less a sum than £20,000 for his Strathspey estate alone. The number of bridges destroyed are thirteen; saw-mills, three; meal-mills, two; and dwelling-houses very many. The loss of the entire crops in the low grounds, belonging to the tenants, falls to be added to make up the grand total; and the mass of human misery that is wrapped up in this last item may be conceived by any one who is in the least acquainted with Highland districts.

CHAPTER 15

THE RIVER AVEN AND THE RIVER LIVET. THE SPEY ABOUT BALLINDALLOCH

THE River Aven, tributary to the Spey at Ballindalloch on the right bank, has its source in the very bosom of the Cairngorum Mountain, a circumstance that sufficiently accounts for the very wide ravage it committed during the flood. Its lonely crystal lake is surrounded by frightful precipices, rising on all sides, sheer up, almost to the very ridges of those towering heaps which are now admitted to be higher than any land in Great Britain. Nothing in our island can approach so near to the wilder and more savage parts of Swiss scenery. Cairngorum and Beinbainac rise almost perpendicularly from its western and northern edges; and the vast foundations of Benmacdui and Bein-main overhang its southern extremity, in frightful masses that seem as if poised for immediate projection into the valley; so that, for several of the winter months, the sun never shines on the surface of the lake. These are the sources of the pure and transparent Aven, the glaciers which hang in their ample bosoms furnishing exhaustless supplies to its stream, by means of the cataracts that continually pour down into it. All traces of man are lost amid the grandeur of these regions. No tree or shrub is to be seen; and no living creature, save when the eagle soars from the verge of the cliff athwart the vacant ether, awakening the echoes with his scream, or when the ptarmigan flutters its low flight across the mountain brow, or perhaps when some straggling deer from the Forest of Mar,

That from the hunter's aim hath ta'en a hurt,
May come to languish.

How terribly grand would have been the feelings excited in the bosom of him who could have sat, on the 4th of August last, by the side of that solitary lake, and to have beheld each furrow in the faces of the frowning cliffs converted into a separate cataract! How sublime their mingled sound, as they blended with the howling of the storm, the hoarse murmur of the agitated lake, and the chilling splash of the sheeted rain, heightened, as these effects would have been, by the conviction that there was probably no other mortal within a circuit of many miles! The Aven issues in a large stream from its lake, and flows with so great pellucidity through its deep and dark glen, that many accidents have occurred to strangers by its appearing fordable in places which proved to be of fatal depth. This quality is marked by an old doggerel proverb:

The water of Aven runs so clear
It would beguile a man of an hundred year.

At *Poll-du-ess*, a little way above the first inhabited place called Inchrory, the river is bounded by perpendicular rocks on each side. There the bed of the stream is 44 feet broad, and the flood was 23 feet above the usual level. Deep as the ravine was, the river overflowed the top of it. From correct measurements taken, the column of water that passed here, with intense velocity, appears to have been about 1200 square feet in its transverse section.

Towards the lower part of the farm of Inchrory, two rills are seen to trickle over the face of the lofty gneiss cliff bounding the glen on the right, bestowing on its dark front singularly striking perpendicular streaks of a beautiful alabastrine whiteness. These are stalactitic incrustations, formed by the evaporation of water holding calcareous matter in solution. A few yards farther down, we found an extensive marl bank reposing on the inclined talus at the base of the hill. This had been evidently laid there by the small burn of *Caochan-saraig*, which descends from the hill through a steep ravine, generally dry in summer. The marl has been deposited in various states according to the reduced or swollen condition of the burn at the time of its deposition. In some parts it appears like a stalactite, the burn having spread weakly over the bank, and produced it thus by evaporation, and it is found in this form in all stages of induration, some specimens being easily crumbled between the fingers, whilst others yield to a hammer with great difficulty. But the great mass of the bank consists of a fine powder, mechanically brought down by the burn, and left there, as any other soil might be. Amongst this levigated matter, I found a number of shells of the genus *Helix*. These approach the globular in shape, and measure about seven-tenths of an inch in their widest diameter. The volutions are four in number, rounded, and delicately striated, diagonally and transversely, the angle of the fossa between the volutions being obtuse. The aperture is ovate. Most of the specimens I picked up are bleached white, but there are individuals among them beautifully marked with four chestnut brown spirals on each volution. That towards the base is about the twentieth part of an inch in breadth; that immediately above it is merely a line. The next above this is of the same width as the first, and the fourth is like the second. These shells are different in size, shape, and confirmation, from the common *Helix putris*, or from the *Helix tentaculata* of Gmelin, and others; animals which abound in our ditches and ponds in the lower part of the province of Moray, and which have originated all our marl-beds. Indeed, I have not been able to discover any *Helix* quite agreeing with them in any author I have had it in my power to consult.* The streams I have

* *I have transmitted specimens to Dr. Fleming, the highly scientific author of 'British Animals,' and hope that his acquaintance with the detail of this branch of natural history may enable me to discover the precise name of the creature alluded to in the text.*

mentioned descend from a moss covering the flat summit of the hill, where there is doubtless an extensive marl deposit. If the insect could be found there alive it would be an interesting fact, as it would raise the thermal line of existence, of this species at least, to a point greatly higher than I have been able to discover the *Helix putris*, or any other, in this country. And, if the exuviæ alone are to be met with, the circumstance that it did once exist alive there would go far to establish a deterioration of climate. The whole right side of the glen, for two or three miles, so far as it sweeps around the hill where the marl manifests itself, is covered with one unvarying emerald carpet of the richest possible grass; whilst the slopes of the hill on the left, though they afford what may be called good hill pasture, are uniformly covered with brown heath.

In the Hill of Dellnalit, near Inchrory, several openings appeared, evidently from the same cause as those of Bein-a-chavirin and Tomanurd. A number of considerable landslips have also taken place. One of these, below Dalestie, has brought down about 500 yards of the hill, measuring from above downwards, till it reach the haugh. No less than 15 acres of the haugh have been carried away or ruined by the river. At the upper end of it stood a tall stone, called *Clach-na-Tagart*, or the Priest's Stone, where tradition said that a priest was burned for some scandal against the Church. The flood has swept away this monument of infamy which had stood for so many ages. Another great landslip appears above Torbain, near which place, at *Alt-tre-chaochan*, there is an inexhaustible rock of fluor-spar.

The Haugh of *Della-vorar*, or the Lord's Haugh, is so called from Montrose having encamped here on his return from his expedition to the North, during the Covenanting times of 1644 and 1645. Some remains of iron still denote the spot where the army forges were placed. Graham of Claverhouse, Viscount Dundee, also encamped here fourteen days before the battle of Killiekrankie, and made a day's march to Braemar where he encamped on another haugh, also since named *Della-vorar*. Five acres were carried off here.

Captain MacGregor has ordered a mark to be cut in the Rock of *Inbher-cor-du*, to mark the height of the flood which was 18 feet above ordinary level, where the breadth of the channel was 86 feet. The farm of Keppoch lost six acres of ground, and the river opened an entirely new channel through it. Immediately opposite to it, 250 yards of the face of a very steep hill shot right down through a birch grove, carrying part of the trees along with it. A boy was driving home his cattle at the time it gave way, and he and they narrowly escaped being buried in the ruins. "When I see'd it comin' doon," said he, "I thought the hill was fa'in'. The grund and stanes gaed dancin' ower the taps o' the trees, an' the beasts war sae fleggit that they cantered awa' through the corn, ilk ane his ain gate hame." The

Mill of Delnabo was completely sanded up by the tributary burn called The Alnac. "Indeed," said the miller, "the height the burns rose to that day was just *a'thegither ridiculous*" The good man had no sooner repaired his damage than the subsequent flood again demolished everything.

We may form some idea of the tremendous nature of the fall of rain, high up among the mountains, from what was observed even at Tomintoul, where the farrier told us that, from two slates having been blown out within two rows of the ridge of his roof, which created a hole of something less than 18 inches square, 80 Scotch pints, or about 40 gallons of rain water entered during the twelve hours between the morning and the evening of the 3rd of August. The whole valley was covered by the flood, the river appearing like a vast moving lake, where it was impossible to distinguish the real channel except from the greater velocity of its current.

The scenery immediately above the Bridge of Campdale is very beautiful. Abrupt rocks, covered with rich wood, rise from the right bank, whilst that on the left recedes, forming a lovely little nook of retirement, surrounded by green slopes, and knolls bedropt with trees. In this delightful spot an industrious retail shop-keeper, called Tom Meldrum, took up his abode, building, digging, and planting, till he had converted his residence into a little paradise. He was thriving, as his industry merited; and, to crown his comforts, he married a very nice-looking woman. His substantial stone and lime house was placed 15 yards from the brink of the river, and 12 above its level. My attention was attracted to it by the heaps of sand that environed it and from which it seemed to have been dug out; by the bundles of straw that were laid on the roof in lieu of the thatch which had been torn off; and by the cracked and undermined appearance of the walls (Plate 45). Tom was from home, but I accosted Mrs. Meldrum, who was walking about with a melancholy

PLATE 45. TOM MELDRUM'S HOUSE, AFTER THE FLOOD

and depressed air. "It was about six o'clock on Monday night that the flood cam' on us in ten minutes time," said she, "an' we had aneuch ado to escape to the brae-side. It took eight o' the stoutest men in the hail country, wi' the risk o' their lives, to get oot my kist. We syne saw the waters rise ower the eaves o' oor thatch, an' that wus the way that a' thing wus till ten o'clock neist mornin', when we cam' back, an' fund that a' the sma' kinkind o' articles had been floated oot at a back wundo'. But waur nor a' that, the hail o' Tam's goods, tea, sugar, an' siclike, war a' gane; an' the sugar a' meltit! A hunner pound wudna mak' it up till us. An' oor comfortable hoose, too, see hoo its ruined, an' it biggit but twa years ago; an' the gairden new ta'en in; an' a' destroyed, as ye see! But it's the Lord's wull, an' we maun submit. An' syne, the wee puckle furniture that wus saved, Tam an' me, we grew sae frightit that when we saw the Awen begud to rise on the twenty-seven, he wud try to get it across the water. Weel, he buckles it a'thegither on a raft, pits a tow till't, an' tries to pu' them to tither side, whan, just as they are i' the midds o' the water, whup! doun she comes, like the side o' a hill, breaks the rope, an' aff they a' gaed to the sea! An' see noo, sir, the hoose is as bare as a barn, an' a' sand an' weet! Oor bit comfortable hoose! We canna leeve ony langer here, that's for certain, an' whar we're to gang, I'm sure I dinna ken!"

PLATE 46. BRIDGE OF CAMPDALE, AFTER THE FLOOD

The Old Bridge of Campdale, built by General Wade, of two arches of 48 and 20 feet span, had the smaller one carried off, a circumstance that saved the larger (Plate 46). The height of the flood here was not less than 21 feet, where it floated over a breadth of nearly 200 feet.

Much destruction was committed by the Conglass, a large tributary from the right. A great extent of new channel had been formed at the point where we crossed it. A large part of the glebe of

Kirkmichael was carried off by the Aven. It also cut away 3 acres of the Kirktonhaugh, and inundated the dwelling of Thomas Cameron. Leaving it and its furniture to their fate, the inmates fled to the house of Peter Grant, the boatman of Dalnagarn, which was conceived to be so far from the river as to be perfectly secure. There some masons were lodged, with the intention of commencing the piers of a bridge next day; and they looked at the rising river with scientific eyes, in the hope of getting some instruction from it as to how they should make their work most secure. The flood speedily deluged this house, too. All fled from it, and in less than five minutes it was tearing up the trees, and rolling them so furiously down that the people were compelled to abandon all hope of saving the furniture, horses, and cattle on the premises. When night fell, the tops of the houses were still seen above the stream, but when day broke in the morning, not only the whole houses were gone, but the ground they stood on was cut away to the depth of many feet, and to the extent of 60 or 80 yards beyond them. The main body of the stream was running in a channel 200 or 300 yards from its former bed, directly through the spot where they had stood. Above 4 acres of land were lost at this point. The most remarkable circumstance of all was that the horses and cattle, which they had left in the stalls the previous night, were found quietly feeding on the hill side in the morning. The Lochy, a tributary on the left bank immediately opposite, ran quite through the garden belonging to the house of Inverlochy, cut away and destroyed 7 acres, and made a new channel for itself. At Milton of Inveroury, too, a new channel was created, an island of 8 acres formed, and 12 acres of valuable arable land carried away.

The houses Ballaneillan, on the left bank, though standing on an elevated site above two hundred yards from the Aven, were yet surrounded by the flood, which sent a powerful stream between them and the hill. Had this not eventually burst a passage for itself through a field, not only the buildings, but the whole farm, must have gone.

A small burn, entering on the left, forced the river over against the beautiful wooded bank of Dalrachney, on the right, of which it cut away two hundred yards in length, and 15 yards in horizontal breadth, leaving a sandy precipice, 90 feet high, *from which a mass of little less than 90,000 cubic yards was removed!* We met with a Mr. and Mrs. Yeats here, an amusing couple. When a question was put, the woman opened her mouth to reply, like an impatient turkey, but, before she could get out half a dozen words, she was silenced by the sharp "haud yer tongue, woman!" of her husband, who proceeded to deliver the response himself, with the gravity of an oracle. He told us of a small lake on his farm which, he assured us, contains a plough-man, his plough, and a yoke of oxen. The man was ploughing in the very field where Mr. and Mrs. Yeats were then reaping when, scared by a thunderstorm, the animals galloped off with plough and man into the loch. As the oxen are always heard bellowing in bad weather, their tremendous routings on the 3rd and 4th of August last may be conceived.

The Reverend Charles Macpherson of Tomintoul estimates the average breadth of the strath completely excavated into a river channel at 250 yards. The length of the inhabited and cultivated part of it is about sixteen miles, which would leave about 1220 acres totally useless. But, deducting one half of this for what usually lay under the river, there remains above 600 acres of the best soil destroyed, great part of which, however, was in lines and patches of pasture and wood, hardly recognizable in an estimate of loss, and which can be only brought into view by such a general calculation as this; for, in the usual summation of damage, nothing is taken into account but such pieces of land as have been swept, *en masse*, from particular fields; but even from this latter mode of calculation, the Duke of Gordon's factor, Mr. Skinner, makes out a loss, on the Aven alone, of from sixty to eighty acres of arable, belonging to His Grace.

In the afternoon of the 1st, Mr. Skinner, who lives at Drumin, immediately above the junction of the Livet, observed an unusually dark cloud on the top of Cromdale Hill, that rises to the north between the Aven and the Spey. It was so very remarkable in its appearance that it excited universal notice. The barometer stood with him at thirty on that day, but gradually fell till the 3rd, when it stood at 28·2.

The River Livet was very destructive. It rose at the bridge of Nevie twelve feet above its ordinary level. It was towards evening that it came down, in a few minutes, and broke directly through the middle of the house of John Grant, shoemaker, above the bridge, on the right bank, sweeping the centre of it entirely out, and leaving the ends; after which it assailed the arch, of forty-six feet span, and tore down the upper part of it. Grant's wife and four children, and his apprentice, were saved with great difficulty; but his account books were lost, and all his furniture was carried away, except a few articles that were arrested by the fall of the roof on them. His watch was buried by the fall of a gable, and was afterwards found with no other damage than a broken glass. Nothing could be more miserable than the situation of this poor man and his family, harboured as they were in a temporary hovel patched up at one end of the ruins, with the miserable remains of his furniture piled up on the sand heaps that half buried the place, whilst a lately purchased skin of bend leather, now all his stock-in-trade, was hanging without, over the end of a shed, as there was not room for it within (Plate 47). But it is truly delightful to record that I beheld a neat new cottage, of substantial stone and lime, rising on the face of the bank out of reach of the river, built by a general, voluntary, and gratuitous turn out of his neighbours. John Grant and his family fled for refuge from the flood to the house of Alexander Innes, below, but to the right of the bridge. Thither the deluge pursued them. Both families were placed in the greatest hazard, and had again to flee for their lives. Innes, anxious to save some papers, returned to the house and was met, as he came out again, by a tremendous rush of water, four or five feet deep. He was only rescued from drowning by the intrepidity of Lachlan Macpherson and John Grant, two stout blacksmiths, who, at the risk of their lives, plunged in to his aid.

PLATE 47. JOHN GRANT THE SHOEMAKER'S HOUSE, AT BRIDGE OF NEVIE, AFTER THE FLOOD

The Bridge of Livet, near Minmore, supposed to be as old as the ancient hunting-seat of Castleton, on the left, consisted of three long straggling picturesque arches, hopping, as it were, from one group of rocks to another, rather than springing boldly from bank to bank, its very plan sufficiently marking its extreme antiquity. Nothing could be more lovely than this little scene when I saw it formerly. Three neat clean-looking cottages, built in a row, lined a magnificently constructed new road in front of them. Beside and behind them were gay little gardens, intermingled trees, and the river rushing clear and sparkling, in little rapids, among the ledges of the smooth worn schistose rock, the whole scene being beautifully closed in by banks of hanging wood. It was but a few days before the flood, that Mr. Macpherson Grant, and the party from Ballindalloch, were struck by the picture of happiness and contentment exhibited by a woman, one of the cottagers, who was seated in a sunny nook of her smiling garden, knitting, and carolling a merry mountain ditty to her children. "About six o'clock on the fatal night of the 3rd," said a woman I conversed with, "the waters cam' doon in a moment, whan we waur a' oot gatherin' sticks in the brae yonder, and filled the road. A whilie after that it fell a wee, an' some o' Smith the merchant's goods were gotten oot, but doon it cam' again, swept awa' Smith's gable, an' a'thegither, and we didna' get oor fit in ower the door again till sax o'clock on Tuesday evening." Immediately after the flood, the party from Ballindalloch found the same woman they had formerly seen so happy, wringing her hands, and loudly lamenting the ruin that had befallen them. The metamorphosis produced by two devastating days was sad, indeed. The old bridge was much demolished, and one of its arches gone; the trees torn away and the gardens annihilated; the new road in front dug into a great ravine filled with water; the gable of the houses gone and all of them injured. As all surrounding circumstances pleasingly harmonized during its prosperity, so now those of its adversity were without one point of relief (Plate 48). An immense breach had taken place in the road, immediately opposite to the burial-ground of Dounan, situated on a picturesque point of rock overhanging the Livet. There the river rose 26 feet in the ravine. It would be well that this failure should be speedily repaired, for as strange sights are said to be sometimes seen in the little field of the dead, filling the space between the road and the river, the Glenlivet farmers returning from market may require to use the spur here, to flee from others than "the inhabitants o' the earth."

PLATE 48. OLD BRIDGE OF LIVET, AFTER THE FLOOD

Wide as the waterway is below the rocks, the river rose 12 feet, swept off a wooden bridge on stone pillars, rushed impetuously on the three dwelling-houses of the Milltown, and carried them and their outhouses away. Widow MacWilliam's house was so suddenly filled that she very narrowly escaped with her life, losing everything else, even her watch and money. A few effects of John Macpherson, merchant-tailor, were saved by great boldness, and by breaking a hole through the roof; but much the greater part was lost. All the tailor's substance had not departed from him, however, for I saw a very superior range of new buildings rising on the side of the hill, to contain a house and shop which, I doubt not, will yet be the wonder of the twin glens of the Aven and the Livet. The flood excavated a new channel for the Livet, which now enters the Aven 100 yards lower down than it did formerly. Nearly 50 ostensible acres have been destroyed by the Livet on the Duke of Gordon's property; but I shall notice His Grace's total damage in an after part of this work.

The old house of Kilmaichly, on Mr. Macpherson Grant's property, on the left bank of the Aven, occupies the flat summit of a green knoll, embosomed in a grove of ancient trees, and overlooking a rich assemblage of wooded banks, and long withdrawing terraces and haughs. The old fir trees are still prominently observable, and the house and its accompaniments, though somewhat in decay, yet remain in a state sufficiently fresh to recall the author's fascinations. The old lady and her ancient butler are, indeed, no longer here in corporeal existence; but blunt must be the fancy of that individual who could visit this classic spot without finding it haunted by their venerable forms.

The flood of 1768 cut a channel through the lower ground of Kilmaichly, isolating a part of it from the rest of the farm, and that of the 3rd and 4th of August last restored the river to its old bed. A remarkable hill, long, flat-topped and steep-sided in form, stretches down through the haughs, from the junction of the Livet with the Aven. It is evidently the remnant of a plain, in which the rivers once met at a much higher level. On this there is a Druidical circle and, on the top of the wooded hill of Craggan, near the lower termination of the Duke's property, there are large remains of cairns, and rude walls of fortification.

The farm of Haughs of Kilmaichly lost two acres; some steep banks of wood have been cut into precipices above the burn of Tomore, and the farm of Craigroy, on the left bank, has had two acres swept off.

The rapid Burn of Tomore descends from the mountain of Benrinnes on the right. John Cly, the meal-miller of Tomore (Plate 49), a sturdy, hale, independent minded old man of seventy-five, has been singularly persecuted by floods, having suffered by that of 1768, and by three or four inundations since, but especially by that of 1783, when his house and mill were carried away, and he was left pennyless. He was not a little affected by that calamity which fell upon him, and on no one else, but his indomitable spirit got the better of everything. Over seven years he undertook to improve a piece of absolute beach, of two acres, entirely covered with enormous

PLATE 49. JOHN CLY, MILLER OF TOMORE

stones and gravel. But John knew that a deep rich soil lay below, buried there by the flood of 1768. He removed the stones with immense labour, formed them into a bulwark and enclosure round the field, trenched down the gravel to the depth of 4 or 5 feet, and brought up the soil which afterwards produced most luxuriant crops. His neighbours ridiculed his operations while they were in progress, saying that he would never have a crop there. "Do ye see these ashen trees?" said John, pointing to some vigorous saplings growing near, "are they no thriving?" It was impossible to deny that they were. "Well," continued John, "if it wunna produce corn, I'll plant it wi' ash trees, and the laird, at least, will hae the benefit." The fruits of all John's labours were swept away by the direful flood of the 3d of August. But pride of his heart, as this improvement had been, the flood was not able to sweep away his equanimity and philosophy together with his acres. When someone condoled with him on his loss, "I took it fae the Awen," said he, with emphasis, "and let the Awen hae her ain again." And, when a gossiping tailor halted at his door one day, charitably to bewail his loss, he cut him short, by pithily remarking, "Well! if I have lost my croft, I have got a fish-pond in its place, where I can fish independent of any one." After the year 1783, he built his house on a rock, that shewed itself from under the soil at the base of the bank bounding the glen of the burn. During the late flood, the water was dashing up at his door, and his sister, who is older than he, having expressed great terror, proposed that they should both fly for it. "What's the woman afeard o'?" cried John, impatiently, "hae we no baith the rock o' nature an' the Rock o' Ages to trust till? We'll no stir one fit!" (Plate 50). John's first exertion after the flood was to go down to Ballindalloch, to assist the Laird in his distress. There he worked hard for three days before Mr. Grant discovered that he had left his own haystack buried to the top in sand, and insisted on his going home to disinter it. When Mr. Grant talked to him of his late calamity, "Od! Sir," said he, "I dinna regaird this matter hauf sae muckle as I did that slap i' the auchty-three, for then I was, in a manner, a marked man. Noo we're a' sufferin' thegither, an' I'm but neebourlike." Mr. Grant says that the people of this district bear misfortunes with a wonderful degree of philosophy, arising from the circumstance of their being deeply tinged with the doctrine of predestination. I was much gratified by my interview with honest John Cly. Whilst I was sketching him unperceived, Mr. Grant was doing his best to occupy his attention. "Well now, John," said Mr. Grant to him, pointing to an apparently impracticable beach of stones a little way up the glen, "if you had improved that piece, as I advised you, it would have been safe still, for you see the burn hasn't touched it at all." "Na, fegs!" replied John, with a most significant shake of his head, "gin I had gruppit her in wi' the stanes that cam' oot o't, whaur wad she hae been noo, think ye? Odd, I kent her ower lang." The flax-miller's croft shared the same fate as John Cly's, and the mill, full of flax, was sanded up to the beams of the first floor.

PLATE 50. JOHN CLY'S HOUSE, MILL OF TOMORE

Even the more elevated arable land on the Aven has not escaped, for some very high banks have been undermined on the left, and large masses of the upper fields hurled down. The farm of Lagmore has lost three acres, and the whole haugh of Dalnashach, of six acres, has been carried off.

The entrance to the pleasure grounds of Ballindalloch is on the right bank of the Aven, at the south end of the noble bridge. There the river is bounded on either side by schistose rocks, and the approach, running along the brink, commands occasional peeps of the clear river through the trees below, whilst it is shaded by the foliage of those that climb the hill above. The rocks terminate at the upper end of the lawn, the river sweeps away to the left, and the approach continues to thread its way through the trees at the base of the wooded bank, stretching to the right, and forming the boundary of the plain on that side. The lawn thus forms an angle at its upper extremity, between the line of the bank and that of the river. Its surface, though apparently level, has in reality a slight inclination towards the house, the antique and massive sewers of which rise about half way down its length, having little more than the breadth of the garden between it and the bank to the right. The lawn, especially below the house, is finely wooded with timber trees of great age, dropped singly in some places, and thickening into groves in others. Below the house, the line of bank on the right and the course of the Aven on the left continue to diverge from each other, and the general form of the whole plain may be said to be that of an obtuse-angled triangle, the obtuse angle of which lies between the Aven and the Spey, subtended by the bank which forms the long side of the figure. The extensive part of the plain below the lawn was laid out in a rich and very highly cultivated farm, enclosed with fine old hedge-rows.

About seven o'clock in the evening of the 3rd, the Aven suddenly overflowed its banks, for 900 yards along its course from the point where it leaves the rocks. Covering the lawn and rushing down towards the house, surrounding it, it flooded the lower storey and outhouses. The garden, of four acres, embraces the house on the side looking up the lawn, as well as on that side fronting the bank. The water forced a passage through the upper garden door, increased till one o'clock in the morning, partially subsided, and then again increased till seven o'clock. The situation of the house, on the morning of the 4th, thus became very alarming; and the garden wall between it and the river having given way, large pieces of it continued to fall in, and a body of water, of 25 yards in width and of immense force, rushed for twenty-four hours through the aperture, tight against the house. The situation of the family, thus shut in by a raging deluge, was dreadful. The ground-floor, where the dining-room is, had above three feet of water in it; streams were pouring violently through all the vaulted passages of the old mansion, and a great part of this period of dread was veiled in the thickest darkness, whilst the rain and the tempest continued to add to the other horrors. All manner of exertion was used to save the furniture, as well as the horses which were standing three and four feet deep in the stables.

A boat was sent from the ferry, some miles below, to remove the inhabitants, but the flood had already so far abated that it was not made use of.

When the waters subsided, it was discovered that the river had taken a slice out of the lawn, and established itself 50 yards nearer to the house. Its operations seemed to indicate a determination to cut its way directly through towards it. Its former bed beyond was filled with gravel and enormous stones, proving that here, as in most other places I have visited, the flood was in reality in a great measure composed of such materials. Part of the lawn was cut into chasms, and the rest covered with sand, trees, and wreck. The garden was filled 4 feet deep with sand, leaving the tops of the fruit trees alone visible, which, as they were loaded with apples and pears, presented a strange and melancholy spectacle. A deep ravine was excavated between the house and the bank. The whole shrubbery stretching along the base of the bank below the house was demolished. And, finally, the flood, bursting across the rich enclosures of the farm, spread devastation over 180 acres of the finest land bearing the heaviest crops of all kinds of produce. It cut away much of the ground, deeply scarifying the soil from other parts, digging some places into holes, covering others with gravel and utterly annihilating its promising fruits. Besides the land injured, which is nearly to the extent of the whole surface, above 18 acres are calculated to be irrecoverably lost.

It is a singular fact that the small birds, of which there was rather an over-abundance at Ballindalloch, all left the place after the flood. The lawn trees, too, which had been flooded round the roots, were immediately struck with the chill of autumn, and prematurely assumed its variegated livery. Here, as everywhere else, fish were strewed over the deluged grounds. This flood is calculated to have exceeded that of 1768, at Ballindalloch, by six feet. At the Bridge of Aven, where the water-way of the two arches is 105 feet, the rise of the river was 23 feet; and, at the upper end of the lawn, where it first escapes from the rocks, the rise was 10 feet on a water-way of 222 feet.

The farms of Delnapot and Pitcroy, on the left bank of the Spey, suffered severely. On the latter, a fine haugh of fifteen acres was utterly ruined, and the river is now working a new channel through it. The rapid burn of Aultyoulie, entering from the left, carried away the corn-mill and saw-mill of Pitcroy. These were built about fifty years ago, and never excited the smallest suspicion of risk. The bench of the saw-mill, 12 feet long, 5 feet broad, and 4 feet high, containing two circular saws, and 100 weight of iron attached to it, was carried down the Spey for twelve miles, and landed on the Heathery Isle, above Arndilly, quite uninjured.

Below Ballindalloch stands the Church of Inveraven, which was so environed by a burn on one side, and the Spey on the other, that it threatened to yield to the fate predicted for it in the old prophecy, *"the Kirk of Inveraven will gang doun Spey fu' o' folk."*

The flood of 1768 isolated a great tract of ground which was taken as a farm, seven years ago, by James Macpherson. This spirited young man erected buildings on it, and improved and limed the ground, which produced great crops. Macpherson, his sister, a carpenter, and a neat herd-boy remained on the island till the greater part of the ground was covered, and the water was flowing in a stream towards the house. At seven o'clock in the evening of the 3rd, they all committed themselves to a small boat, and Macpherson, being an expert timber-floater, effected a landing on the left bank. Next morning, nothing was visible but his houses and a hay stack. He resolved to make a desperate attempt to save his cattle and horses and, accompanied by a young man of the name of Clark, he, at five o'clock in the morning of the 4th, crossed to the island through the mountainous waves. A man who witnessed the daring exploit declared "That it made him blind to look at them." Having reached the houses, he found the cattle and horses standing up to their backs in the water, perfectly cramped with cold. Their only resource was to force hay or straw in underneath their feet, and so to raise the animals by degrees above the water. They had no sooner accomplished this, than the creatures lay down, being quite exhausted with their twenty-four hours immersion. The most extraordinary part of their history was that they actually slept for three days afterwards without intermission.

A line of majestic oaks, skirting the water's edge but high above it, were swept away from the farm of Wearach, and most of them landed on that of Dandaleith, 12 miles below. To pass over smaller injuries done to other farms, Dalvennan had 12 acres, a croft adjacent to it 5 acres, and Delgarvon 15 acres, utterly destroyed. The sum total of Mr. Macpherson Grant's loss amounts to £8000. That experienced by his tenantry was great, afflicting, and productive of much misery; but, in so overwhelming a calamity, it is pleasing to remark the Christian temper with which it is borne. Mr. Grant says, in one of his letters to me, that "they talk of nothing but how they are to recover and restore their farms, and have never mentioned the word abatement, leaving that to my own decision.* Our friend John Cly has already begun the restoration of his croft, which, he says, *"was a great deal waur i' the seventeen hunner and auchty-three!"* Eleven families have been made destitute in the parish of Inveraven: some have lost property to the extent of between £100 and £200 each.

* *Mr. Grant has since fully warranted the confidence reposed in him by making abatements to the full extent of their losses, thus taking them entirely upon himself, in addition to all he has suffered as proprietor.*

CHAPTER 16

THE KNOCKANDO BURN. THE RIVER SPEY TO LOWER CRAIGELLACHIE. THE RIVERS DULLAN AND FIDDOCH

THE Knockando Burn, entering from the left, is extremely small, but it was swollen by the flood to a size equal to that of the Spey in its ordinary state. The high promontory, on the neck of which the manse of Knockando stands, shoots forward towards the steep opposite banks of the burn, interrupting the continuity of its haughs by a narrow pass, leaving room only, at the base of the precipice, for two cottages, a small garden and a road. Where the glen opens, a little way above, there stood a carding-mill, a meal-mill, and the houses of their occupants. Of the two cottages at the bottom of the promontory, one was inhabited by the old bellman, his wife, and daughter, and a blind beggar-woman who had that night sought quarters with them. The other was tenanted by a poor, lame woman, who keeps a school for girls and young children. On Monday evening, the 3rd, the bellman's daughter came running to the manse. "For the love o' gudeness come an' help my father and mother! The burn's like to tak' awa' baith themsel's and their hoose. The mistress has cruppen oot at a wundo, an' is stan'in' i' the yaird amouw the kail-castocks, an' she binna whirled awa' else," and, hastily shuffling a small parcel into the hands of the lady of the house, saying, "Keep that, mem, for it belangs tae the mistress", she disappeared. The parcel contained the hard-earned trifle the schoolmistress had gained by teaching, and was all that had been saved from her house. By the time the Reverend William Asher reached the spot, a stout, determined fellow had succeeded in carrying the poor schoolmistress to the face of the precipice, where she stood on a sloping ledge, leaning on her crutch, exposed to the fury of the elements. The same gallant fellow, at the risk of his life, ventured in for the bellman's wife, and took her up on his back, but if it had not been for the aid of the bystanders, both would have been lost. To return again was impossible, and yet there the bellman and the blind beggar-woman stood, linked together, with only their head and shoulders above the current. A long ladder at the manse was thought of, but ere it arrived the house had so given way that there was no place to rest its end on. Ropes, therefore, became the only alternative. A stout man, who had early made his way into the place, secured one end of them to a post near the cottages, and the other being drawn tight was attached to a tree on the precipice. The man then, grasping the bellman firmly by the collar, and holding hard by the rope, dragged himself and his charge through the furious current, where he had no footing. By wonderful exertion, both were landed safely, and the poor beggar woman was rescued in a similar manner, and in a half drowned state. "Nae wonder that oor teeth are chatterin," said the bellman, "seein' that we war stan'in' sae lang yonder, wi' the water up to the sloat o' the breast, in dread a' the time that the neist jaw wad whirl us awa' to yeternity."

After the flood the prospect here was melancholy. The burn that formerly wound through the beautiful haugh, above the promontory, had cut a channel, as broad as that of the Spey, from one end of it to the other. The whole wood was gone, the carding-mill had disappeared, the miller's house was in ruins, and the banks below were strewed with pales, gates, bridges, rafts, engines, wool, yarn, and half-woven webs, all utterly destroyed. A new road was recently made in this parish, and all the burns were substantially bridged; but, with the exception of one arch, all yielded to the pressure of the flood. Mr. Grant of Wester Elchies' damage is estimated at £820. The parish of Knockando returned twelve cases of families rendered destitute by this calamity.

The flood, both in the Spey and its tributary burn, was terrible at the village of Charlestown of Aberlour. On the 3rd of August, Charles Cruickshanks, the innkeeper, had a party of friends in his house. There was no inebriety, but there was a fiddle; and what Scotsman is he who does not know that the well jerked strains of a lively Strathspey have a potent spell in them that goes beyond even the witchery of the bowl? On one who daily inhales the breezes from the musical stream that gives name to the measure, the influence is powerful, and it was that day felt by Cruickshanks with a more than ordinary degree of excitement. He was joyous to a pitch that made his wife grave. I have already noticed the predestinarian principles prevalent in these parts. Mrs. Cruickshanks was deeply affected by her husband's unusual jollity. "Surely my goodman is daft the day," said she gravely, "I ne'er saw him dance at sic a rate. Lord grant that he binna *fey*!"*

When the river began to rise rapidly in the evening, Cruickshanks, who had a quantity of wood lying near the mouth of the burn, asked two of his neighbours, James Stewart and James Mackerran, to go and assist him in dragging it out of the water. They readily complied, and Cruickshanks, getting on the loose raft of wood, they followed him, and did what they could in pushing and hauling the pieces of timber ashore, till the stream increased so much that, with one voice, they declared they would stay no longer. Making a desperate effort, they plunged over head, and reached the land with the greatest difficulty. They then tried all their eloquence to persuade Cruickshanks to come away, but he was a bold and

* *"I think," said the old gardener to one of the maids, "the gauger's fie"; by which word the common people express those violent spirits which they think a presage of death. (Guy Mannering).*

experienced floater, and laughed at their fears; nay, so utterly reckless was he, that, having now diminished the crazy ill-put-together raft he stood on, till it consisted of a few spars only, he employed himself in trying to catch at and save some haycocks belonging to the clergyman, which were floating past him. But, while his attention was so engaged, the flood was rapidly increasing, till, at last, even his dauntless heart became appalled at its magnitude and fury. "A horse! a horse!" he loudly and anxiously cried, "Run for one of the minister's horses, and ride in with a rope, else I must go with the stream." He was quickly obeyed, but ere a horse arrived, the flood had rendered it impossible to approach him.

Seeing that he must abandon all hope of help in that way, Cruickshanks was now seen, as if summoning up all his resolution and presence of mind, to make the perilous attempt of dashing through the raging current with his frail and imperfect raft. Grasping more firmly the iron-shod pole he held in his hand, called in floater's language a *sting*, he pushed resolutely into it. He had hardly done so when the violence of the water wrenched from his hold that which was all he had to depend on. A shriek burst from his friends as they beheld the wretched raft dart off with him, down the stream, like an arrow freed from the bow-string. But the mind of Cruickshanks was no common one to quail before the first approach of danger. He poised himself, and stood balanced, with determination and self-command in his eye, and no sound of fear or of complaint was heard to come from him. At the point where the burn met the river, in the ordinary state of both, there grew some trees, now surrounded by deep and strong currents, and far from the land. The raft took a direction towards one of these, and seeing the wide and tumultuous waters of the Spey before him, in which there was no hope that his loosely connected logs could stick one moment together, he coolly prepared himself and, collecting all his force into one well-timed and well-directed effort, he sprang, caught a tree, and clung among its boughs, whilst the frail raft hurried away from under his foot, was dashed into fragments, and scattered on the bosom of the waves. A shout of joy arose from his anxious friends, for they now deemed him safe; but he uttered no shout in return. Every nerve was strained to procure help. "A boat!" was the general cry, and some ran this way and some that, to endeavour to procure one. It was now between seven and eight o'clock in the evening. A boat was speedily obtained from Mr. Gordon of Aberlour and, though no one there was very expert in its use, it was quickly manned by people eager to save Cruickshanks from his perilous situation. The current was too terrible about the tree to admit of their nearing it, so as to take him directly into the boat; but their object was to row through the smoother water, to such a distance as might enable them to throw a rope to him, by which means they hoped to drag him to the boat.

Frequently did they attempt this, and as frequently were they foiled, even by that which was considered as the gentler part of the stream, for it hurried them past the point whence they wished to make the cast of their rope, and compelled them to row up again by the side, to start on each fresh adventure. Often were they carried so much in the direction of the tree as to be compelled to exert all their strength to pull themselves away from him they would have saved, that they might avoid the vortex that would have caught and swept them to destruction. And often was poor Cruickshanks tantalized with the approach of help, which came but to add to the other miseries of his situation, that of the bitterest disappointment. Yet he bore all calmly. In the transient glimpses they had of him, as they were driven past him, they saw no blenching on his dauntless countenance, they heard no reproach, no complaint, no sound, but an occasional short exclamation of encouragement to persevere in their friendly endeavours. But the evening wore on, and still they were unsuccessful. It seemed to them that something more than mere natural causes was operating against them. "His hour is come!" said they, as they regarded one another with looks of awe; "our struggles are vain." The courage and the hope which had hitherto supported them began to fail, and the descending shades of night extinguished the last feeble sparks of both, and put an end to their endeavours.

Fancy alone can picture the horrors that must have crept on the unfortunate man as, amidst the impenetrable darkness which now prevailed, he became aware of the continued increase of the flood that roared around him, by its gradual advance towards his feet, whilst the rain and the tempest continued to beat more and more dreadfully upon him. That these were long ineffectual in shaking his collected mind, we know from the fact, afterwards ascertained, that he actually wound up his watch while in this dreadful situation. But, hearing no more the occasional passing exclamations of those who had been hither-to trying to succour him, he began to shout for help in a voice that became every moment more long drawn and piteous as, between the gusts of the tempest, and borne over the thunder of the waters, it fell from time to time on the ears of his clustered friends, and rent the heart of his distracted wife. Ever and anon it came, and hoarser than before, and there was an occasional wildness in its note, and now and then a strange and clamorous repetition for a time, as if despair had inspired him with an unnatural energy. But the shouts became gradually shorter, less audible, and less frequent, till at last their eagerly listening ears could catch them no longer. "Is he gone?" was the half-whispered question they put to one another, and the smothered responses that were muttered around but too plainly told how much the fears of all were in unison.

"What was that?" cried his wife in delirious scream. "That was his whistle I heard!" She said truly. A shrill whistle, such as that which is given with the fingers in the mouth, rose again over the loud din of the deluge, and the yelling of the storm. He was not yet gone. His voice was but cracked by his frequent exertions to make it heard, and he had now resorted to an easier mode of transmitting to his friends the certainty of his safety. For some time his unhappy wife drew hope from such considerations, but his whistles, as they came more loud and prolonged, pierced the ears of his foreboding friends like the ill-omened cry of some warning spirit; and, it may be matter of question whether all believed that the sounds they heard were really mortal. Still they came louder and clearer for a brief space; but at last they were heard no more, save in his frantic wife's fancy, who continued to start as if she still heard them, and to wander about, and to listen, when all but herself were satisfied that she could never hear them again.

Wet, weary, and shivering with cold, was this miserable woman when the tardy dawn of morning beheld her, straining her eyeballs through the imperfect light towards the trees where Cruickshanks had been last seen. There was something there that looked like the figure of a man, and on that her eyes fixed. But those around her saw, alas! too well, that what she fondly supposed to be her husband was but a bunch of wreck, gathered by the flood into one of the trees, for the one to which he clung had been swept away.

The body of poor Cruickshanks was found in the afternoon of next day, on the haugh of Dandaleith, some four or five miles below. As it had ever been his uniform practice to wind his watch up at night, and as it was discovered to be nearly full wound when it was taken from his pocket, the fact of his having had self-possession enough to obey his usual custom, under circumstances so terrible, is as unquestionable as it is wonderful. It had stopped at a quarter of an hour past eleven o'clock, which would seem to fix that as the fatal moment when the tree was rent away, for when that happened, his struggles amidst the raging waves of the Spey must have been few and short. When the men who had so unsuccessfully attempted to save him were talking over the matter, and agreeing that no human help could have availed him, "I'm thinkin' I could ha' ta'en him oot," said a voice in the circle. All eyes were turned towards the speaker, and a general expression of contempt followed, for it was a boy of the name of John Rainey, a reputed idiot, from the foot of Benrinnes, who spoke. "You!" cried a dozen voices at once, "what would you have done, you wise man?" "I wud hae tied an empty anker-cask to the end o' a lang lang tow, an' I wud hae floated it aff fae near aboot whar the raft was ta'en first awa', an' syne, ye see, as the stream teuk the raft till the tree, maybe she wud hae ta'en the cask there too. An' if Charley Cruickshanks had ance gotten a haud o' the rope..." He would have finished, but his auditors were gone. They had silently slunk away in different directions, one man alone having muttered, as he went, something about "wisdom coming out of the mouths of fools."

The Manse of Aberlour was inundated and, in the confusion that occurred, the cellar was drained in more ways than one by some officious assistants. Part of the glebe was swept away.* The boatman's house at Wester Elchies was in imminent danger, the outhouses were carried off, and 50 acres of valuable haugh land, in crop, were covered with above two feet deep of sand and gravel. A row of venerable trees were rent away from Easter Elchies, where the stream altered its course and threatens farther injury to a place ornamented more than a century ago by the father of Lord Elchies, the distinguished judge.

The haugh above the bridge of Lower Craigellachie was very much cut up, and the house and nursery at the south end of the arch are gone. The widow of James Shanks, amidst the loss of her furniture, house, and her son's garden ground, lamented nothing so much as her deceased husband's watch, and his fiddle, on the strings of which hung many a tender recollection. That fiddle, the dulcet strains of which had come over her "like the sweet south** breathing upon a bed of violets," stealing the tender affections of her virgin heart, till they all centred on her Orpheus, Mr. James Shanks; that fiddle, to the sprightly notes of which she had so often jerked out her youthful limbs, and whirled round in the wild *pirouette* of the Highland fling, to the animating tune of *Bog-an-Lochan*; that fiddle, in fine, which had been the fiddle of her fancy from the hey-day of her youth upwards, "was gone with the water, and was now, for ought she knew to the contrair, in Norrawa or Denmark!" The grief of Mrs. Shanks for the loss of this valued violin was more than I shall attempt to paint. Great artists often envelope the heads of their chief mourners in drapery, from a conscious inability to do justice to the passion, and so must I hide the lachrymose head of Mrs. Shanks. And how, indeed, shall I describe her joy, some days afterwards, when an idle loon who had been wandering about the banks of the river "finding things," as he said himself, appeared before her astonished and delighted eyes, with the identical fiddle in his hand. The yell of Mrs. Shanks was said, by those who heard it, to resemble the wild shriek with which her husband was wont to inspire additional fury into the heels of the dancers, already excited by the power of his wonderful bow hand. She kissed and hugged the fiddle, and, as if its very contact had music in it, she laid hands on the astonished loon, and went a full round of the floor with him, ending

** The Presbytery of Aberlour are said to have taken up this case. It is not the only one of the kind. The question is, What remedy has the minister in such circumstances?*

*** Publisher's Note: This quotation has been faithfully reproduced from Sir Thomas's original text, and is evidently based on the words of Orsino in Act 1, Scene 1, of Shakespeare's 'Twelfth Night'. The exact quotation from that work, however, is "Oh! It came o'er my ear like the sweet* ***sound*** *that breathes upon a bank of violets..."*

with a fling that surprised every one. The fiddle had been found in the neighbourhood of Arndilly, whither it had merrily floated on the bosom of the waves. But what was yet infinitely more extraordinary, the watch, which had hung in a small bag suspended by a nail to a post of her bed, was found - watch, bag, post, and all - near Fochabers, eight or ten miles below, and was safely restored to its overjoyed owner.

The flood was 15 feet higher than ordinary at Craigellachie Bridge, where the river spread over the whole haugh. This beautiful iron arch, of 150 feet span, springing boldly from the buttress on the low right bank to the high cliff on the left, was in some jeopardy, and was only saved by the works of approach yielding to the force of the stream.

The River Fiddoch enters from the right a short way below the bridge. It, and its tributary the Dullan, were by no means harmless, and all the oldest people agree that no such flood was ever seen in either. The Reverend Morris Forsyth lost a considerable part of his glebe at Mortlach, by the Dullan. The church, which was the ancient Cathedral of Mortlach, existed in the days of Malcolm Canmore, who added three lengths of his spear to the nave, in fulfilment of a vow he made previous to a battle with the Danes, in which he entirely routed them. Some of their heads were built into the wall, where their skulls may yet be seen. This is a lovely spot, combining all the richness of England with the scenery of a Highland glen. Immediately above the junction of the Dullan with the Fiddoch, a woollen manufactory and dye-work, established by Mr. Stewart, were entirely destroyed with all their materials. From the magnificent old Castle of Balveny downwards, the beautiful haugh lands were much cut up, and a flax-mill on the estate of Kinnivie was left in a very picturesque state, one side having fallen in, whilst the machinery hung on pegs, as if self-suspended. Kinnivie is a highly interesting old house, with towers and narrow gables and roofs, old trees, thick hedges, Dutch parterres, terraces, bowery shrubs, and intricate labyrinths, and the greatest good taste has been displayed in keeping it up entirely in its original style. The damage on this small property is £750. Below the ruins of the Castle of Gauldwell, the palace of the Bishop of Mortlach, the Fiddoch rooted out a plantation belonging to Mr. Shearer of Buchromb, and terminated its devastations by sweeping away the bridges of two arches, one of 50, and the other of 10 feet span, immediately above its junction with the Spey.

CHAPTER 17

THE RIVER SPEY, FROM LOWER CRAIGELLACHIE TO THE PASS OF SOURDEN, INCLUDING THE PLAIN OF ROTHES

WE now enter on the once beautiful Plain of Rothes, presenting, since the flood, a scene of utter devastation. The first farm on the left is that of Dandaleith, a stretch of level land, which had been rendered, by the skill and capital of Mr. MacInnes, the boast of Speyside. And well it might be called so, for land in higher cultivation, or more perfectly fenced, was nowhere to be met with. But the flood burst over it from Lower Craigellachie, the Spey being forced to the left by the Fiddoch, and converted it into a desert that seemed as if it had never been tilled by man. At least 26 acres of very fine land were carried entirely away, and not less than 50 more were covered with sand and gravel to the depth of about 3 feet. Immense river channels were cut in various places, the fences were levelled, and the whole crop was destroyed. The ground was strewed over, when I saw it, with enormous trees, including one immense oak from Ballindalloch, weighing, with its root, not less than 3 or 4 tons (Plate 51). A cow-herd boy in the area, being asked if he lost anything, "Aye," replied he, "I lost twa sarks, an' ane o' them was clean too." As I walked over the farm, I was

PLATE 51. OAK TREE FROM BALLINDALLOCH, STRANDED AT DANDALEITH

suddenly arrested by observing a longitudinal cairn of small stones, about the dimensions of a man's body. This was a frail and melancholy monument, placed there by the friends of poor Cruickshanks, to mark the spot where they had found his body.

Mr. MacInnes estimates his damage, as tenant, at £2000.*

** He has already commenced trenching down the sand and gravel, which he wisely considers the best plan, as the surface of the field is thereby raised just so much higher above the river than it was before. The expense is great.*

Opposite to Dandaleith is the Heathery Isle, among the trees of which there were found spinning-wheels, chairs, tables, beds, chests of drawers, and all manner of cottage furniture and farming utensils, from the cradle to the cart; and, among other things, as already noticed, the bench and saws of the saw-mill of Pitcroy.

The Valley of the Spey may be said to be about a mile wide at Rothes. The river there keeps entirely over towards the right bank, and the large and populous village is built along the base of the high ground bounding the valley on the left. Two burns descend from glens opening directly on the village, cross it, and find their way to the river through the intervening plain, which was entirely occupied by the potato grounds, and patches of corn, rented by the villagers. The village consists of one long street, running N.E. and S.W. along the base of the hill, and of another crossing it diagonally. One burn has its course in the line of this last mentioned cross street, and the other passes by the N.E. end of the long thoroughfare. By five o'clock in the afternoon of the 3rd, these rose tremendously, and that at the end of the town swept away its bridge. The upper and under divisions of the cross street, and the north-eastern end of the main thoroughfare, were instantly converted into rivers, the water bursting open the doors, and rushing into the houses. A large proportion of the inhabitants of these three streets were now in the utmost danger, and those who were themselves in safety flew to succour their friends and neighbours who were in peril. Then were the stout and active of both sexes seen wading in, at the risk of being carried away by the stream, and dragging the young, the aged, and the infirm, some of whom had not for years been from under a roof, out at their windows or doors, as they best could, and carrying them, some on their backs, some in their arms, through the deep and powerful currents. Peats in black masses, firewood, poultry, and pigs, were seen tumbling along, and every now and then the young fellows were dashing in and hauling out huge hogs by the hind legs, or plunging to the middle after some other live or dead object. Fortunate it was that all this confusion occurred during the light of day, and that the whole of the people were placed in safety before nightfall; but, as the burns increased, and the bridge in the centre of the village gave way, darkness brought with it a night of dreadful suspense. There was a partial subsidence here as elsewhere; but, after twelve o'clock next day, the flood again rose, and to a still greater height, and either totally demolished, or partially destroyed, fifteen dwelling-houses of as good and substantial masonry as could possibly be built.

A remarkable corroboration of what I have stated in the preliminary chapter, that our floods of modern days must be greatly augmented by the increase of drainage of all kinds, is furnished by these burns of Rothes. Mr. Brown of Dunkinty, factor for Lord Seafield, tells me that after some extensive draining operations had been executed at the head of the burn of Rothes, the tenant of the mills applied for an additional mill-dam, because the drains had the effect of running off the water so quickly that the mills ceased to be supplied with the same regularity as formerly.

It was a truly fortunate circumstance that Mr. Brown happened to be at Rothes during the inundation. Soon after sunrise on the morning of the 4th, the Spey was at its extreme height, and flooded the greater part of the wide plain. Mr. Brown then became alarmed for the safety of some of the inhabitants of the farms above the village. He left the inn and, on reaching a point on the turnpike road, opposite to the farm house immediately below that of Dandaleith, tenanted by Widow Riach, he was shocked to see the water five feet up on the walls, though many hundred yards removed from the ordinary channel of the river, and the stream that swept along between the buildings and the bank where the road ran, was of itself at least four times as large as the Spey in its ordinary state. Other currents rushing through the smoother water from the main run of the river, set right against the houses and forced violently through between the gable of the dwelling-house and the offices, so that it was evident that the upper end of the former must soon fall. But what was Mr. Brown's horror, when he perceived a woman looking out at a small window, in that very gable, waving a handkerchief as if imploring for speedy aid. There was no retreat from that end of the house, for that was the only part of it that had an upper room. In an agony of apprehension, Mr. Brown hurried off to the village of Rothes, to make inquiry about a boat which he knew was in possession of some one in the town, and, after being teased by a thousand delays and disappointments, he at length found it in a shed, buried under an immense heap of peats. It was soon got out, however, and there was something peculiarly good in the feeling of that bystander who said, "Don't take it up to the spot to raise hopes by its appearance, until you are certain that you have hands who will man it, and realize them." "I will go!" "And I," cried two lads of the name of Riach, though, I believe, not connected with her of the same name whom they were thus volunteering to risk their lives to rescue. Not a moment more was lost; the boat was instantly carted, carried to the place, and launched off the turnpike road. The flood was still going on increasing; for, as they were in the act of lowering the boat into the water, a cart was observed to float away from Mrs. Riach's farm-yard; and, before the men had seated themselves at the oars, the corn stacks from Dandaleith passed down the stream quite entire. The boat put off, and a nervous and agitating spectacle it was; for the current ran so strong and rough, that they were carried several hundred yards down before they could shoot into the less violent water, where, after a long pull up, they passed round by the front or farther side of the buildings, and were altogether hid by them for a time from the anxious eyes of those on shore. There, as they afterwards learned, the two men made fast the boat to some part of the dwelling-house (Plate 52), and the water covering it nearly to the eaves, they were enabled to get upon the roof, whence they shouted down the chimney to the inmates. It is unnecessary to say how thankfully they obeyed the summons.

PLATE 52. WIDOW RIACH'S HOUSE, DURING THE FLOOD, SOUTH SIDE

The women were first taken out, with great difficulty, from a small window and, after a hazardous passage, were safely landed amidst the congratulations of all those who witnessed this trying scene. The boat then returned for the men, and for two of Mrs. Riach's grand-children, and disappeared, as formerly, behind the intervening buildings. While the spectators were anxiously looking for its re-appearance, the upper gable of the house, which had been so long undermined by the press of currents combined against it, gave way all at once, and carried half the building along with it. "Oh! my brother! - My brother is gone!" cried a young man in a voice of agony, alluding to one of the lads who had taken an oar. Half-uttered ejaculations burst from the shuddering crowd of spectators, the poor widow was paralyzed, and Mr. Brown was overwhelmed by the horror of the scene. A tremendous splash of water mingled with the cloud of dust that arose from the crumbling ruin. It cleared away and, to the unspeakable joy of all the beholders, the little boat was disclosed to view, through the gap in the building, with the remainder of the family seated in it; and, as it made for the land, it actually floated directly over the fallen and submerged materials of that house which they had occupied but a few seconds before. There was a shout of joy, and an offering up of short, yet sincere, thanks to God, by those on shore, for so signal an interference of His providence; and the whole of the rescued, consisting of eight grown persons, and two children, were soon happily united, beyond the reach of danger, after having remained in that awful situation for nine hours during the night. Mrs. Riach's mental sufferings were infinitely the most severe, for, having been urged to remove the previous evening, her attachment to her home led her to refuse, in the belief that it was out of all possibility the flood could come so many hundred yards beyond where the Spey has ever been seen or heard of. She therefore felt that she had been the cause of the peril in which her grand-children, and some of her friends, who had kindly come to lend her assistance, were so unfortunately placed. She had her Bible in her hand, apparently the only wreck of property she had saved, but in that she had found consolation. Her soul had been already well attuned to affliction. In this her widowed state, she had recently lost her son, and now nearly her all was gone; for, when I visited her farm, not a vestige of new or of old crop was left. The house had indeed been built up, but the offices were still in ruins, a great ravine was dug out between them and the dwelling-house, and the surface of the farm was reduced to one waste of devastation. Yet, with all this, pure religion had produced its effect and the pale, mild countenance of the widow, lighted by a celestial smile, met me at her unpretending threshold, wearing the expression of Christian resignation and gratitude for the merciful salvation which had been vouchsafed her. There was no lisp of complaint, and every word she uttered was expressive of the deep sense she entertained of the goodness of that God, who is ever the widow's friend, who had so wonderfully preserved herself and those whom she held most dear. One sight of that woman's face, after having seen and heard the sum-total of her afflictions, was worth a volume of sermons. It is pleasing to think that her lot is cast on an estate where the hearts of both the manager and his constituent are too much fraught with the finer feelings of humanity not to show the tenderest mercy towards 'the shorn ewe.'

From Dandaleith to the Pass of Sourden, where the Rothes Plain terminates, 70 or 80 acres of very fine land, on the left bank of the Spey, were either carried off entirely, or so laid over with sand and gravel, as to render it extremely doubtful whether they can ever be reclaimed. Of these nearly 40 acres were rented in small patches by the poor villagers of Rothes. While the loss of the land falls heavy on the proprietor, the utter destruction of the crops creates incalculable misery to these unfortunate people. There are no less than 107 cases of destitute families produced by the flood in this parish. Mr. Brown visited the village two days after the flood. At the first glance he threw along the street as he entered it, he was led to believe there was a fair in the town. But he soon saw that the crowd, and the occupation of the people, and the display of goods, arose from a much more melancholy cause. Some were actively engaged in moving out the mud and gravel that had filled their houses 5 feet deep, and choked up the entrances; and the furniture that had not been absolutely lost, and beds, bedding, chairs, tables, and all such articles, were ranged along the streets, to allow the water they had imbibed to evaporate by exposure to the air. Among other things so exposed were the goods belonging to the shop-keepers; but the utter loss in tea and sugar was very considerable. The most afflicting spectacle of all was that of the people assembling, in the solemn garb of woe, to convey the remains of poor Charles Cruickshanks from the Church of Rothes, where they had been lodged, to the place of interment at Knockando.

On the Arndilly property, lying along the right bank, the river carried off a bulwark of great length and strength opposite the house, ran through the fine haugh below the garden, converting it into a perfect waste, and carried off a beautiful belt of wood, and many clumps of trees. A little lower down, another haugh, and the plantations adjoining it, shared the same fate.

CHAPTER 18

THE RIVER SPEY, FROM THE PASS OF SOURDEN TO THE BRIDGE OF FOCHABERS

AT the Rock of Sourden, where the width from the site of the old Castle of Aikenwalls, on the right bank, to the hill on the left of the Pass, is 237 feet, *the river was 20 feet 10 inches above its ordinary level,* and 15 inches above the mark made to record the rise of the Spey in the much-talked-of flood of September, 1768. This is a great difference over so extensive a space. But I am disposed to think that the real difference was much greater than this. It is probable that, in 60 years, a very considerable change may have taken place in the depth and capacity of the river's bed, especially in a narrow pass of this kind, where there must be a great rush at all times when the river is full. Besides, it is not easy accurately to measure inches in a tumultuous body of rolling water. But however large the flood of 1768 might be, it is probable that its duration was comparatively short, otherwise we should have had more ample records of the mischief produced by it.

Immediately below the Pass of Sourden, Lord Seafield's saw-mill of Dundurcus was carried off, and sailed down the river like a great ship. The whole works about it disappeared; nay their very site was eradicated, and the ground left not only as if no such thing had ever been there, but so that nothing of the kind could ever be placed there again. The island of Dundurcus, too, of 13 acres, was completely obliterated. The tremendous damage done here is much to be attributed to the concentration of the force of the flood at the Pass. At Boat of Brig, where the haughs were much flooded, the river was 17 feet above the ordinary level at nine o'clock in the morning of the 4th. By midday it was down to 12 feet, at which height it remained till six o'clock in the evening, when it rapidly subsided.

The Burn of Mulben, tributary to the Spey, on the right bank, at Boat of Brig, is generally almost dry in the summer season, but, in the afternoon of the 3rd, it rose 20 feet, damaged the plantations of Auchluncart, the glebe lands, and Lord Seafield's property. Opposite to Auchluncart, it undermined a bank, and water having accumulated in the under strata, an extent of ground containing 800 square yards of surface composed of hard compact gravel, and crossed by a smaller burn, slipped and subsided in one mass, more than a foot, carrying with it two houses, 200 yards of a dry stone wall, 200 yards of the turnpike road, and a bridge, all unbroken! The Burn of Mulben also destroyed a bridge on the turnpike road worth £250, and materially injured many others. Lord Seafield's wood-manager at Boat of Brig says that "it came down, as it were, in a bank of water, destroying everything but the rock in its progress." It carried off the dam of the saw-mill here, choked up the mill-run, demolished a 50 feet wooden bridge, cut away an acre of land, and floated off several hundred pounds worth of timber from the depot.

The wood-manager says that the Spey "began to appear in earnest," between seven and eight o'clock on Monday evening the 3rd. In three hours it rose 10 feet, on a surface of not less than 500 yards wide. The manager's neat cottage of Delfur, newly finished, and its garden and shrubberies, laid out with great taste, stood at the foot of a wooded bank at about a furlong from the Spey, having a fine haugh, with belts of wood stretching between it and the river. The flood first attacked the offices, where the horses were taken from the stable swimming; and, by the time they were safe, two cows, in an adjacent cow-house, could not be got out, from the increased strength and violence of the stream, and, as a last resource, they were drawn into a porch at the kitchen door, where they remained, with the water almost over their backs, until the forenoon of the 4th, when a cut was made in a steep precipice up which the poor, half-drowned animals were drawn by ropes. The manager's family were expelled from the house at eleven o'clock at night. When daylight appeared on the 4th, the barn, the cart-shed with four carts, the stable, with all its harness, the cow-house, the poultry-house, with all its inmates, the washing-house, with copper-boiler and tubs, were gone as if they had never existed, together with a whole year's provision of fuel. About nine o'clock the kitchen gable was broken down, and all the kitchen furniture swept away. The water was 3 feet 2 inches deep in the house, destroying everything it contained, especially books, which were rendered completely useless; and considerably above £100 of damage was done in this way. To sum up all, the beautiful haugh, containing 10 acres of fine land under crop, was destroyed for ever.

The Spey, by cutting 365 feet laterally from its old channel, uncovered a stone-work, running across its course 3 feet below the surface of the field, exactly similar in direction, formation, and size, to those used at present in what is called 'Cairn-fishing,' in the River Spey, and evidently intended for that purpose. This is a parallel case to that of the iron-mill of the River Nethy, and, from the facts we know regarding that, it is reasonable to conclude that salmon may have been taken here by this apparatus, at no very ancient period. This terminates Lord Seafield's Rothes property, where his damage is given in at £8000, which, with the £20,000 for Strathspey, already mentioned, and the injury done by the Lossie near Elgin, and the burns at Cullen, &c., will bring up his total to above £30,000. The loss suffered by the tenantry is immense, the whole crop within reach of the river being ruined. There were three cases of families rendered destitute by this calamity in Boharm parish.

On Mr. Wharton Duff's estate of Orton, the Burn of Garbity, coming from the left, swept away the western approach to its bridge, with the ground it stood on, and also the arch, leaving nothing but a whimsical and picturesque fragment of the eastern abutment (Plate 53). It carried off 6 acres of land, and £200 worth of crop from the farm. The whole plain below Orton, of a mile broad, was covered by the flood, which was running 6 feet deep within 30 yards of the house, and 4½ feet deep in the garden, destroying fruits, flowers, and vegetables.* The farm of Mains of Orton had 106 acres of crop under water, and the tenant's loss is estimated at £800. So great has been the destruction of ground there, that, in a new arrangement with the tenant, Mr. Wharton Duff has been obliged to deduct from 50 to 60 acres from the actual extent. The whole landlord's damage on the Orton estate is given in at £3100.

PLATE 53. BRIDGE OF GARBITY, AFTER THE FLOOD

A widow lady, mother-in-law to Mr. Cameron of Mains of Orton, had her house, near Mr. Wharton Duffs garden, surrounded by ten o'clock in the evening of the 3rd. The water rushed into it, and might have drowned a servant girl, and her little charge, a daughter of Mr. Cameron's, had not the old lady roused them from the bed, into which it was rapidly advancing. They fled up stairs to the garret, where they remained, screaming for help, till three o'clock in the morning of the 4th. Mrs. Cameron's anxiety for her mother and her child during that dreadful night may be imagined. But Mr. Cameron, assisted by the Orton gardener, at the risk of the lives of both,

The accuracy of a salmon-fisher's eye, as regards the rise and fall of the river, is remarkably exemplified in an anecdote told me by Mr. Brown of Dunkinty. Having expressed his fears for the safety of Garbity, when talking to a Rothes fisherman, during the flood, at a point some miles above, "Garbity is the safest farm in a' Spey, Sir," replied the man, "but I'll warrant she's aboon four fit up in Mr. Wharton Duff's garden."

pushed to their aid in Mr. Wharton Duff's boat, and succeeded in rescuing them by pulling them through the garret window, the house door being entirely under water.

Below Orton, the Duke of Gordon's small tenants of the Ellie were clustered together in a little hamlet, or, as a boy emphatically called it, *"a bourrach o' hooses."* Some of these dwellings were not more than 6 feet above the level of the Spey, and between these and the houses on the higher grounds there is an old river course. The flood made its way into this on the evening of the 3rd, and whilst some escaped at the risk of their lives, it unexpectedly cut off all chance of retreat from others. About seven o'clock, the water began to spread over the fields, and to approach the houses. That of a poor and very industrious man, called John Geddes, built on a somewhat elevated spot, had entirely escaped in the floods of 1768 and 1799, when the neighbouring cottages were inundated to a considerable depth.* Alarmed by the rapid growth of the river, the people of the other cottages crowded as night fell towards that belonging to Geddes, firmly believing that they should be perfectly safe in it. There nine men and women, and four children, sat shivering over the fire in their wet garments. The faggots were heaped high and, as John Geddes himself says, "We soon begud to grow braw an' hearty, whan John Forsyth an' me gaed oot to big up the stable door, an' saw the water growin' terrible! 'Ye're a' very merry, Sirs,' said I, as I gaed in, 'but ye'll no be lang sae. Ye had better stir your stumps an' put things oot o' the gate, an' look till your ain safety.' The words were hardly oot o' my mouth, whan in cam' the river on us. We lifted the meal-kist, pat the wife an' her bit weane and the bairnies into the bed, an' the rest got up on kists and tables. We pat the fire on the girdle, hang the girdle on the crook in the lumm, an' stuck the lamp up on the wa'. But the water soon drooned oot the fire, and rose into the bed. I then pat twa chairs i' the bed, an' the wife sat upon them wi' the little anes in her lap, but the water soon got up to them there. Syne I cut the ceilin' aboon the bed, pat a door atween the twa chair backs, laid a caff-bed on the door, set the wife an' little anes aboon that, and then gaed up mysel' to the couple-baulk, an' held the door firm wi' my feet, an' had an axe ready to cut the hoose roof in case o' need. The rest o' the fouk stowed themsel's awa' fae the water as weel as they could, on chairs on the tap o' tables an' kists. We waur lang in this way, an' I cheered them the best I could, an' tell't them the hours every noo an' than by my watch, that I hang up on the couple-leg i' my sight. But the water raise and raise, till about twa o'clock, whan it drooned oot the lamp, an' left us a' i' the dark thegither. There was a groan, an' a cry that

* *What follows sufficiently proves how much the flood of the 3rd and 4th of August last was greater than those of 1768 or 1799.*

there was naething for us noo but death. 'Trust in Providence,' says I till them, 'trust in Providence, neebours. But dinna think that ye can be saved unless ye mak' use o' the raison an' the faculties that God has bestowed on ye. I'll cut the roof the moment I see that naething else will do.' But, in trouth, it was an' a'some night, what wi' the roar an' ragin' o' the water, the howlin' o' the wind, an' the blatterin' o' the rain without, an' the cries an' prayers o' the terrified fouk, an' the greetin' o' the bairns within, an' a'thing dark, an' we, as a body might say, hangin' atween the twa warlds, ilka moment expectin' the hoose to gie way bodily, an' the very tables an' chairs the fouk waur stan'in' on shakin' an' floatin' anaith them. Auld Jean Stronach, fourscore years o' age, sat the hale night amid a' the jostlin', wi' a clockin' hen an' a wheen chuckens in her apron. Some ane said till her that she might hae ither things in her mind than a hen an' chuckens, when she was on the brink o' yeternity. 'Poor things,' quo' Jean, 'I couldna think o' lettin' them be drooned.' Aweel! when we waur a' in the height o' despondency, Maggy Christie heard tongues thereoot, an' wi' very joy, she jumpit doon fae the kist she was stan'in' on, but, I trow, she gat sic a gliff o' the water, that she gied a roar, an' lap upon the hearth, gruppit at the crook to save hersel', an' wi' that she climbed up the lumm, an' pat her heid oot at the tap, wi' her face as black as a sutty-man's. 'Oh! Jamie Mill, Jamie Mill,' cried she, 'ye're the blythest sicht that ever I saw!' 'Keep us a'! is that you Maggy?' quo' Jamie Mill, 'weel, I've seen blyther sichts than you are at this precious moment, but, black though ye be, I maun hae ye oot o' that.' An' sae he crap up the roof an' pu'ed her oot o' the lumm into the boat. Whan they cam' round to the door, the hoose was sae deep wi' water that there was barely space to thrust our heads atween the stream an' the door-lintel, so that I was forced to dip the bit bairnies i' the water afore I could get them oot. That did gang to my very heart! Poor Jean Stronach lost five o' her chuckens, as they were draggin' her oot through the water into the boat, an' we waur a' sae benumbed wi' cauld an' weet that, I'm sure, she an' the bairnies wad hae died had we been muckle langer there." The boat was so full that, to prevent its sinking, some of the men were compelled to creep on the house top, and to wait there till it could return.

In the house whence one family had escaped the previous evening, there was a young man who, having come in the afternoon, tired and tipsy, after eighteen hours' hard labour in fishing, threw off his wet clothes, shirt and all, and went to bed, and, laughing at the danger that alarmed the rest, he refused to move. Early in the night he was awakened by the water creeping into his bed. Starting up in a fright, he made for the door, but the moment he opened it a torrent burst in upon him, breast high, and he was glad to climb into a small garret where he sat shivering, until he was pulled out, by great exertions, through a very small window in the roof, like a periwinkle from its shell, to the great laceration of his flesh, and was conveyed by the boat, benumbed and bleeding, to a neighbouring house.

The Ellie presented a miserable scene after the waters had subsided, the houses, furniture, and crops being ruined, buried, or swept off. Among the cattle carried away and drowned was poor John Geddes's cow; "but the thrawsome brute," as he said himself, "was drooned by her ain obstinacy, for she wad gang nae gate but what she liket."

Below the Ellie, the Haugh of Dipple, containing nearly 500 acres, was inundated, the crop destroyed, and the soil scarified in some places and irrecoverably ruined by deposits of sand and gravel in others. At Beathill, the people were in a similar state with those at the Ellie. At Greens a boat was rowed up to the parlour window, when the water was 3 feet deep in the house, and the boat-rope was actually tied to the grate in the chimney until the rowers had loosed the drowning cattle from their stalls. The calves and pigs were carried up to a corn loft, whence they looked down with astonishment and dismay on the flood below. An immense number of rabbits were drowned, and many were found, as on the Findhorn, alive on the tops of the trees.

CHAPTER 19

Bridge of Fochabers, and the left bank of the Spey to the sea, with Garmouth and Kingston

THE Bridge of Fochabers consisted of four arches, two of 95 feet, and two of 75 feet span each, making a total water-way of 340 feet. The view from it on the morning of the 4th presented one vast undulating expanse of dark-brown water, from the foot of the hill of Benaigen, on the one hand, to the sea on the other, about 10 miles in length, and in many places more than 2 miles broad. The floating wrecks of Nature, and of human industry and comfort, were strewed over its surface, which was only varied by the appearance of the tufted tops of submerged trees, or by the roofs of houses to which, in more than one instance, the miserable inhabitants were seen clinging, whilst boats were plying about for their relief. And still the elements raved with unabated fury, so that not a bird could dare to wing the air.

By eight o'clock the flood was 17 feet up on the bridge, but still its giant limbs magnificently bestrode the roaring stream, which, disparted by the opposing piers, closed around them in perfect vortices, forming a high curved crest from one bank to the other. The Duke of Gordon, who was on the bridge several times during the morning, had reined up his horse to the parapet, pointing out to his party the cauldrons that boiled about the pillars. He had then ridden away whilst Lord Saltoun and Mr. Macdowal Grant, Younger, of Arndilly, crossed on foot. The crowds of people who had been looking over the parapets at the wreck, carcases of dead animals, and other bodies which were hurried through, had all run off to the south end to see the forester and his men drive piles for the protection of the mound of approach.

Mr. Gordon MacEwan, a teacher at Fochabers, and seven others, were on their way back from the toll-house, on the red sandstone rock at the north end. It was now about twenty minutes past twelve o'clock. Suddenly a crack, no wider than the cut of a sword, opened across the roadway, immediately over the second arch from the toll-house, about 3 yards before them, and backwards, parallel with the parapet. "Good God!" cried Mr. MacEwan, "the bridge is falling; run for your lives!" With one cry of alarm, he and his companions sprang forward in the direction of Fochabers. The crack yawned wide ere Mr. Russell, one of their number, could step across it. He leaped from the falling ruins, and alighted on that part which was yet firm, with one foot hanging behind him in vacancy. Down went the whole mass of the two arches next the left bank, falling with the loose, shattered, and cloud-like appearance of an avalanche into the foaming surge below. For the fraction of a moment the furious stream was driven backwards with impetuous recoil, baring its channel to the very bottom, and again rushing onwards, its thundering roar proclaiming its victory, and not a vestige of the fallen fragments was to be seen.

At the time the alarm was given, William Sivewright, mason; John Cuthbert, slater; and John Anderson, a lame young man, only son of Widow Anderson, the toll-keeper, were leaning over the parapet wall. Mrs. Anderson, and one of her daughters, had quitted the bridge only a few minutes before. She was sitting by the fire when she heard the terrible crash. "Oh, my son! my son!" exclaimed she, starting up, "he's gone! he's gone! my son! my son! I shall never see him again!" And, rushing out, she stared with a frenzied air on the frightful chasm, wildly repeating the same exclamations. Some of those about her would have persuaded her that her son was on the other side of the river; but the awful truth was too apparent to permit so well-meant a fraud to take effect.

"I saw them running and waving their hats," said Sivewright, when narrating the circumstances, "but before I could guess what they meant, the parapet wall folded round before me, and parted from the roadway, which then seemed whole; but, ere I had time to cry out, it was falling in a thousand pieces, cracking end-long and across from the centre. I sprang sideways past Anderson and Cuthbert, and leaped from fragment to fragment of the falling roadway, as if I had been flying. When I reached the rock I was blind for a moment; and, when I recovered and looked round, Anderson and Cuthbert were gone." In my confusion, I had not at first seen Cuthbert, who now appeared crossing the road. I congratulated him on his escape, and asked him the particulars. "When the brig begud to fa'" said he, "I made a jump to get past, but the shake jostled me ower to the ither parapet. A stane struck me, and the road gaed awa' anaith my feet. I then made a claught wi' my hands at the gravel." Luckily for him, it was nearly as hard as a rock, though he did leave the mark of his fingers in it. "When I made the loup," continued Cuthbert, "poor Anderson made a claught at the tail o' my coat. He missed it, and fell on his back. The parapet wall tumbled doon aboot him, an' I never saw him again." The poor youth's body was found in the evening, about a quarter of a mile below, lying on his back, his greatcoat entangled among some brushwood, and his hands held up, as if to save himself.

The shriek that spread along both banks of the river, when the bridge fell, was loud and agonizing. People ran in all directions, clamorously inquiring for friends and relatives. Signals and shouts were exchanged from either bank, to tell of the safety of individuals, and many were the joyous recognitions that took place. The Duke rode in great anxiety to the bridge; but, on seeing Lord Saltoun and Mr. Grant on the opposite bank, he waved his hat and gave them a hearty cheer. During the afternoon, the people crowded to the spot from all quarters, and many could not be persuaded that the "Brig o' Spey" had actually fallen, until they beheld its ruins with "their ain een." (Plate 54).

The piers of the bridge were founded on the surface of a rock of red sandstone, shelving down stream, instead of being laid, as they ought to have been, in a box hewn out of it, to give stability to the building. The materials were not jointed throughout, but only cased with jointed stones, for a rod has been thrust 10 feet into one of the remaining pillars since the flood. Those who saw the fall agree in describing it as having been precisely like that of a man who is thrown down by the application of a force against his legs, the whole mass of the masonry having gone up stream, from which I have no doubt that, after the foundation was worn away by the vortex that boiled around it, the pillar slid down the stream, and so produced the destruction of the superstructure.

PLATE 54. BRIDGE OF SPEY AT FOCHABERS, AFTER THE FLOOD

Pursuing the left bank of the river, the farm of Newton had all its low ground flooded, above £400 worth of crop destroyed, and a great deal of land ruined. Essil also suffered severely; and the whole lands from that farm to the river's mouth were inundated and devastated, and the losses of the Garmouth feuars and the Duke's tenants about Garmouth have been immense. The families of John and James Lamb, living a little below Essil, were alarmed by the rise of the river, and some of them who drove away the cattle found it impossible to return. An old man, his wife, daughter, and grand-child were left all night in the house, where the water rose several feet up in the lower rooms, and compelled them to sit in a small loft, listening with horror and apprehension to the flood beating against the walls of their dwelling, and to the fall of the farm-offices, which were from time to time tumbling piecemeal. At length part of the building they were in gave way, and their dread of instant destruction became agonizing. Day dawned, but then light only served to make their danger more manifest. At length a boat was brought, with much toil, from Kingston, by Mr. P. Thomson, Lord Seafield's wood-agent. It was conveyed on men's shoulders to the top of a bank, launched, and manned by a gallant crew who, with great hazard, reached the premises, took out the inmates, and landed them safely at Essil. They had hardly left the house when the whole walls gave way, and the roof fell in. The buildings, furniture, and crop were completely annihilated.

The alarm at the Mill of Garmouth, occupied by George Scott, induced his wife and daughters to wade away, driving their cattle before them, whilst the miller and his lad remained to put something to rights about the premises, with the intention of following the family. But the flood increased, and the tempest still raged, and neither came. After relieving the family of the Lambs next morning, the boatmen pulled for the miller's house. They rowed several times round it, and among the ruined out-buildings, calling loudly on the miller. Receiving no answer, they turned away, in the sad conviction that the unfortunate inmates had perished. As they were in the act of leaving the place, the wall of the house gave way in a moment, and great part of it fell into the rushing waves. The boatmen pulled off, in dread of being overwhelmed by the fall of the remainder of the building, when, to their no small surprise, they espied Mr. Scott's head, and red night-cap, thrust through the broken roof, and heard him calling loudly for help. They gladly returned, lowered him and his lad down into the boat, and placed both of them in safety. Mr. Scott's own account was that, having gone from the mill into the house to dinner, they were surrounded by the water, "which," said he, "gaed on growin' an' growin' till between eleven an' twal' o'clock. We got up on a table on ane o' the beds, and syne on chairs aboon the table, till we proppit oursel's up to the ceilin' o' the hoose. Ilka ither thing was floatin' aboot. The water was full five feet deep, an' mysel' but five an' a hauf, an' the loon five feet high. I was hearin' the rummel o' the oot-hooses as they war fa'in', an' sae I began to be frightit that the farrest up end o' oor fire-hoose might tummel doon an' kill us baith. So mysel' and the loon got a haud o' a rope, and swung wi' the help o' it to a bed at the ither end o' the hoose, whar there was nae ceilin', an' we had hardly gotten there, wi' the Providence o' God, whan the upper end o' the hoose that we had left gied way, an' cam' doon wi' sic an awfu' rummel that my heart lap to my mouth wi' fright. I thought surely the end we waur in wad gang neist. But whan I put my head oot o' the roof, an' saw a' the hooses in ruins, an spied the boat, I trow I praised the Lord for oor salvation. What think ye o' my swine, only sax months auld? Ane o' them sweemed doon to the bar, an' then 4 miles east, through the sea to Portgordon, whaur the poor beast landed safe, an' I sauld him there. Ither three o' them teuk a sea voyage 5 miles to the wast, an' landed at the Blackhill. See, they's them i' the sty there.* A' my furniture was ruint, an' I thought I wad hae been ruint too, if no killed or drooned. But wi' some fash I got a hand o' my watch, an' my bit pickters,** an' some ither usefu' papers, and rowed them i' my naipkin, an' pat them aboot my throat. I thought, whan the water should come there, I wad soon hae little need o' them. But feggs! I saved them that way." Strange as it may appear, the miller assured his deliverers that he had "got a glimmer o' sleep aboot five o'clock i' the mornin'."

The populous village of Garmouth stands about a quarter of a mile above the embouchure of the Spey, occupying the base and slope of a gently rising ground. It consists of several winding streets. The houses, many of them three storeys high, are built of clay, kneaded up with straw in a frame, as practised in the south of France, at Roanne, for example, the whole of which town is of these materials. Here they are plastered, or roughcast, with lime, so as to present an extremely good exterior. The smaller village of Kingston stands on a ridge close to the sea-shore, composed of rounded pebbles brought down by the river, and again thrown up by the tide. It has its name from the historical fact of Charles II having landed here from Holland in 1650. The descendants of a man of the name of Milne, who carried His Majesty ashore, are still in existence; and the family have been distinguished ever since by the appellation of *King Milne*, from the service then performed by their ancestor.

Thomas Milne, or, as some will have it, John Milne, was ferryman here in 1650. The vessel which brought Charles to Scotland could not come into the harbour, but rode at anchor in the bay, whilst a boat was sent to land the King. The boat could not approach the shore sufficiently near to admit of Charles landing dry-shod; and Milne, wading into the tide, turned his broad back to the King at the side of the boat, and, resting his hands on his knees, very quietly bade His Majesty "loup on." "Nay, friend," said the King, smiling, though somewhat alarmed at the proposal, "I am too great a weight for so little a man as you." "Od! I may be wee o' stature", replied Milne, looking up and laughing in Charles' face, "but I'se be bound I'm baith strong an' steedy; an' mony's the weightier burden I've carried i' my day." Amused with the man, and persuaded by those around him that there was no danger, the King mounted on Milne's back, and was landed safely on the boat-green. It does not appear that Milne received any reward for this piece of service. The present

* *These well-authenticated instances of swine swimming to distances so wonderful, quite contradicts the popular error that, when thrown into the water, they speedily destroy themselves by cutting their throats with their own feet.*

** *Meaning his bank-notes.*

representative of the family is Mr. William Milne, ship-master at Banff, a very respectable man, who is great-great-grandson to King Thomas. Mr. Milne has a son, a half-pay surgeon of the Royal Navy, and he still possesses the small property in Garmouth on which all his predecessors lived. It is now occupied by his brother-in-law, Mr. John Wilson. The old dwelling-house was taken down, and a new house built by the present occupier. With the exception of the present King Milne, all the descendants of the original King Thomas have lived and died here, maintaining their families by salmon fishing in the Spey, a right enjoyed by all the feuars or proprietors of houses in this place till a comparatively recent period.

It is well known that some Irish auxiliaries were sent by the Earl of Antrim, in 1646, to the west coast of Scotland. Their commander was Alister Mac-Coll-Chiadoch, son of old Coll Chiadoch, who was executed at Dunstaffnage by Argyll, and who was himself afterwards taken and executed in Ireland. Having formed a junction with Montrose, and fought in all his battles, these Irish ultimately partook with him in the affair of Fyvie, and in the retreat that succeeded it. Some of the stragglers from the camp traversed the country till they reached Garmouth, where they burnt houses, carried away property and spread a general alarm.* Milne, at the head of a few of his neighbours, bravely endeavoured to resist them, with no other weapon but his boat-hook or *sett*; but being beaten by numbers, after a stout resistance, he was pursued by five or six of the party, eager to put him to death. Having got considerably ahead of them, he forced a door off its hinges, reared it on his shoulders, hurried to the river, threw it in, and jumping upon it, and poising his body, he pushed it off. Guiding it with his *sett*, he crossed the stream, and escaped from his enemies who, in attempting to pass after him in a cart, were swept away and drowned.

With one exception, all my informants agree that Charles II was not only received on his landing by the then Knight of Innes, but that the King also dined with him in a house of his then occupied by his son. Many still alive remember to have seen the house entire. It was two storeys high, built, like the others, of clay and straw, with an outside stair, and contained three rooms and a kitchen. The upper apartments were panelled all round.** It was in this very house that the Clergy of Moray presented Charles with the *Solemn League and Covenant*, which he signed. This fact is slightly alluded

**Sir Walter Scott tells us that these Hibernians actually begged of the good citizens of Aberdeen to step out of their clothes, before putting them to death, lest the garments might be injured by the wounds or the blood.*

*** Part of the gable is still standing, 16½ feet wide, and 5 feet high. The door the King entered by is now built up. The premises are the property of John Geddes, wright, and are styled in his titles 'The Laird's Toft'. The lairds of Innes were superiors of the village.*

to in the title to it, as given in the printed copies of the Confession of Faith of the Scottish Church, where it is said that it was *"taken and subscribed by King Charles II at Spey, June 23, 1650, and at Scoon, January 1, 1651."*

Notwithstanding the breadth of the plain on the right bank of the river, great part of the lands of Garmouth were under water by seven o'clock on the evening of the 3rd of August; yet none of the inhabitants had any dread of damage, far less of danger. Not so those of Kingston, who began to fear that the rolling tide, increased to mountains by the furious north-east wind, would sweep away the lower end of that village. Mr. Thomson, becoming alarmed for Lord Seafield's wood depot, hastened to the stacking ground, which he found inundated. There he kept his people working hard, till the water rose so rapidly on them that their danger became too apparent. They tried to escape in the boat, but they found it impossible; for some of the huge piles having given way so covered the surface with pieces of timber as to render it impossible to propel the boat through the water. They had now no alternative but to clamber over the timber stacks, still standing between them and land, a hazardous attempt, from the wood being slippery with the wet, from the extreme darkness of the night, and, above all, from the danger there was of the whole being lifted up at once by the force of the current, and scattered abroad on the waters like those which had gone before them. But no time was to be lost. They mounted the piles of wood, on the stability of which their lives now depended, whilst the water was rushing through and under them with an ominous and dismaying sound, and most providentially they reached the land. In one instant after they were all safe, the water made a breach 40 yards wide through the stacks they had travelled over, and soon afterwards dug out a new channel in that direction, which destroyed Lord Seafield's wood-pond, but saved Kingston, by opening a new vent for the flood. Mr. James Geddie was employed, with three of his men, in saving some timber that lay within the flood-mark, and he and they were swept away by the sudden violence of the stream. Mr. Geddie and two of the men fortunately made their way out, after being carried down for 200 yards. But the fourth individual was in deeper water. For some minutes they heard his heart-rending cries for help, but were able to render him no assistance. The cries ceased and, chilled with horror at his sudden and melancholy fate, they hurried to Garmouth to apprize their friends. But the joy of all assembled may be easily conceived, when, as they were bewailing his loss, the young man appeared among them, having, by an extraordinary exertion, swam ashore, greatly exhausted, but without injury.

So great was the body of water that rushed into the sea, that no tide could enter; whilst, on the other hand, the river was stemmed, and raised as far up as Garmouth. The people of that village, for the greater part of a respectable rank in life, were already almost all in bed on the evening of the 3rd, when the water began partially to inundate the houses. Even then it was difficult to persuade them that there could be any danger, so far above where any inundation had ever come. But, by 12 o'clock at night, the houses in the lower quarter of the village were deeply flooded; and, by half-past two o'clock, the first building yielded to the force of the flood and fell. Then it was that the doubters became suddenly converted. Those who were quite incredulous before were now ready to believe anything. The confusion and bustle became great beyond conception. Some fled immediately; others, suddenly roused from sleep, leaped from their beds to the knees in water, and found their furniture floating around them. Their noise and clamour waked the inhabitants of the other quarters, and uproar and alarm spread everywhere. The danger, great in reality, was magnified by fear, and by the intense darkness of the night. Lights burst out here and there from windows, and lanterns and torches gleamed on the obscurity of the streets; whilst signals of distress were flashing from the vessels in the more distant port. Property was at first forgotten in the anxious solicitude of all to save human life. Parents were heard entreating for the rescue of their children, and the middle-aged imploring for help to the old and infirm. Now were men seen wading into the deep currents that ran through the streets, carrying out women, children, and old people of both sexes, from their houses, half dressed; the surprise and terror of their countenances partially betrayed by the momentary influence of some accidental light, as they appeared and vanished like spectres. Then followed the incessant rumbling of carts, carrying off furniture, the continual crashing of which sufficiently told the ruin that was going forward, had not that of the frequent fall of houses spoken in a language of a louder and more tremendous tone. And all this was blended with the roar of the elements, the unremitting plash of the rain, and the screams of the timid; and, when the gusts lulled for an instant, the voices of the seamen, toiling in laborious chorus for their lives, came sad and fearfully from the sorely distressed vessels.

When I visited Garmouth, I beheld many houses of two, and even three storeys, half thrown down, with the nicely painted walls and ceilings of what were snug and comfortable rooms now laid open perpendicularly, and appearing tier above tier. But what must have been the spectacle, when day dawned on the 4th of August, while the torrents still filled the streets, and the extent of that night's destruction was revealed, and fresh ruin was every moment working? When, as far as the eye could reach, the neighbouring plain was covered with water, and the beach, the harbour, and along the sweep of the bay, was studded with stranded vessels and covered with one heap of wreck from river and ocean, composed of immense quantities of wood; dead bodies of animals, furniture, and an endless variety of heterogeneous articles, strangely tossed and blended together in one common ruin.

The mouth of the river, which, previous to the flood, was not above 20 yards wide, had a breach of 400 yards opened through it, by which the vessels in the harbour were exposed to the greatest danger. The schooner *Pursuit* was driven from her chains out to the bar, and the fury of the rush of water may be judged of from the fact that her salvation was effected by her being kept dreadfully balanced between it and the opposing force of the violent north-east wind, to which her crew crowded all her canvas. The *Barbara and Anne* was swept from her moorings, and carried the *Unity* along with her. The one was driven ashore within the bar, and the other, having no one on board, was forced to sea, drifted to the eastward, and thrown up on the top of the beach. The *Good Intent* was also driven on the east beach. The *Elizabeth* held by her moorings, but was upset by the current, and her crew only saved by desperately leaping ashore. Two vessels went on shore between the Spey and Portgordon; and two others, the *Lizard* and the *Lively*, which left Leith together, were stranded within ten yards of each other, four miles to the eastward of Speymouth. The *Robert*, of Limekilns, foundered beyond Spey's Bay, and all on board perished, but fortunately no lives were lost in any of the other vessels, most of which were afterwards saved from utter wreck.*

The scene for miles along the beach was at once animated and terrible. Crowds were employed in endeavouring to save the wood and other wreck with which the heavy rolling tide was loaded, whilst the margin of the sea was strewed with the carcases of domestic animals, and with millions of dead hares and rabbits. Thousands of living frogs also, swept from the fields, no one can say how far off, were observed leaping among the wreck.

It would be quite hopeless to attempt to give any minute detail of the damage done at Garmouth. Eight dwelling-houses and seven other buildings were utterly or nearly destroyed, and there was scarcely a house in the lower quarter of the village which was not injured, or a garden-wall which was not swept away. Opposite to the saw-mill of Garmouth, where the width of the inundation was fully a mile, the flood rose 10 feet 2 inches above the ordinary level; and at Kingston Port, where the width was about half a mile, it rose 13 feet 9 inches. These measurements, of course, refer to the Spey in its ordinary state.

The kind and charitable exertions of the inhabitants of such

* *The harbour, formerly very safe, has been rendered very much the reverse by the flood. Every succeeding stream-tide now sweeps away a fresh portion of the beach of gravel, between the river and Kingston, so that serious apprehensions are entertained that the sea will encroach and carry off the lower end of the village.*

parts of Garmouth as were safe, towards providing for the comfort of their less fortunate neighbours were most exemplary. A party of gentlemen from Gordon Castle were to have dined on the 4th with Captain Fyfe, but the fall of the bridge of Spey prevented any of them from appearing. The gallant Captain did not lack guests, however, for he went about and indiscriminately invited the families and individuals who had been forced from their homes, and who now depended for food and shelter on the hospitality of their neighbours, and had the satisfaction of presiding over a numerous and grateful company. As the losses in Garmouth fell chiefly on the wealthy, only eight cases of destitute families were produced here.

CHAPTER 20

THE RIGHT BANK OF THE SPEY, FROM FOCHABERS TO THE SEA. THE RILL OF TINET, BURN OF BUCKIE AND CULLEN RIVER

THE damage done to the plantations and ducal grounds of Gordon Castle was very great. One breach of 186 yards was made in the park wall, which was likewise demolished in many other places, and free access being thus permitted to the flood, it tore up a number of beautiful trees, and spread over the grounds to within 125 yards of the Castle. The inundation covered the whole lower part of the park, and the cultivated lands beyond, destroying the plantations and crops in that direction, and utterly ruining large fields of grass, turnips, and corn, levelling the walls and other fences, ploughing up and scarifying the ground in some places, and covering it with sand and gravel in others. The deluge then burst over the plain of Bellie, annihilating the whole crop, and much injuring the greater part of the land.

Mr. James Scott's house, being situated on ground rather more elevated than the surrounding plain, was filled with guests who had fled from their own houses to what was deemed a place of undoubted security. It was soon hemmed in by the water, however, but Mr. Scott had taken the precaution to build up the door with sods, by which means the interior remained dry after it was several feet deep on the outer walls; but, as its vertical pressure increased, it gradually began to force itself through the sand under the foundations of the house, and burst up in springs through the floor. There were no less than 24 persons in the company, yet all their exertions were unequal to subdue their insidiously obtrusive enemy, to which they were compelled to yield up the ground floor, and to take refuge upstairs. In the morning, the people who saw their hazardous situation sent for boats. A ship's yaul was first procured, but, after it was taken to the spot, it was found too small to encounter the flood that raged widely between the shore and the house. A large boat was then brought with great difficulty from the fishing station called The Tugnet, launched, rowed with considerable risk to the house, and the prisoners were taken from the windows into it, and safely landed. Mr. Scott alone remained to watch over his infirm mother, of 85 years of age, who was in too delicate a state of health to be removed. A signal was agreed on, in the event of his considering the house in danger of falling, but it was not found necessary to employ it. The poor old woman did not long survive the flood. Mr. Scott's horses and cows stood half covered with water, the cows bellowing with terror, and the calves, pigs, and sheep swimming about like ducks. But this description applies equally to all the farms in this neighbourhood. Early on the morning of the 4th, about half a dozen of hares were observed in a little elevated spot in front of Mr. Scott's house, completely encircled with water. The creatures were seen running round, making the wildest efforts to escape; but, alas! the water continued gradually to narrow the little space that was left to them, until it finally closed over them and swept them away. Many thousand rabbits and hares were destroyed among the furzy patches of ground. Twenty-five large English sheep were carried off from the farm of Burnside.

In the Milltown of Bogmoor the houses had 5 or 6 feet of water in them. I talked to John Geddes, a poor man, who rents a small patch of land on Bogmoor. With a face the picture of woe and misery, he was scraping from the sand a few straggling heads of oats, little better than chaff as to substance, of a dark colour when rubbed out, and so filled with dust and dirt that I certainly think even rats and mice would have refused them. He told me that the whole extent of plain between him and The Tugnet is occupied by people who hold little possessions like his own, and the description given of his crop may serve for the whole. Yet this is all they have to look to as a year's provision for themselves and their beasts! What a sum of misery would be here, were it all reckoned up! Yet John Geddes was bearing his affliction with a spirit not unbecoming a Christian; and his neighbours were no less patient under the chastisement they had received.

At Carsemoor the water was 9 feet deep and upwards. It carried off a house and its furniture, and all the stacks of corn. A man I met with there, told me that the flood came upon them quite unexpectedly, "i' the middle o' the dark night, an' they had eneugh ado to escape awa', by widin' up to their middles, in an awfu' terrification." One young man was roused from his slumbers by the water rushing into his bed. He leapt out into it 3 feet deep, among floating furniture. On looking abroad from the door, and beholding the strange and frightful deluge, he alarmed his wife, and each snatching up a blanket and a naked child, they, with no other clothes than they had slept in, entered the water together, and waded in the darkness of night through the flood, where they frequently sank into holes that threatened to drown them and the trembling innocents they carried. After struggling thus for more than a quarter of a mile, they providentially reached Dalachy in safety. And fortunate it was that they risked this desperate attempt to escape, for their house was swept away soon after they left it, and everything they possessed in the world went with it.

Near them lived Alexander Gray and his family, and as the place was at so great a distance from the river as to remove all suspicion of its ever coming there, they had gone to bed, and were sleeping soundly, when Mrs. Gray, as she said herself, "wus waukened by a' the things i' the hoose *knap, knap, knappin'* against each other through the floor." Alarmed by the water coming into her bed, she stretched out her hand to rouse her husband; but his place was vacant. She screamed with affright, and jumped into the water, where her daughters soon joined their cries with hers. Everything was dark, there was no means of procuring a light, and consternation and clamour prevailed. They called on old Gray, but in vain. They listened, and nothing reached their ears but the howl of the tempest, and the flood roaring around the house, as if loudly telling them what his fate had been, and what their own was soon likely to be. One of the sons, who had been employed in herring fishing, had gone very tired to bed, in an apartment somewhat removed from the house. He was awakened, as he said, "by them *skellachin'* i' the main hoose. I faund the pillow dooblin' round my heid wi' the jaw o' the water," said he; "I louped oot, an' swattered to the door; an'. the first thing I saw, when I cam' round the corner, was a great lump o' meal oot o' the meal kist, which the water had turned ower, an' then I kent that a' was wrang i' the hoose."

Whilst the mother and her daughters were pouring forth lamentations for the fate of old Gray, interrupted only by shrieks when that which impended over themselves more immediately pressed itself upon them, the family of another son, who lived in an adjoining cottage, made their way to them with great difficulty, from a yet more imminent peril; and the cries of the whole were redoubled. The flood was still gaining on them, and the miserable women were obliged to stand in the beds, and to hold up the naked children, as well as they could, to keep them from being drowned. The son, brave though he was, had no means of doing any thing either for himself or for those he held so dear. He wished to attempt to get to the stable, resolving, that if he should find the old mare still safe, he would endeavour to breast the stream with her. But Mrs. Gray had already lost a husband, and the rest a father, and they now clung about a son and a brother, to prevent what must have ended in his certain destruction. And yet, what but certain destruction awaited them all? The waters were still rising, and every hope seemed to be extinguished.

It was now three o'clock in the morning. Their situation was becoming every moment more critical, and they were expecting the arrival of that awful period that was to sweep them into eternity, when the gladdening sound of other human voices than their own came upon them. They listened eagerly, and old Saunders Gray's well-known tongue was heard calling to them; and in a short time the dripping women and naked children were dragged on board a boat. Saunders had had some rather strange adventures. He, too, had been disturbed by the *"knap, knap, knapping,"* of the furniture, but somewhat earlier than the rest. Surprised at the sound, and at the gurgling noise that came about the bed, he arose to ascertain what was the cause, and immediately found himself standing in 2 feet of water. He had the wonderful presence of mind to remain silent, and to allow his wife to sleep on, till he could assure himself of the real extent of the danger. Quietly slipping on part of his clothes, he gently opened the outer door, and was astonished to see nothing but water as far as the darkness allowed his eyes to penetrate. Being a resolute man, he at once determined to make the best of his way to land, and thence to The Tugnet to procure a boat for the relief of his family. Wading with some difficulty to the stable, therefore, he extricated his old mare Meg, mounted her and, without a moment's hesitation, dashed boldly into the rough stream that opposed him. Meg was instantly swept from her footing, and carried rapidly down. But Saunders kept her head to the stream, and both master and mare being of stern stuff, they struggled toughly against it, till, after swimming above 100 yards, Meg again recovered her footing and waded with her rider to the shore. So deep was the stream, that Saunders swam over a wall 4 feet high; and, on being asked how he had done this, "Guid kens!" replied he; "for trouth I ne'er faund it i' my road."

Saunders had a rich harvest of golden hopes swept away on that woeful night. Never did the poor man's croft give promise of a more abundant crop, and he did not gather one boll of good grain where he expected 40. He lately thrashed 52 shocks of oats, from which he obtained 3 pecks of dressed corn, of the most wretched description. But this, as I have already shewn, is but a sample of the whole crop hereabouts. His potatoes, invaluable in a poor man's family, and his turnips, are quite gone, his furniture spoiled, his out-houses levelled, and his little all destroyed.

The families of Bogmoor were removed from their houses by a boat; but there was no case of personal danger among them. One woman, who was snugly tucked into bed with her husband, being suddenly disturbed by the crying of a child, jumped out of bed. "Eh! Oh! Ech! Echeigh!" cried she, with a long drawn sigh, "Eh, God preserve me, I'm up to the henches in boilin' water!" Coming directly, "hissing hot," from her bed, the sudden chill she experienced, thrilled through every fibre like fire, and produced this whimsical exclamation.

I have no means of ascertaining the number of families rendered destitute on this side of the embouchure of the Spey. They must be very numerous. His Grace the Duke of Gordon has given in his losses at £16,494.

After leaving the Spey, the natural rampart of water-worn pebbles I have elsewhere noticed, runs regularly along the shore towards Portgordon; not far from which place the small rill of Tinet has undermined and ruined a salmon-house belonging to the stake-net fishery, though standing high upon the bank, and most substantially built (Plate 55).

PLATE 55. SALMON-FISHING HOUSE, DESTROYED BY THE BURN OF TINET

In riding eastwards, along the turnpike road, we found the bridge over the Burn of Buckie gone; and on reaching Cullen House, we learned that the stream which runs through the magnificently wooded glen there had done a world of mischief. In a beautiful spot, nearly encircled by one lovely link of the little river, was situated one of the most fairy flower gardens I ever beheld. It was swept over by the flood, and covered with ruinous wreck. But the same potent spells which originally called it into being had already restored it, and no eye could have supposed that so fell a devastation had ever visited it.

CHAPTER 21

RIVERS BOGIE, DEVERON AND ISLA, WITH DUFF HOUSE AND BANFF

THE Deveron, and its tributaries, rise in Aberdeenshire among the second-rate hills of the Cairngorum group. The course of the principal stream to Banff, where it throws itself into the German ocean, is about 50 miles in extreme length. As nothing of any importance has reached me regarding the Deveron above Huntly, I shall begin with the burn watering and animating Mr. Gordon's romantic residence of Craig, which, uniting itself at some distance below the house with the Burn of Clova, forms the River Bogie. The whole of the wooden bridges were swept from Mr. Gordon's pleasure walks. One of these, immediately under the house, rested on a huge mass of the basaltic rock, which I measured to be 8 feet long, 5 feet wide, and 4 feet deep, dimensions that would make it weigh something between 7 and 8 tons. Yet this ponderous and angular body was removed by the flood full 300 yards down the stream! The inclination of the channel of the burn is considerable: but it had not

PLATE 56. MASS OF ROCK, OF SOME 7 OR 8 TONS, TO THE LEFT OF THE TREE IN THE FOREGROUND, BROUGHT DOWN BODILY, WITHOUT TUMBLING, BY THE BURN OF CRAIG

been rolled; for I particularly remarked some delicate plants of maiden-hair fern (*Asplenium Rata muraria*), still growing unharmed on its upper side, which would have been destroyed by the least friction against the rocky bottom of the burn. Its progress, therefore, must have been effected by the water gradually sliding it forward. The last exploit performed by this errant mass was a leap over a cascade of some 30 feet of fall. In executing this, it did not select the lower part of the ledge, but the higher part of it, that is rarely covered but in great floods; and, as nobody happened to witness its feat, it chipped a large triangular piece out of the sharp edge of the shelf of rock, that, viewed in conjunction with its present resting-place, removes all doubt as to the circumstances attending its descent (Plate 56).

Mr. Gordon informs me that the shock of an earthquake was felt in this neighbourhood towards the morning of the 4th. After the ruin we have been contemplating on the banks of the more northern rivers, the injury done by the Bogie, and its tributaries, to the land and crop, is really not worth notice. But no less than 7 important bridges were swept away, and one much injured, by these streams. On the Deveron, two bridges were carried off; that near the ruins of Peterkirk was of 56 feet span. Besides these, 7 other bridges, in different parts of the district, were much damaged. Mr. Murdoch, at Huntly Lodge, informs me that the whole of these have suffered, not from lateral pressure, but from the water ruining the foundation where there was no rock. To prevent this evil in future, he very properly recommends a substantial pavement to be carried, from a point 10 or 20 feet above the bridge, round the pillars, under the arch, and to a distance of at least 10 feet below it, to be defended by rows of good piles at both extremities.

At Huntly, the flood was 22 feet above ordinary level at the old bridge of Deveron, only 6 feet of the arch being left unoccupied. A mass of the rock, rent out by the roots of a tree that grew in it, was carried about 60 or 80 yards down, and now lies in the middle of the stream. The park-wall, to the west of the old Castle of Huntly, is about 7 feet high, yet the water rose 2 feet over it, and made its way through the park towards the Bogie, isolating the noble ruin. The whole of the fertile haugh above the wall, which is let out in acres to the inhabitants of Huntly, was flooded half a mile wide, and from 3 to 9 feet deep. Through all this meadow, hay-cocks might be seen sailing along. Those belonging to Dr. MacColl, with a hay-stack at their head, looked like a fleet of merchantmen under convoy. They weighed from their anchorage at the upper extremity of the park-wall, the line of which ran at right angles to that of the flood; and, sailing along its whole length, they wore, and turned in at the park gate, in very regular order, and took up a new position on the bank opposite to the castle. From its situation between its two rivers,

Huntly was almost surrounded by water; but the current was gentle, and tore away little soil, except from a few turnip fields. The Bogie flooded the distillery at Pirie's Mill, and destroyed a great quantity of malt; and some other houses and mills were inundated, but none were carried off. The house of Thomas Leslie, fisherman to the Duke of Gordon, was almost filled by the Deveron. All the family left it on the evening of the 3rd, except the man's daughter, who perched herself on the top of a chest of drawers, made by a favourite brother, resolving to save the beloved piece of furniture, or perish with it. Both were fortunately preserved. Six fine heifers belonging to the Marquis of Caermarthen, which were grazing in a little paddock, railed in from the park and immediately within the park wall, already mentioned, were nearly drowned. Their lowings, expressively speaking their terror, were extremely affecting. A breach was made near the end of the wall towards Huntly, and some boys, by first wading to the neck, and then swimming, got behind the poor animals, and drove them out. There was a prodigious commotion among the hares, rats, mice, and moles, an immense number of which were drowned. At one place, not less than 50 weasels were dislodged from a deep covered drain. The creatures ran anxiously about, rising occasionally upon their hind legs, and looking as if amazed at what had befallen them.

The House of Avochy, on the right bank, stands about 10 feet above the level of the river, yet the inundation was $3\frac{1}{2}$ feet deep all over the lower storey, and the furniture was floating about. In more confined situations on this property it rose fully 18 feet, exceeding the great flood of 1768 by from 15 inches to $1\frac{1}{2}$ feet, and that of 1799 by 2 feet or $2\frac{1}{2}$ feet. The garden was flooded 4 feet, and the offices 3 feet deep. The flood was at its height on the morning of the 4th, between seven and eight o'clock.

The Isla, which joins the Deveron from the left bank, destroyed several dwelling-houses and other buildings. The mill and brewery at Keith would have been demolished by it, but for the exertions of those on the spot. The destruction of vats, casks and beer was great; and the whole winter stock of coals was carried away.

On Lord Fife's property of Rothiemay, on the left bank, a few acres were carried off. Some of the smaller streams hereabouts rose 15 feet, and swept away great numbers of pigs and other animals. On the morning of the 4th, three men who went out to cut grass in the haughs at Rothiemay, were suddenly surrounded by the water breaking out upon them from several different parts of the river at the same moment. They had a horse and cart with them; and, after driving the animal to the highest accessible ground, and being pursued thither by the inundation, they unyoked him and got into the cart. The water rose around them, luckily without much current, till it reached their shoulders; and, in this condition, they sat until next morning at eight o'clock. A boat was at last carried from a distance of six miles to effect their rescue. When landed, they were so benumbed and exhausted as to be unable either to stand or to speak.

At the Bridge of Marnoch, I learned from some masons that the Deveron had risen 14 feet above the usual level there.

Sir George Abercromby had two acres of soil carried off at Forglen, worth £120; corn crops destroyed and damaged, £80; pasture and hay injured, £34; and growing wood lost, £40; in addition to which it is calculated that £500 will be required to make the whole banks secure. I mention these particulars to show how much less the scale of ruin on the Deveron was than that of the Spey or Findhorn, where the damage on such an estate as that of Forglen would have been 10 or 15 times as much. Sir George's cattle were surrounded, but they all got safe out. The height of the flood here was 19½ feet above the usual level of the river.

At the Craigs of Alvah, where the Deveron enters the beautiful grounds of Duff House, under the noble bridge of Alvah, the rocks cross the valley exactly like the dam of a mill-pond, above which the flood formed a lake nearly a mile long, by above a quarter of a mile wide. This natural compensation-pond was of various depths, from 10 feet on the haughs, to 40 feet at the entrance to the Craigs. It was well for Duff House, and the good town of Banff, that this immense body of water was so arrested; for, if it could have been otherwise, their disasters would have been greater. The water above the Craigs was smooth and unruffled. On looking towards the bridge from the haughs, with the eye placed on a level with the water, a very small segment of the arch was visible. The fall, therefore, immediately above the bridge, resembling the escape of the water from a sluice, was not less than 15 feet. So great was the rapidity in the narrow pass among the rocks, that some aquatic birds were literally dashed to pieces by it; and its impetuosity at the entrance was sufficiently displayed by the whole of the trees and bushes being overturned and thrown with their tops downwards. Had the bridge been situated at the upper part of the rocky pass, it must have been inevitably swept away. The crop that lay under so great a depth of water was, of course, almost entirely destroyed.

The Bridge of Alvah, consisting of one grand and lofty arch, reminds me more of a Roman work than anything of modern times (Plate 57). To have stood in the midst of its beautiful scenery, when the mighty lake above was discharging itself between the Craigs, would have been to enjoy a spectacle of the most sublime description. From the rocky nature of the banks for some miles down, little damage was done to the upper part of the grounds of Duff House. But, in the lower part of the park, and at Banff, the effects of the storm and flood were both severely felt.

PLATE 57. BRIDGE OF ALVAH

Towards the afternoon of the 3rd, the water-bleared horizon dimly showed a number of vessels struggling hard to keep off the iron-bound coast on their lee, and apparently in fearful distress. As some of them were evidently fast yielding to the storm, parties of the Whitehills fishermen patrolled the beach all that dark and tempestuous night, to be ready with their help, if aught of help might yet avail. The fears and the pious hopes of these praiseworthy fellows were soon alike realised; for, about one o'clock in the morning, the coal brig, *Success*, came ashore among the rocks to the eastward of the Knockhead, and six men and women, all in an exhausted state, were safely landed by their intrepid and well-directed exertions. So furious was the surf, that it instantly beat the vessel to pieces, and literally pounded her cargo to a powder that blackened the white waves around. As day broke, two sloops were seen among the breakers, rapidly driven towards the Sands of Boyndie, where the men of the Preventive Coast-Guard had joined the Whitehills fishermen. As they drifted on, the toil-spent crews were seen clinging to the rigging, as if in preparation for the coming shock. One of them, the *Katherine*, was immediately thrown on her beam-ends on the sand, and the spray that dashed over her left it doubtful whether the men were swept away. But she partly righted, and the crew again became visible. A rope was thrown over her by Captain Manby's apparatus; but the poor people were so worn-out and benumbed that upwards of an hour was lost before they could draw in and adjust the cable and reeve-rope, after which they were all safely landed. The other vessel, called the *Active*, being new, leaked less, and maintained her upright position, so that the crew remained dry on board of her till the tide fell.

The lower part of the town of Banff is bounded on the south by the gardens of Duff House. The wall, partly built of stone and partly of brick, extends along the whole of Bridge Street, the market place, and thence eastward till it joins the bridge. Above the gardens, and in the middle of the expanded part of the valley, stands the Earl of Fife's residence. At a bend of the river, about half-a-mile above the house, there was a strong embankment. Over this the flood poured with tremendous impetuosity on the morning of the 4th, overspreading the extensive park and lawn around Duff House, and, in a few minutes, deluging the gardens below, to the depth, in some places, of 14 feet. The wall was now the only barrier between the immense inundation above it, and the nether quarter of the town below it. For a short time it most wonderfully resisted the weight of water that pressed upon it. But it soon began to betray symptoms of weakness, in a thousand little jets that played through it in all directions, till the waters, becoming impatient of longer restraint, burst a large breach in it, and rushed onwards into the market-place. Terrific was the scene that now ensued. At that early hour, many of the houses were occupied by unconscious sleepers, and such of these as were in the lower apartments received the first intimation of the disaster from the water that approached them in their beds. To think of saving furniture where life was so immediately at stake, was impossible. Those in houses of more than one storey fled for safety to the upper rooms, abandoning every description of property below, and there they remained trembling with apprehension lest the foundations of the buildings might be undermined by the furious flood. Those in humbler dwellings, being compelled to make their way into the street, many of them almost in a state of nudity, and many of them with infants in their arms, were seen struggling for their lives in the midst of the raging waters.

And now the alarm was given, and down ran the population from the upper streets of the town, mingling their shouts and exclamations of astonishment with the cries of those who wrestled with the peril that had so suddenly environed them. Help was speedily lent by such as were best able to give aid and, after the rescue of all who were in immediate jeopardy, some attempt was made to save a few articles of furniture, shop goods of all kinds, and whatever valuables could be most easily snatched up. As the day advanced, the water still increased till the strong bulwark forming the eastern boundary of the town, having been partly cut, gave way. The water rushed in with unparalleled force, demolished one house completely, and very much injured several others. By twelve o'clock, the flood had attained its greatest height, being 18 feet and 4 inches above the ordinary level of the river, at low tide. This was ascertained from an accurate measurement made in the market place. By this time, the view from the upper part of the town was truly grand, if the destruction of the property, and the perilous state of those who still remained in the higher apartments of their houses, could have been forgotten. The streets below appeared like canals. Lord Fife's park and gardens formed one immense lake, studded with islands and clumps of trees; and the beautiful Bridge of Banff, though nearly engulfed, was still withstanding the mighty force of this otherwise overpowering deluge, whilst boats were plying everywhere across the flat, from the Palmer's Cove, near Macduff, almost all the way to the top of Bridge Street.

An alarm was given that a number of cattle were drowning in a field above Duff House, and that some men who had gone on horseback to their relief, were now participating in their danger. A boat was hastily dragged to the place, and the men and the animals were seen clustered together on a knoll, in the midst of the flood. The boat was launched and pushed off, and on reaching the isolated spot, the first creature that sought safety in it was a poor hare, which had survived the fate of hundreds of her tribe. A number of live rats were also collected on the knoll. The people and the cattle were all saved. In the kitchen and eastern wing of Duff House, the water rose to the height of 4 feet. Mounds of clay and sods were raised to keep it out of the western rooms, but the water forced itself up, in powerful springs, through the floors and pavements, and compelled the factor to remove the furniture to the rooms above. A tame eagle, long a favourite, was drowned.

The mail coach had found it impracticable to proceed south, in the morning, by its usual route, and had gone round by the Bridge of Alvah. It was therefore supposed that the mail for Inverness, which reaches Banff in the afternoon, would take the same road. But what was the astonishment of the assembled population when the coach appeared, within a few minutes of the usual time, at the farther end of the bridge of Banff. The people who were standing there urged both the guard and coachman not to attempt to pass where their danger was so certain. On hearing this, the passengers left the coach, but the guard and coachman, scorning the idea of danger in the very streets of Banff, disregarded the advices they received, and drove straight forward along the bridge. As they turned the corner of the butcher-market, signals were made and loud cries were uttered from the nearest houses, to warn them of the danger of advancing; yet still they kept urging the horses onwards. But no sooner had they reached the place where the wall had burst, than coach and horses were at once borne away together by the raging current, and the vehicle was dashed violently against the corner of Gillan's Inn. The whole four horses immediately disappeared, but rose and plunged again, and dashed and struggled long and hard for their lives. Loud were the shrieks of those who witnessed this spectacle. A boat came almost instantaneously to the spot but, as the rowers pushed up to try to disengage the horses, the poor animals, as they alternately reached the surface, made desperate exertions to get into the boat, so that extreme caution was necessary in approaching them. They did succeed in liberating one of them, which immediately swam along the streets, amidst the cheering of the populace; but the other three sank to rise no more. By this time the coach, with the coachman and guard, had been thrown on the pavement, where the depth of water was less. There the guard was seen clinging to the top, and the coachman hanging by his hands to a lamp-post, with his toes occasionally touching the box. In this perilous state they remained till another boat came and relieved them, when the guard and the mails were landed in safety. Great indignation was displayed against the obstinacy which had produced this accident. But much is to be said in defence of the servants of the royal mail, who are expected to persevere in their endeavours to forward the public post, in defiance of risk, though, in this case, their zeal was unfortunately proved to have been mistaken.

In running off, the flood broke down the walls of the slaughter-houses, and the house of the tacksman* of the customs. A good deal of water still remained in the market-place on the 5th, and the cellars were not emptied on the 8th. Trouts, flounders, and eels were taken in them and in kitchens. The loss of property was very great, as may easily be imagined when it is stated that no less than fifty houses and seven shops, containing perishable merchandise to a great amount, were flooded. Two men narrowly escaped drowning, their boat having been driven into a frightful vortex at the river's mouth.

Mr. William Robertson, of Banff, has some memoranda regarding floods in the Deveron in the years 1739, 1768, 1772, and 1779, but none of these appear to have equalled that of last August. The notice regarding that of 1739 is worth recording. *"In January this year, and on a public market day, a great flood took place in the Dovern, when William Haddo, with two men and three women, crossing in a ferry-*

* *Publisher's Note:* ***tacksman*** *(Scot) a lessee; in the Scottish Highlands, a person who holds a lease and sublets.*

boat, were forced down the river by the impetuosity of the current, and carried out to sea. The two men and two of the women unfortunately perished; but the other woman, of the name of Shand, was miraculously saved, owing to her having a large sack of wool on her back, which buoyed her up, until a Doune boat reached her in the bay, and picked her up. Some will have it that she floated about during part of a day, and all the following night, but it rather appears she was rescued from her great peril almost immediately on being seen in the bay."*

The Rivers Ugie and Ythan, though flooded, were productive of nothing worth notice.

* *Now Macduff.*

CHAPTER 22

THE RIVER DON

THE River Don rises from the hills bordering on the higher mountains of the Cairngorum group. Its windings give it a course of about 62 miles, but the straight line of country it waters is not above two-thirds of that extent. Although much more flooded on the 3rd and 4th of August than it ever was known to have been before, yet it was less extravagantly so than any of the other rivers. The rain that fell, though very great, was considered by many as quite inadequate to account for its rapid and uncommon increase. *"It didna come oot o' the cludds,"* was an observation frequently made with a grave face, and a significant shake of the head, by those who had seen many floods, but nothing like this.

Mr. Watson, landlord of the New Arms Inn, Strathdon, was awakened, between the hours of one and two o'clock in the morning of the 4th of August, by the shock of an earthquake. He could not speak with any degree of accuracy as to its duration or direction, but he says that it set all the glasses and tumblers in a cupboard a-ringing, and threw down the key of a clock that was placed on the top of the clock-case. At the same hour, the School-house of Strathdon was also felt to shake by several persons.

At Milltown of Allargue, the house of a shoemaker was so instantaneously and unexpectedly swept away by the bursting of a mill-dam, that the poor occupant only escaped by wading and plunging for his life, abandoning his whole stock of leather, lasts, and awls to the raging torrent. Even his very lap-stone was not left behind. But sometimes the proverb of "an ill wind" may be applied with equal justice to the water. A strolling brother of the craft, who, but a few days before, had earnestly, but vainly, solicited him for the loan of a few lasts, procured an immediate supply by searching among the wreck on the banks of the river.

The water so rapidly surrounded the farm-house of Dalachash, on the right bank, opposite to the church of Loinorn, that all possibility of retreat was cut off before the danger could be perceived. The tenant's wife had just had an accouchement, and her husband was in the greatest anxiety regarding her. With the utmost haste he built up the door and windows with turf, and having erected a temporary platform, as near the roof as possible, he lifted his wife and new-born babe with great tenderness and care, and placed them upon it. There they spent that cheerless and dismal night, amidst the mingled roar of the waters and the tempest, awaiting the result with trembling anxiety. Most providentially, the house resisted the furious stream that beset it on all sides, and neither the woman nor her infant suffered materially from all they had been subjected to.

The house of a widow lady at Glenconry was so distant from the river, and so much elevated above it that, deeming herself perfectly safe, she only felt for the danger of others. But her dream of security was disturbed by the flood first sweeping away some fine trees that stood between her and the river. Then her washing-house, with all its contents of boilers and tubs, vanished amid the waters, and next, a large peat-stack, containing her whole stock of fuel, melted into the stream. The deluge then advanced on the house, with the threat of undermining it, and induced her to remove all her furniture, but, fortunately, it ultimately subsided without doing further injury.

Three miles of turnpike-road were destroyed near Inverernan, and the Bridge of Naughty was swept away by the tributary stream of that name. The Bridge over the Don at Castleton of Corgarff, built in 1749, and that across the same river at Poolduilie, which is as old as 1715, both resisted the violence of the flood. Indeed, the number of *'auld briggs'* which have stood, whilst new erections have been swept away, is rather a reproach to the boasted superiority of modern masons. Early in the afternoon of the 3rd, and long before the Don had risen to the unwonted height it afterwards attained, Mr. Alexander Thompson, assistant schoolmaster of Strathdon, reached its banks about a quarter of a mile below the church, on his return from a visit to his relations at Drumblade. A strange infatuation seems to have attended this man. Within a few yards of the ford there was a wooden bridge, along which he might have passed with perfect safety, for it remained uninjured throughout the whole flood. But he was observed to push his horse into the water without a moment's pause. Both were engulfed at once. The horse rose to the surface, and struggled to the farther bank, but the rider was gone. Nearly an hour elapsed before the body could be recovered. The moment it was found, it was carried to a poor old woman's humble cottage near the spot, but, strange to say, she stood in her doorway and peremptorily refused to admit it over her threshold. Let not the reader suppose, however, that her conduct proceeded from any uncharitable feeling. The poor creature was overwhelmed by the superstitious dread, by no means uncommon, that the admission of a drowned person into her house was certain to be followed by some fearful calamity. But those who were vainly anxious to use every means to restore animation, would have taken the frail tenement by assault in their eagerness. She was, therefore, compelled to come to immediate terms with those who besieged her. A capitulation was the consequence, and she agreed to yield immediate admittance, on condition that the evil effects of her compliance should be guarded against, as far as possible, by the usual charm provided for such occasions. This was judged reasonable by all, and highly necessary by many, and accordingly the corpse was carried with all due ceremony completely around the outside walls of the house, after which it was permitted to enter. But this mysterious conjuration was not enough, and it is somewhat surprising that any one of the years and knowledge of this ancient dame should have allowed it to be so inefficiently performed. The effect was never held to be complete until the magical number of three circles had been performed around the dwelling. A charm never can be available unless its terms are executed to the veriest letter. It is, therefore, not to be wondered at that the result, in this case, should have been unfortunate, and that the poor woman's frail cottage was utterly destroyed, in the course of the night, by the river. Her own escape was a miracle. But if she has lost her house, she has, at least, gained a hard-earned experience, enabling her to assure her neighbours that she never will again admit the body of a drowned person within the walls of the house she occupies.

A party of people were guiding Mr. Forbes of Edinglassie to shooting quarters, after the flood had considerably subsided on the evening of the 4th. They had reached a spot near Forbes Lodge, when one of the guides, in making his way through the inundation, suddenly began to flounder and plunge in a very unaccountable manner. The fellow was known to be a wag, and his companions being accustomed to see him play tricks for their amusement, laughed heartily at his supposed freak, and wondered what it would end in. But Mr. Forbes, becoming alarmed at his strange mode of diving, rushed forward to his assistance, and drew him to land. Most fortunate it was that he did so, for the man had slipped into a newly formed hole, of great depth, and would have been drowned but for Mr. Forbes's prompt and humane aid.

These dangerous excavations were so frequent, and the panic against fording streams became so general, that a medical practitioner, called on an express occasion which compelled him to cross the river Naughty on horseback, carefully fastened a strong rope round his body, and committed the other end of it to a trusty person posted on the bank he was quitting, notwithstanding the repeated assurances of the bystanders that it had been previously crossed on foot with perfect safety.

Opposite to the Manse of Towie, the river completely altered its course, and left the bridge quite dry.

Another life was lost in this neighbourhood, in a yet more foolish manner than that of Mr. Thomson. A blacksmith undertook, for a bet, to swim across the flooded river, near the Mason Lodge of Glenkindy. If his strength had been like that of Hercules, it would have availed him nothing in such a stream. He was whelmed beneath the raging billows, and sank to rise no more. If he who tempted him to so wilful a provocation of Providence has any human feeling in his bosom, I should say with Douglas, that *"happy in my mind was he who died."*

The flood appeared to me to have been about 12 feet up on Alford Bridge, a handsome structure of three arches, where the valley was flooded for some hundred yards wide. The bridge is said to have been considerably shaken, and even rendered insecure.

At the house of Monymusk, where the haughs are flat and very extensive, the Don rose about 10 feet; and, at Tillyfour, where the banks are contracted, its height was about 14 feet above ordinary level. The meal-mill at Ramstone, the saw-mill at Ordmill, and the malt-mill in the distillery at Monymusk, all sustained injury by the flood. Several bridges were damaged, and some soil carried off, but to an extent not worth naming, after the devastations of the Findhorn and Spey. The loss of crop was everywhere considerable.

At Kemnay, the terrors of the storm were heightened, about six o'clock in the evening of the 3rd, by tremendous thunder and lightning. The flood was at its height about seven o'clock in the morning of the 4th, having risen, opposite to the manse, 18 feet above ordinary level, and 15 feet at a point about a mile below, where the ground on both sides is elevated. Several houses were flooded 4 or 5 feet deep. Half the mill-house of Kemnay was swept away, and the wooden part of the machinery carried down to Inverury and Kintore. The millstone was moved several yards, and left on a little island. In the parishes of Oyne, Monymusk, Kemnay, and that part of Inverury and Kintore lying above the Inverury Bridge, all the best land was flooded to the extent of at least 600 acres, averaging 42 shillings an acre of rent. Many acres were covered with sand and gravel, and the crop, being all in a state of immaturity, was very much injured. To give some idea of the loss in the grain crop, one farmer carried to the mill the whole produce of four acres of his best land, and brought home four bolls of very bad meal.

Mr. William Williamson, butcher, of George Street, Aberdeen, was riding between Kemnay and Monymusk when his horse started at some wreck that was floating on the road, near a bridge, then completely flooded over by the Burn of Ton. The animal leaped over the end of the bridge, and disappeared with his rider in the stream, then raging along 10 feet deep. His companion was Mr. George Williamson, grandson and nameson of the great cattle-dealer so called, well known at every market from John O'Groat's to Smithfield, by the name of *Stately*. With a bravery not often paralleled, he leaped to the ground, stripped, and in defiance of the furious flood, plunged in, and dived in several places. He did succeed in getting hold of the horse's rein, and dragged him out, but the rider was irrecoverably lost. This is perhaps the most gallant action I have had to notice, and Mr. George Williamson would indeed richly merit some distinguished mark of the approbation of his fellow-men. The body was not found until next morning.

For a day or two before the storm, the haugh land was observed to be so unaccountably loose and wet that the feet sank into it at every step. The Reverend Dr. Mitchell of Kemnay has lived to see all the floods of the Don since 1768. He says that of August last was at least 2 feet higher than that of 1768, which was much greater than any other he ever witnessed.

At Inverury, the furious rain and wind was attended, in the afternoon of the 3rd, by the loudest thunder, and the most vivid lightning that had ever been seen there. The Don and the Ury join about three-quarters of a mile below the town. The churchyard lies by the side of the road leading to Keithhall, close to the singular green knoll called *The Bass*, and the Ury runs on the north side of both. But, on the morning of the 4th, the rivers united close to the town, and inundated some of the houses 4 feet deep. As in the case of that near Grantown, this churchyard was completely covered, the tops of two or three of the tallest tombstones only being visible; and one of these frail memorials of the dead was actually carried off by the force of the stream, and deposited on the haugh grounds below Kintore, a distance of four or five miles down the river! More than once during the day a boat was seen to sail over the churchyard. The Bass is an artificial mount, being a very regularly shaped truncated cone of about 40 feet in perpendicular height. A smaller mount, of less regular shape, and half the height, rises to the east of it. The Bass is one of those *moot hills*, or places for holding courts, not unfrequently found in Scotland. This is the Bass alluded to in Thomas-a-Rhymer's prophecy:

The Dee and Don shall run in one,
The Tweed shall run to Tay;
And the bonny Water of Ury
Shall bear the Bass away.

As the first part of the prophecy has been fulfilled by the formation of the Aberdeenshire Canal, which is fed from the Don at Inverury, and discharges itself into the Dee at Aberdeen, I felt very desirous to know whether the fate of The Bass had been, in any degree, hastened by the operation of the late flood, but I am happy to say it remains untouched. The inundation stood high on it, and even left a wooden bridge upon it, but the water was rendered dead and harmless by the force of the Don damming it back. The destruction of crops on the Don and Ury was very considerable, but the injury done to the properties on the banks has been comparatively little. The bridge on the Ury, at Williamston, was carried off; and those at Pitmachie and Pitcaple were so injured that the former has been taken down.

The flood of 1768, which seems to have stood next to that of August last, left a small spot of the haugh ground visible below

Inverury, whereas on the 4th, a paling 4 feet high, standing on the same piece of ground, was completely hid.

At Fintray, on the Skene estate, the tenant was engaged with three of his servants repairing an embankment when the flood burst out about a mile above them and surrounded them. Fortunately, their alarming situation was observed, horses were sent in for them, and they were removed, with the greatest difficulty and danger, from a high earthen fence, where they had taken refuge.

At Kintore, where the environs are flat, a number of people were taken out of their houses, at the upper windows, by means of boats. At Dyce, the roads were so flooded on both sides of the river, that it was impossible to cross by the bridge, so that the Banff mail was obliged to find its way to Aberdeen by the old road. A good many cattle were swept from the haughs of Bedlestown, and utterly lost.

The flood was at its height at Mr. Pirie's Stoneywood paper-mill, near Aberdeen, about noon on the 4th, and continued unabated till between four and five o'clock in the afternoon. The water made a breach in the bulwarks, between eleven and twelve o'clock, swept them entirely away, and, rushing with resistless fury through the premises, carried off some of the smaller houses, with a considerable quantity of paper and rags, destroyed the water-courses, and made a new channel for the flood-water of the river. At this point, the bed of the river is confined by rocks. The current is consequently very rapid, and the height of the flood was from 12 to 14 feet above ordinary level. The houses of the workmen, near the mills, were under water, and part of their furniture was washed out and carried away. Five men, employed in a drying-house situated between the mill-lead and the Don, were intercepted in their attempt to escape, and obliged to take refuge in the highest part of the haugh, of which about half an acre had remained uncovered. Their situation was distressing and hazardous. Captain Manby's apparatus was sent for, and speedily brought to the spot by Lieutenant Sanderson of the Preventive Service, and the men of the Don station under his command. A small line was sent over to the men on the island, who fixed the end of the rope to a pole there; but, in a few minutes, the fury of the flood loosened the pole, and swept it away. In the course of the afternoon, however, the people on shore, by means of the small rope of the apparatus, contrived to send over some refreshments to the poor fellows, which served to enliven their spirits, and enabled them to bear up under their misery. At length, as the river subsided, all fears for their safety ceased; and, about four o'clock on the morning of the 4th, they were brought out in a state of great exhaustion.

Much damage was also sustained at Mr. Davidson's paper-mill. A house occupied by Mr. Watson, junior, was reduced to a heap of ruins, and Mrs. Watson, who remained in it until part of the furniture had floated out, had nearly perished. Another house, immediately adjoining, was also swept away. Considerable damage was done by the water entering the lower storey of the Printfield. At Persely bleachfield, the sluices of the mill-lead gave way on the forenoon of the 4th, and, in a few moments, the field and the workmen were surrounded by water. The mill-lead, which runs 12 feet above the level of the river, was confounded with it in one stream. Boats were procured, and the people were relieved; but many of the dwelling houses were injured, and their furniture destroyed. Some damage was likewise sustained at Gordon's Mills, Bleachfield, and at Messrs. Smith & Company's paper-work. The flood also rose to the lower windows of the Grandholm works.

The park at Seton House was nearly covered, and the flood rose 4 feet in the ground-floor of the house, that was about 16 feet above the level of the river, and it was 18 feet higher in the gorge below. The gardener here recollects the flood of 1768 perfectly well. It took place in the end of September. He says it was not so high as that of the 4th of August last.* Lady Die Middleton, who then lived in Seton House, was rescued by means of a ladder applied to a window of the second storey.

The river's channel becomes narrowed by the rocks on both sides as it approaches the ancient Brig of Balgownie. The waters rose opposite to the centre of the arch, somewhat in the form of an arc, the extremities of which touched the foundations of the piers on both sides. From this height they poured down in a cascade of many feet to the lower side of the bridge, where they produced a frightful whirlpool. "I have seen the waves of the Atlantic rolling down the Pentland Firth," says my informant, Mr. George Tulloch, "and wasting their gigantic strength on the bold and iron-bound coasts of the north; but, even there my impression of power was less vivid. The united exertions of the whole human race seemed but a feeble conception compared with it, and I recurred to the sublime language of the Psalmist: *'The floods have lifted up, 0 Lord! the floods have lifted up their voice! the floods lift up their waves! The Lord on high is mightier than the noise of many waters, yea, than the mighty waves of the ocean.'*"

* *This is doubted by some, from the height of the flood of 1768 being marked by a notch in a stone at the mill of Dyce, which the last flood did not reach by 8 inches. But we must not forget that the very effect of a flood is to enlarge the permanent capacity of the river's bed, so that, if precisely the same volume of water were to return, it would not nearly fill the altered channel. The excavations in the Findhorn and Divie, in certain places, were such that the same body of water would not rise within many feet of the height attained by the flood that occasioned them. If, therefore, we find a modern flood rise above any such old flood mark, we are well entitled to argue that it has been larger, but when the fact is the other way, we cannot with equal certainty draw an opposite conclusion. In the present case, the general opinion and facts regarding the Don are all decidedly with the old Seton gardener.*

The history of this old Brig of Balgownie, which stood firm amidst assault so terrible, is extremely interesting (Plate 58). Henry Cheyne, Bishop of Aberdeen, nephew of the Cumin who was killed by Bruce at Dumfries in 1305, fled to England after that event, and remained there for several years. Being later reconciled to the King, he was allowed to return to his See of Aberdeen. The Bishop was so gratified by this indulgence, that he proposed to the King to apply the revenues of his bishopric, accumulated during his absence, to the erection of this bridge over the Don, and he accordingly built it in the year 1320. It is therefore above 500 years old, and presents a singular specimen of the Gothic arch. Lord Byron, who long lived near it, thus notices this ancient bridge, in the tenth canto of *Don Juan*:

As "Auld lang syne" brings Scotland, one and all,
Scotch plaids, Scotch snoods, the blue hills and clear streams,*
The Dee, the Don, Balgownie's Brig's black wall,
All my boy-feelings, all my gentler dreams,
Of what I then dream't, clothed in their own pall,
Like Banquo's offspring; floating past me seems
My childhood, in this childishness of mind:
I care not; 'tis a glimpse of "Auld lang syne."

PLATE 58. BRIG O' BALGOWNIE

* *Publisher's Note: a band for the hair, once worn by unmarried women in Scotland as the badge of virginity.*

"The Brig of Don," adds he in a note, "near the Auld Toun of Aberdeen, with its one arch, and its black deep salmon stream below, is in my memory as yesterday. I still remember, though perhaps I may misquote, the awful proverb, which made me pause to cross it, and yet lean over it with a childish delight, being an only son, at least by my mother's side. The saying, as recollected by me, was this, but I have never heard nor seen it since I was nine years of age:

Brig o' Balgownie, black's your wa',
Wi' a wife's ane son, and a mear's ane foal,
Doun ye shall fa'!

It must be particularly gratifying to Mr. Gibb, the contractor for the beautiful new bridge over the Don, that although it was not quite finished at the time of the flood, it sustained no injury.

CHAPTER 23

The River Dee to Crathie

THE Dee takes its rise from the very bosom of the Cairngorum Mountains, and therefore it is not wonderful that it should have been largely affected on the late occasion. Its course to Aberdeen is not less than 90 miles in length, during which it receives a great number of tributaries. The scenery of the upper part of this river is so grand as strongly to recall to my mind many parts of the Alps. I do not speak of those regions bordering on the glaciers and eternal snow, which the savage aspect of the lonely Loch Aven so much resembles, though the mountains about the source of this river possess many such specimens, but I allude to the magnitude of the features of Braemar, where the immense extent of its pine forests, and the huge bulk of its timber, give quite a Swiss character to the country. The rapidity and wildness of many of the streams, their craggy channels, the infinite variety displayed in the grouping of their birches and picturesque firs, often partially interposing their deep green mantles before the white foam of the waterfalls, and the accidental glimpses of the misty mountain-tops caught between them, combine to form an endless variety of pictures, such as are to be met with among the upper Alpine ravines. About Mar Lodge, Invercauld and Ballater, we have the wide and cultivated valley, the sublime outline of bounding mountains, their bold and rocky fronts starting forward into individually prominent masses, hung with woods, their deep and shadowy recesses, and their levels and slopes, and varied knolls, where even the very buildings are found to complete compositions well calculated to bring back the recollection of many a lovely Swiss valley.

The 2nd of August was a remarkably fine day at Braemar. Towards night it began to rain a little, but the barometer never fell below 29½ inches, and nothing appeared to lead to the anticipation of any approaching deluge. Throughout the morning and forenoon of the 3rd, there were heavy intermittent showers, with strong gusts of wind from the north-west. During the afternoon the wind and rain gradually increased, and about five o'clock it blew a perfect hurricane, driving clouds of rain before it of that comminuted description that somewhat resembled snow-drift. It was during one of these violent gusts of wind that the first flash of lightning occurred. It was intensely vivid, and was instantaneously followed by a deafening peal of thunder. It was not the common long, loud, continued, rolling thunder; but it was as if whole batteries of the pieces of Heaven's ordnance had been discharged in rapid succession. The lightning appeared like a broad stream of liquid fire, widely diffused, and fearfully glaring over the hemisphere. About seven o'clock in the evening the thunder ceased, but the wind and rain continued undiminished, and many of the smaller streams, already swollen to an unusual height, had commenced their havoc.

A night of pitchy darkness followed this dismal day and, between one and two o'clock in the morning, the shock of earthquake experienced in the neighbourhood of Craig, and at the head of the Don, was sensibly and simultaneously felt here by different individuals, in different places. William Rattray, boatman at Monaltrie, who was up during the whole night, said that "he felt the earth hobblin' under him." A lady at Aldourie Cottage was awaked by a singular noise at the time mentioned, which she immediately referred to an earthquake. At Allanquoich the same noise and sensations were noticed and, at Crathie, three of Dr. Robertson's men-servants, who were sleeping in a loft, started from their beds, felt the house shake, and heard a noise as if the slates were falling from the roof. The combined horrors of this dreadful night led many in Braemar to imagine that the end of the world was approaching. One individual, in particular, remained a whole night in a corner of his house, and would not go to bed, in full persuasion that the termination of all things was at hand.

The rain on the northern mountains was infinitely more tremendous than that which fell in the valley; and whilst the tributaries from that quarter were swollen to an unparalleled height, those from the south, in the Braemar district, were not more raised than they are every year by spring and autumn floods. Instances of outbursts of subterranean water were very frequent in the northern mountains. The red granite hill of the *Muckle Glashault*, 9 miles to the north-west of Invercauld, is about 3000 feet high, and of steep ascent on all sides, the surface being covered with immense masses of stone and granitic sand. On the north side, and at about a third of the way from the summit, no less than 15 or 16 of these openings have been made, varying in breadth from 30 to 40 yards. Each of these appears to have had an immense column of water issuing from it, which has cut a track for itself to the very base of the mountain, into the Glashault burn. The ravines are all of very peculiar formation. Their margins or sides are completely defined by a fence of stones, raised considerably above the surface, something like that presented by the track of an avalanche. Dr. Robertson of Crathie concludes, from the appearances, that the water burst from the bowels of the mountain in repeated jets, rather than in one continued stream; and such we know to have been the case at Tomanurd. Some of the stones on the sides are of great size, and must have required a powerful force to have placed them there. None of these appearances existed previous to the 3rd and 4th of August, but were noticed immediately afterwards. They are by no means confined to the *Muckle Glashault*, being observed of greater or lesser magnitude by Dr. Robertson in all the hills he had an opportunity of examining. To have stood in the midst of a solitary amphitheatre of these wildernesses, with all the elements warring around, and to have beheld the mountain sides heaving, and these 'fountains of the great deep broken up,' and their streams sent forth as messengers of Almighty displeasure, would have been inconceivably awful.

The Dee reached its height, at different places in Braemar, between the hours of eight and ten in the morning of the 4th. By correct measurements made by Dr. Robertson at six different points of the river, the average breath of which was 130 feet, the mean rise of the whole was 15 or 16 feet.

Hugh MacDougall, one of Lord Fife's keepers, has his house situated on an isthmus at the junction of the rivers Gouldie and Dee, in a remote part of the forest, several miles from any human dwelling. Being at Inverey on the 3rd, four or five miles from home, he became alarmed at the heavy rain, lest it might swell the Gouldie so as to prevent his joining his family. He ran all the way home, therefore, and did get through the river with some difficulty, but he had no sooner reached his house, than the flood came down with a terrific noise and, in a few moments, he and his family were surrounded by water to a depth that rendered escape, in any direction, quite impossible. The poor people spent the night in a state of the liveliest anxiety and misery, whilst every one who thought of them, as the wind blew and the rain beat, shuddered at what they conceived the certainty of their doom. But, as the daylight came in, the flood most providentially subsided, and they were saved.

At the Linn of Dee (Plate 59), the river forces itself through a deep and narrow chasm in the primitive rocks, over which an Alpine wooden bridge is thrown, for the passage of carts, at a height of 30 feet above the stream. The flood rose 3 feet above this bridge, and swept it entirely away.

The uppermost cultivated farm on the Dee is Dellavorar, the place formerly alluded to as having had its name from Lord Dundee encamping here.* The river surrounded the house on the night of the 3rd with so much rapidity, that the husband, the wife, and seven or eight children, had hardly time to escape by wading, and they were compelled to trudge through the pelting and pitiless storm, by a circuitous route of several miles, to Inverey. The whole of their crop was destroyed, as well as eleven acres of arable land, and the farm is now valued at one third of its former rent.

A little to the westward of Inverey, on the right bank, the river cut its way through the road and came sweeping down on the little hamlet, insulating six families whose houses were built nearer to the Dee, and rather detached from the rest. So suddenly, and to so great

* *See page 143.*

PLATE 59. LINN OF DEE

a height did it rise, that it was quite impossible for the poor people either to escape towards the hill, or to receive the least aid from their neighbours. The flood continued to inundate house after house, until all the families they contained were driven for shelter to one, and the only remaining, hearth. Whilst condoling with each other, and expressing their gratitude that even this had been left to them, the water burst suddenly through the gable upon them, and drowned out their fire. All was instantly terror, and confusion, and shrieking, and lamentation, and they were compelled to flee from this their last hope, to a flat piece of ground of considerable size, now an island, and little elevated above the surrounding waters. There these unfortunate people, men, women, and children, to the number of twenty-two, remained among the young fir trees, helpless infants and all, drenched by the rain and shivering in the tempest. They repeatedly succeeded in lighting a fire but, as they told me themselves, it was as often immediately extinguished by the torrents of water that poured from the heavens, and they were without a morsel of food. In the midst of that dark and stormy night, even the sense of these afflictions was absorbed in the growing dread they felt, as the roar of the flood came louder upon them, that it was gaining an increase that must soon spread it over the ground they stood on, and sweep them to destruction. In this state of misery they were kept till ten or eleven o'clock next day, when the water so far subsided as to admit of their relief.

The glen and river Lui meet the Dee on the left. The Bridge of Lui was founded on the solid micaceo-schistose rock, the foundations being several feet high above the surface of the river in its ordinary state. But the flood actually cut out a cavern in the rock, under the north-east abutment, large enough for a man to shelter himself in. It must be observed that the laminated structure of this rock is peculiarly adapted for being torn up by the force of a stream rushing against its seams.

In our way to the Park of Mar Lodge, we saw three capercailzies, a young cock and hen, kept in one place, and an old cock, who resides in a separate apartment. The hen has laid eggs, but has uniformly destroyed them. Whether this was in obedience to an instinct, leading her to prevent the generation of progeny to live in captivity, may be matter of curious inquiry. What a desirable restoration it would be to the pine-covered districts of Scotland if this noble bird could be introduced! Donald Mackenzie, one of Lord Fife's gamekeepers, who has the charge of them, has had the advantage of paying two visits at Court, and can boast of a reception from Majesty, which many a greater man might envy. He was twice sent by Lord Fife with presents of live roe-deer to the King, who was so much pleased with him, that he gave him more than one audience, manifested towards him repeated proofs of his favour, kept him a considerable time at Windsor, made people attend him to shew him whatever might be supposed interesting, and had it communicated to him that he might stay about Windsor as long as he pleased. "Why did you not remain altogether, Donald?" demanded I. "Hout, what was I to do stayin' there?" replied he; "I had naething to do, an' I tired." But though Donald had no fancy for becoming a courtier, he was not a little proud of a handsome coronation medal, presented to him by His Majesty's express order, which he brought out and showed us with a considerable sparkle in his eye.

The destruction at Mar Lodge is very lamentable. The river broke over the embankment of Poldearg, at a bend of the stream, at the upper part of the lawn, and the whole breadth of the valley was soon afterwards laid under water. A current, 5½ feet deep, set with great force directly against the house, garden, and adjacent buildings, which lie along the base of the northern hill, with the lawn stretching 1000 yards broad in front of them towards the ordinary channel of the river. The garden was completely destroyed, and the beautiful iron railing that fenced it, modelled from that at the Tuilleries,

PLATE 60. STORE-HOUSE AT MAR LODGE, RUINED BY THE FLOOD

though inserted in hewn granite, was broken over and prostrated from one end to the other. The approach was cut into great gulphs, the house was surrounded, the ground-floor filled with water, and the stream that rushed past it was so violent, that it cut away the gravel and exposed an old causeway, 3 feet below the surface, of the existence of which no one was aware, which saved the house by preventing the complete excavation of the ground it stands on. As it was, the corner of the dining-room was taken entirely away, and the room was filled 3 or 4 feet deep with mud. The bow window of the drawing-room was also undermined, and would have fallen, had it not been promptly supported with a dry-stone wall. The foundation of a large store-house, at the back of the garden, was dug under, and a part of the building broken down (Plate 60). The dog-kennel was entirely swept away, and an out-house attached to it, containing some excellent apartments, was completely ruined (Plate 61). The lawn was very much sanded and destroyed, and the handsome wooden bridge of approach across the Dee was carried off completely.

Notwithstanding the breadth of the valley hereabouts, the flood was running over the greater part of the grounds at a depth of 8 or 10 feet. The plantations were much injured, and the roads and walks utterly ruined. In short, a scene of wreck more melancholy than that which the once beautiful spot of Mar Lodge now presents, is hardly to be conceived, and it was impossible to behold it without the most painful feelings.

PLATE 61. KENNEL AND OUTHOUSE AT MAR LODGE, RUINED BY THE FLOOD

The river Cuach,* or Quoich, which falls in from the left bank, committed great havoc. A little way up its rocky and picturesque bed, a handsome bridge, of one wide arch, spanned a most romantic water-fall. The scene here was curious and magnificent. As the water ran completely over the parapet, the arch was quite hidden from above; but when viewed from below, it appeared empty on the under side, and exhibited a dark cavernous appearance. The noise was tremendous, and the shaking of the rocks was so terrific that Mr. Cumming of Allanquoich, factor on Lord Fife's estate here, who has long lived close to the place and has been all his life familiar with such scenes, felt as if he was hardly safe, though standing at a considerable distance. At length the bridge could no longer resist the force of the water, and not only its strong masonry, but immense

* *Cuach is a drinking cup, and the river is so called from the circular holes worn in the micaceous rock near where the bridge stood. Tradition says that the Earl of Mar, and his followers, used to rest here as they returned from the chase, and to drink, mixing their liquors with the pellucid water for which the river is remarkable. One of these holes is still called The Earl of Mar's Punch-bowl.*

masses of the micaceous rock were rent away, and no part of the fabric was left but a small fragment of the western land breast (Plate 62).

Issuing from its gorge, the Cuach swept away three acres of a well-grown young larch wood, surrounded a group of cottages, and manoeuvred with the main body of its stream, now in front, and now in rear of them, so as to keep the unfortunate inmates in a state of distraction. The result was, that, by the providential mercy of God, the mere spot of earth on which the foundations of the houses

PLATE 62. FALL AND BRIDGE OF CUACH, RUINED BY THE FLOOD

stand was left in the midst of a deep excavation, extending for many hundred yards around them, and the river now runs on the side of them opposite to that where it had its course before the flood.

From the point where the houses are situated, the Cuach used to run across a very wide and extensive haugh, for perhaps one-third of a mile, to join, nearly at a right angle, the Dee, that has its course close to the base of the southern hills. The haugh formed Mr. Cumming's farm, and he had just finished a most expensive deer-fence round it, without which agricultural labour is rendered utterly useless in Braemar, owing to the numerous herds of red-deer by which it is tenanted. The flood having brought down an immense slice of a high hill of gravel and stones, not far from the cottages, filled up the channel below, broke out to the left, and rushed across the eastern division of the farm, in a diagonal line, spreading one wide flood of devastation over 150 acres. It then filled up the mouth of this new or second channel, as it had done the first, and, bursting away to the right, it cut a third, still deeper, along the line of Mr. Cumming's wall of enclosure, and then spread itself abroad over the upper part of the western end of the farm, and converted 60 acres of valuable meadow into a permanent lake. Tired with running in this direction, it filled up the new-made channel under the wall, and heaped stones and gravel so high on it as to leave only its cope visible, and completed its operations by opening a fourth bed in a diagonal line between the first and the third, in which I saw it running. All these cruel gambols were performed by this wicked stream in the course of a few hours, leaving two-thirds of the once beautiful and valuable surface of the farm lying in scarified river beds, or covered to a great depth with sand and gravel, and the rest of it in a large lake, where wild fowl may breed. The smell of decomposing matter that came from this scene of desolation was sickening and offensive, and reminded me of what I had experienced after the debacle at Martigny.

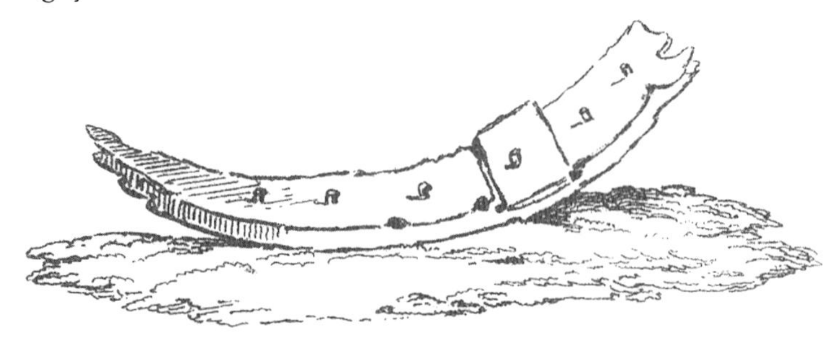

PLATE 63. FRAGMENT OF OLD SAW-MILL BROUGHT DOWN BY THE CUACH

An old fragment of a mill was disinterred and brought down by the Cuach, and lodged on Mr. Cumming's farm (Plate 63). It was ultimately proved to have belonged to a saw-mill that existed in Glenquoich, in Mr. Cumming's father's youth, though for some time it excited yet greater interest, as it was believed to be part of a corn-mill anciently erected in a small plain in the glen. As persons conversant in mechanics were not plenty in the Highlands in the days when this corn-mill was constructed, the laird brought a miller from the low country to manage it. In this neighbourhood, there lived at that time a certain Donald Mackenzie, a far removed branch of the family of Dalmore, a place that once stood where the Lodge does now. This hero, being remarkable for his haughty and imperious manner, was known by the appellation of *Donald Unasach*, or Donald the Proud. Being a native of Glenquoich, he knew as little of the English language as the miller did of the Gaelic. He was an outlaw, addicted to freebooting, and of so fierce and unruly a temper that the whole country stood in awe of him. One circumstance regarding him struck every one with superstitious awe, and created much conjecture and speculation among those around him. He was never known to be without abundance of meal, and yet he was never known to carry any corn to the mill.

But the sagacious miller of Glenquoich soon discovered that, in order to bilk him of his proper mill-dues, the caitiff was in the habit of bringing his grain to the mill in the night, grinding it, and carrying it off before morning. To charge him directly with his fraud was too dangerous an attempt. But the miller ventured to ask him now and then quietly how he did for meal, as he never brought any corn to the mill? To which the freebooter never returned any other answer than *"Is laider laimh Dhe!"* - "Strong is the hand of God!"

Provoked at last, the miller determined to take his own way of curing the evil and, having some previous inkling of the next nocturnal visit of his unwelcome customer, he took care, before leaving the mill in the evening, to remove the bush, or that piece of wood which is driven into the eye of the nether millstone, for the purpose of keeping the spindle steady in passing through the upper stone. He also stopped up the spout through which the meal discharged itself; and, as the mill was one of those old-fashioned machines, where the water-wheel moved horizontally, and directly under the stones, it follows that, by this arrangement of things, the corn would fall into the stream. Having made these preparations, the miller locked his house door, and went to bed. About midnight, Donald arrived with his people, and some sacks of dry corn; and finding everything, as he thought, in good order in the mill, he filled the hopper and let on the water. The machinery revolved with more than ordinary rapidity and the grain sank fast in the hopper, but not a particle of it came out at the place where he was wont to receive it into his bag as meal. Donald the Proud, and his gillies, were all aghast. Frantic with rage, he and they ran up and down and, in their hurry to do everything, they succeeded in doing nothing. At length Donald perceived what even the obscurity of the night could not hide, a long white line of fair provender flowing down the middle of the stream, that left not a doubt as to where his corn was discharging itself. But he could neither guess how this strange phenomenon was produced, nor how the evil was to be cured. After much perplexity, he thought of turning off the water. But here the wily miller had also been prepared for him, having so contrived matters that the pole or handle connecting the sluice with the inside of the mill had fallen off as soon as the water was let on the wheel. Baffled at all points, Donald was compelled at last to run to the miller's house. Finding the door locked, he knocked and bawled loudly at the window and, on the miller demanding to know who was there, he did his best to explain, in broken English, the whole circumstances of the case. The miller heard him to an end and, turning himself in his bed, he coolly replied, "Strong is the hand of God!" Donald Unasach gnashed his teeth; tried the door again; returned to the window; and, humbled by circumstances, repeated his explanation and entreaties for help. *"Te meal town te purn to te tiel! Hoigh! Hoigh!"* "I thought ye had been ower weel practeesed in the business to let ony sic mischanter come ower ye, Maister Anesack," replied the imperturbable lowlander, but 'strong is the hand o' God!'" The mountaineer now lost all patience. Drawing his dirk, and driving it through the window, he began to strike it so violently against the stones on the outside of the wall, that he illuminated the house with a shower of fire, and showed the terrified inmates the ferocious countenance of him who wielded the weapon. *"Te meal to te mill, te mutter to te mailler,"* sputtered out Donald in the midst of his wrath, meaning to imply that, if the miller would only come and help him, he should have all his dues in future. Partly moved by this promise, but still more by his well-grounded fears, the miller arose at last, put the mill to rights, and ground the rest of the corn; and tradition tells us that, after this, the mill-dues were regularly paid, and the greatest harmony subsisted between Donald Unasach and the miller of Glenquoich.

The damage done by the flood to Lord Fife's estate in Braemar, is estimated at £10,000.

The river *Cluanadh*, or *Cluny*, which runs in a deep and craggy bed through the village of Castleton, and enters the Dee from the right, was not swollen to any extraordinary degree. The remains of King Malcolm Canmore's hunting castle may still be traced on the rocky knoll near the south-east corner of the Bridge of Castleton; and the old name of *Ceann-an-drochait*, which once designated the parish of Braemar, was given to it from the bridge, probably of wood, which Malcolm threw across here to facilitate his hunting operations.

The most extensive mischief done by the flood on the estate of Invercauld was by the Burn of Chandlick, which cut away 6000 square yards from a gravel hill, and deposited the debris on the haugh land of the farm of Milton, utterly destroying about 30 arable acres. The stream came directly through the farm house, but fortunately the farmer and his family had gone, some time before, to another farm. In its progress through the park of Invercauld, the Dee was about 400 yards wide and 14½ feet above the usual level. But its greatest havoc was committed where it leaves the park, immediately above the fine old bridge. The lodge is one of those numerous cottages scattered about the grounds, all so exquisitely well conceived, both as to plan and position, as to exhibit a perfect, as well as an exhaustless, good taste. It stands some 30 or 40 yards from the north end of the bridge, and considerably elevated above the river. Its inmates, Kenneth Lamond, his wife, and daughter, were awakened at midnight by the noise proceeding from the stools and chairs knocking about; and, on jumping out of bed, they found themselves knee-deep in water. Undressed as they were, the whole party made for the door, but the moment they opened it they were nearly thrown down by the fury of the torrent that burst in on them. In the midst of all these horrors, old Kenneth reasoned and calculated with perfect presence of mind. To attempt to make a direct course to dry land would probably be certain destruction; but, bethinking him of a line of paling that ran along an elevated ridge, he proceeded, with his companions, linked hand in hand, till he reached it; and, by means of the direction it afforded him, they all gained the houses of Kiloch in safety. The river rose 17½ feet here. It was fearfully grand. A fine nursery above the bridge, and a beautiful flower-garden below it, gave to this spot all the charms of a little paradise amidst the tall beetling cliffs and solemn woods that surround it. These were utterly ruined, together with the smallest of the three arches of the bridge. According to the most accurate observations, the recent flood hereabouts seems to have exceeded that of 1768 by fully 2 feet, in addition to which difference we must not overlook the probable increase of capacity in the river's bed.*

The Swiss character of the scenery about and below Invercauld is much heightened by the larches, which are scattered wildly over the crags among the natural pines and birches. When these begin to shed their seed around, this valuable tree will soon become as much a native here as the Scotch firs, which have maintained their gloomy but sublime dominion for so many centuries.

* *Old Spalding tells us that, on "the 2nd of February, 1642, at midnight, there arose an extraordinary high wind in Aberdeen, with fireflaught and rain. The Rivers Dee and Ythan, through high flood, overflowed their wonted limits, both in this month and January. Dee surpassed in speat the Key-head, and Ythan grew so great that it drowned out the fires in some men's houses in Ellon and Newburgh, far beyond the wonted course, many thinking this to be prodigious tokens. Besides, in Marr, about that part called Banka Fair, the country people heard nightly tucking of drums, beginning about the sky going to, and continuing till eight hours at even. The noise was fearful, for they could hear marches perfectly tucked, as if there had been an army in order. This was not well thought of by honest, peaceable men, as it over well proved by the overthrow of the house of Drum."*

CHAPTER 24

The River Dee, from Crathie to Woodend Cottage

DR. ROBERTSON'S cottage of Crathie stands in a romantic nook, where the brawling little burn of that name hurries into the Dee, from the left bank. During the flood it ran quite over the parapets of the bridge, which resisted all its force. It rose 2 feet on the walls of the house, and 8 feet above its usual level. From an eminence above the house, the valley can be seen for six miles up, where occasional glimpses of the windings of the river are caught through openings in the thick natural woods, and the mountains, on both sides, are seen standing out in high and bold relief. On the morning of the 4th, one wide sea of water, filling the valley from side to side, came rolling on. Houses appeared as if floating on its surface, and groups of birches and alders were tossing about their branches, and labouring to withstand its furious impetuosity. When the flood had passed away, fearful destruction everywhere appeared; 'the land-marks of our forefathers' were gone, and even the angler will now look in vain for the pools and streams of other days.

The damage done at Abergeldie, on the right bank of the river, is estimated at £1000. The house itself, near the Dee and not much elevated above its stream, must have been in some degree of jeopardy. At the base of Craighuis, some 4 or 5 acres were swept away from the haughs, and the whole crops were destroyed. Lower down, the stream of the Girnock, coming in from the right, committed much devastation, and formed two large islands by the new channels it produced.

The river Gairden, which joins the Dee from the left bank, did great damage both to the land and crops along its course. Lord Aboyne's loss here is estimated at £1000. At the bridge where I crossed it, the stream rose from 20 to 25 feet in the narrow rocky bed, and flooded the first storey of the mill.

A little way below the point where the Gairden falls in, the Dee strikes directly against the rocky base of Craigdarroch, and sweeps off suddenly to the right. Here it cut off a considerable promontory, covered with trees, and laid bare two parallel logs of oak, about 15 feet apart, strongly connected by cross bars of the same wood, with two upright posts at the end next the land. Only 10 feet of the logs are visible, the rest being still buried by a sand-bank. There is a tradition that a wooden bridge was erected here, in ancient times, by Gordon, the laird of the Knock, and the baron of the Castle of Glengairden, to facilitate their communication with each other, but that, when it was nearly finished, a flood swept it away. Many suppose that what has thus recently been brought to light formed a part of its foundations, though some think it may be the buried wreck of a bridge brought down the river, and deposited there by some former deluge.

After leaving Craigdarroch, the Dee takes a southerly direction for a mile or more; and then, bending gently round towards the east for perhaps a mile, it gradually assumes a northerly direction, which it holds for about a mile and a half farther, thus encircling three sides of a great plain, the fourth, or north side, of which may be said to be bounded by Craigdarroch. The village of Ballater, formed of regular streets crossing each other at right angles, covers a considerable extent of ground immediately below the bend of the river, and about 12 feet above the ordinary level of the stream. The beautiful stone bridge, designed by Mr. Telford, consisting of five arches with an aggregate water-way of 200 feet, was thrown across from the centre of the great square to the opposite bank, in 1819, at an expense of £5000.

The rain and hurricane on the 3rd of August, at Ballater, was attended in the evening by the brightest lightning, and the loudest thunder, ever seen or heard there; and the same shock of earthquake which was experienced elsewhere was sensibly felt by different individuals in the village and its neighbourhood. The Dee rose gradually till about eleven o'clock at night, when the same partial subsidence took place which was observed in all the other rivers; and the inhabitants, thinking that all cause for apprehension was now over, retired to rest in full confidence. Ballater is always crowded during the summer months, with invalids and other visitors, brought together by the fame of the chalybeate wells of Pananich, which spring from the side of the wooded hill on the right bank of the river; or attracted by the salubrity of the air, and the grandeur of the surrounding scenery. This was the height of the season, and not a house in the village was without some inmate of more than ordinary consequence. Among these was a lady, who was suddenly disturbed, about half-an-hour after midnight, by voices talking loud and earnestly under her window. The ominous words "flood", "deluge", "drooned" and "ha'e mercy on us a'!" having reached her ears, she thought it was time to inquire what had occasioned them. Opening her window, therefore, she asked what was the matter. "The Dee's oot ower bank and brae!" cried half a dozen voices at once, "an' some o' the hooses are surroonded wi' the water, an' they've been cairryin' oot the fouk; sae ye had better get up a'thegither o' ye, for she's comin' roarin' doon jist like an ocean, an' we'll be a' drooned!" Extravagant as all this clamour appeared, there was some foundation for their fears, for an individual in one of the houses the water had made its way into, particularly marked the progress of its rise during a whole hour, in the stair-case, which was at the astonishingly rapid rate of one foot in every ten minutes!

The lady lost no time in dressing, but, as the house she occupied had several others between it and the river, and was, moreover, on rather higher ground, she did not, as yet, think it necessary to leave it.

But, about half-past three o'clock, the flood increased, and swept before it the two northern arches of the bridge at one and the same instant, and, in the course of two hours afterwards, the three others were borne away in succession. Those who saw the first arches go assured me that the noise was tremendous, and that the splash of the water was so great that it was driven over the tops of the adjoining houses. Certain it is that the current was so arrested, for a moment, by the ruins, as to produce a recoil that burst open the doors and smashed many of the windows of the offices belonging to the inn. This dreadful reflux of water alarmed the lady I have mentioned, and she and her party deemed it prudent to move. In doing so, they had to wade more than an hundred yards through the town before they could get to a dry house. But they were fortunate in so escaping, for danger now swept into the village from a quarter where it was least expected. At a point about half a mile to the north-west, the river burst over its banks, and, following the track of an old water-course, a stream of about 4 feet deep came rushing down through the streets. Now was the bustle, the hubbub, the screaming, and the plunging, of delicate and nervous women, all wading for their lives, something too serious for matter of merriment. And yet there were scenes that were irresistibly comic. On most of these strangers the catastrophe came so suddenly, that they were only roused from their sleep to flee from the deluge in drapery that, to say nothing more of it, was at least too scanty for encountering the raging elements in this most tempestuous night. Every horse in the village, and every vehicle that could be made useful, was pressed into active service, to convey the invalids, and the more helpless, to some place of safety. One of the lumbering Aberdeen and Ballater coaches was ferreted out, and horses being yoked to it, the interior was filled, and the outside covered with so great a number of passengers as set the laws at defiance. Nor was there any great ceremony used in the manner of bestowing this overload of human beings. Ladies and gentlemen, young and old, fat and lean, strangers to each other, were all huddled in together, all anxious to escape, but each wishing that the rest had been away, or, at least, that an introduction had taken place under other circumstances. Many a fair creature had her slumbers rudely broken, and a blanket being thrown around her, she was scarcely conscious of what passed till she found herself hoisted in the arms of some hero who, rejoicing at the accident, and proud of his precious burden, was seen gallantly plunging along, middle-deep, with an air that might have done honour to a quadrille. It is impossible to say how many of the tedious out-works of courtship were swept away by the flood at Ballater.

Still the waters went on increasing, and so rapidly did they gain on the village, that the house to which the lady and her party had fled for refuge was so inundated in half-an-hour after they reached it, that they were again compelled to move. Still was the crowd of provincial fashionables to be seen floundering on. In the midst of a terrified group of grown daughters who were hanging around her, one lady clung to her worthy husband and their dear papa, till the good man, who was rather corpulent, had been nearly pressed down into the water by the weight of their united embraces. "Call you this a watering-place?" exclaimed he, as he shook himself good naturedly free of them on reaching a dry spot, and began to get a little freer breathing; "if you catch me coming a-watering again this gate, I'll alloo ye to mak' a water-kelpie o' me!"*

It would be in vain to attempt an enumeration of all the disasters that occurred. Two calves were drowned in Mr. Smith's barn, and one of them was found within the hopper of the corn-fanners, 5 feet 6 inches from the ground; and certainly it is not easy to imagine a more singular place for an animal to have met with a watery grave. One of Mr. Smith's pigs was afterwards found alive on an island, two miles below Ballater, grunting in his liberty. A great quantity of grain and meal was carried off. The lower storey of the inn near the end of the bridge was flooded to the depth of 5 feet 3 inches; the furniture carried away from the kitchen; two hogsheads of porter from the cellar, one never again heard of and the other found uninjured on the island with Mr. Smith's pig; and one anker** of whisky was laid hold of by a stout young fellow as it was in the act of making its exit at the door.

Mrs. Mitchell, her child, and servant, were sleeping in the kitchen, which is sunk several feet below the level of the street. They were awakened about one o'clock, by the noise of the door bursting open, and the dreadful sound of the water rushing into the place. Snatching up her infant, Mrs. Mitchell jumped out of bed, followed by the maid, and found the water already more than knee deep. Undressed as they were, they struggled to the stair leading upwards to the first floor. Having gained it, the servant attempted to return for their clothes, but it was already impossible and, in half an hour, the kitchen was filled to the ceiling. Had the warning they received been but ten minutes later, they must have been drowned in that apartment, the very name of which is designative of dryness, warmth, security, and substantial comfort.

Few of the houses of the village suffered much, but many of them were filled from 4 to 6 feet deep of water, and a great deal of furniture was destroyed. The most deplorable loss was that of the

** Publisher's Note:* ***kelpie*** *or* ***kelpy****, a malignant water-sprite haunting fords in the form of a horse (Scot. folklore).*

*** Publisher's Note:* ***anker****, a Dutch word for an old measure for wines and spirits used in Northern Europe, the exact volume varying considerably (that of Rotterdam being eight and a half imperial gallons).*

magnificent bridge (Plate 64). The appearance of the ruins, when I saw them as viewed from the window of the inn, with a ruined flower-garden in the fore-ground, was truly lamentable; nothing remaining but the two land-breasts of the north and south arches, and a tall spectre-like fragment of a central pier, rearing itself from the midst of the triumphant stream, as if quivering from dread of its utter annihilation. The whole crops of the fertile plain below the village were, of course, completely destroyed.

PLATE 64. BRIDGE OF BALLATER, RUINED BY THE FLOOD

The view of Ballater, from the lower extremity of the plain, is something quite exquisite. I do not speak of the village itself, which, at that distance, presents little more than the indication of a town with a steeple rising from it; but I allude to the grand features of nature by which it is surrounded. The very smallness of the town indeed adds to the altitude of the mountains; for, when seen from the point I mean, it might be a city for aught the traveller knows to the contrary. It stands, half hidden among trees, in the rich and diversified vale. On the north rises the mountainous rock of Craigdarroch, luxuriantly wooded with birch and divided off from the bounding mountains of that side of the valley by the wild, and anciently impregnable, Pass of Ballater. Beyond the river, amidst an infinite variety of slopes and woods, is seen the tall, old hunting-tower of Knock; and, behind it, distance rises over distance, till the prospect is terminated by the long and shivered front ridge of Lochnagar, the nurse of the sublime genius of Byron, who, in his beautiful little poem, so entitled, still *"Sighs for the Valley of dark Loch-na-gar"*.

On my way down the left bank of the river, I stopped for a few minutes at the door of a neat little inn, called Cambus-may, kept by a respectable couple, Mr James Ogg and his wife. The spot is beautiful.

The house is situated in the pass forming the eastern entrance to that enchanting and heart-expanding scenery of which the upper part of the Dee exhibits one uninterrupted series. Here the woods present a delightful intermixture of birches and oaks, and the ground is diversified with knolls and little plains, and bounded by friable granite mountains, the decomposing rocks of which assume the most picturesque shapes imaginable. The bank of the river here is 8 or 10 feet high, and Mr. Ogg's house stands on a small level haugh, having little more than the breadth of the road between it and the stream. Mr. Ogg told me that the river burst suddenly in on the upper end of the haugh at one o'clock on the morning of the 4th, surrounded the house, and rose 5 feet up in it. Mr. and Mrs. Ogg were roused from their slumbers by the rushing noise of the waters as they entered, and had not time to remove anything to the upper storey. "Troth, sir," said Mr. Ogg, "we waur glad aneuch to escape awa' as fast as we could, widin' up to oor middles, to the hill yonder, whaur we got shelter in a neebour's hoose." When they returned next day, after the water had subsided, they found the house half filled with mud and sand. "Ay, sir," said Mrs. Ogg, "and we lost three ankers o' whisky an' ane o' rum, an' a deal o' oor furnitur'." "Ay," said Mr. Ogg, "an' oor corn an oor cairts an' a'! Sixty pun' wadna cover oor loss!" "An' what think ye, sir?" said Mrs. Ogg, "the very first thing I fand whan we cam back was a bit trootie in the plate-rack." "That was something, Mrs. Ogg," said I, "did you fry it?" "Eh, na!" said Mr. Ogg, "the peer beastie wasna deid; it was soomin' aboot amang the dishes; she couldna hae fund in her hairt to hae hairmed it, whan it had come, as it were, to oor vera hairthstane for shelter, sae I took it an' pat it into the reever again, an' it soomed awa'." Mr. Ogg told me that, at the Haugh, a farm a little way lower down, a fine island of three acres was swept entirely away.

After quitting the Pass of Cambus-may, I crossed a wide and dreary heath-covered plain, which was not so once, nor is it now, without interest. It was here that Sir Andrew Murray of Bothwell, William Douglas of Liddesdale, and the Earl of March, with 800 of the lads of Lothian and the Merse, attacked David de Hastings, Earl of Athole, where he and the Cumins lay under cover of the Forest of Culblane. They routed his troops, slew him and Walter Cumin, and took and beheaded Walter Cumin's brother Thomas.

"Thare, by an ake, deyed Erle Dawy, And syndry of his company."

Wyntown gives a very accurate description of the ground. But the '*akes*' (oaks) have all fled, like '*Erle Dawy*'s' troops, and have ensconced themselves within the Pass of Cambus-may, leaving no object to break the monotony of the heath but the huge grey cairn marking the spot where '*Erle Dawy*' fell.

CHAPTER 25

The River Dee, from Woodend Cottage to Aberdeen

MAJOR Leith Hay's residence of Woodend Cottage stands on a haugh of four acres, on the left bank of the Dee, elevated about 16 feet above the ordinary level of its stream, that runs about 30 yards in front of the house. The haugh is backed to the north by a long and rapid rise, is terminated to the west by wood and a garden, part of which is on a level with the cottage, and part on a slope also rising to the north, and is bounded on the east by a semi-circle of rocks and single trees, beyond which is the wood of Trustach. The Dee runs from west to east, forming the southern boundary of the grounds at all points. The rain and tempest at Woodend were quite tremendous, and were accompanied by thunder and lightning. The water rushed in streams down the opposite bank, where none had ever been visible before; and the ground giving way in several places, an enclosure of trees, with all its paling, was completely swept away by the precipitate fall of earth and rock from the height above, and a cataract of 50 feet high was formed. By six o'clock in the morning of the 4th, the river surmounted the lowest part of the ground near the garden, and soon afterwards ran in a strong current to the north of the haugh, through a hollow at the back of the house. At seven o'clock nothing remained uncovered but the ground the house stood on. The stable, coach-house, washing-house, and larder were flooded to the depth of several feet; and the boat belonging to the proprietor having been carried away, all egress from the cottage was rendered impracticable. Meanwhile the river went on to increase, and, in an hour afterwards, it rushed into the house in every direction. A very formidable current swept round the south-west angle of the house, and threatened to undermine it; and it was discovered, on investigation, that it had laid it bare nearly to the depth of 3 feet. At this time the lower panes of a French window in the dining-room gave way, by which a great addition of water was admitted into the house, and the windows to the east were opened to allow it to escape. The family took shelter in the upper storey, and now the strength of the masonry, the shelter afforded by the trees, already matted with wreck so as to form a kind of bulwark, and the hope that so unnatural an inundation could not long endure, were the only circumstances which could inspire confidence in a situation so distressing, from which escape had become impracticable.

By eleven o'clock, the flood had reached its height, and there was little perceptible alteration in it for an hour. At this time the depth of the water was above 18 inches in the front rooms and passages of the house, 3 feet in the servants' hall, 5 feet in the larder, and 5½ feet in the washing-house. The extreme height above ordinary level of the river was $17^{1}/_{2}$ or 18 feet, and 20 feet above the lowest summer level. In the memory of man, the Dee was never before known to cover the ground the cottage stands on, nearly an acre having remained dry on former occasions. The flood of August 4th had exceeded all those preceding it, by at least 2 feet perpendicular. "It appears to me," says Major Leith Hay, in a letter I received from him, "that the inhabitants of this country were never before acquainted with the irresistible power of water, particularly in mountain streams. My impression is that the power of the ocean is nothing to it."*

Mr. Douglas, Sheriff of Kincardineshire, was awaked at his cottage of Maryfield, on the right bank of the Dee, at three o'clock in the morning of the 4th, by the dreadful noise of the river, and found that it had risen about 25 feet above the ordinary level. The cottage, which stands 28 feet above the stream, seemed to be in imminent danger of inundation. Curiosity having tempted him to go to look at the cascade at the Bridge of Feugh, he found the turnpike road impracticable, and was compelled to ascend the high grounds and take a circuitous route to an elevated spot, from which he could view the scene below. The stream was dashing entirely over the parapets of the bridge, which soon gave way with a terrible crash, leaving the centre arch totally bare. An adventurous baker from the village of Banchory walked along one of the parapets, through the spray, immediately before they gave way. A huge fragment of rock, many tons in weight, was disengaged from its solid bed by the force of the current, and carried down several yards, to a position where it still remains conspicuously poised. The interest of the scene was augmented by the appearance of a number of people, most of them driven from the neighbouring cottages by the intrusion of the stream, and the whole effect was highly grand and picturesque. The arches of the Bridge of Banchory over the Dee were nearly full, and a small island, a little way below, which was pastured by sheep, being wholly submerged, the wretched animals were seen floating helplessly down the river. One ewe reached Maryfield Cottage in safety, and, when driven homewards by the turnpike road, after the island had again become visible, the poor creature plunged into the water, and swam to the spot where she had been so lately severed from her lamb, which, alas! all her piteous bleatings could not recall.

Mr. Moir of Park, on the left bank of the Dee, was attracted to the window by the noise of the flood, about three o'clock in the

** This remark of Major Leith Hay's is perfectly in accordance with my own observations. I have already endeavoured to draw the distinction between the two forces, by comparing the agitated ocean to a heap of gunpowder set fire to on an open plain, whilst the intense velocity and power of a flooded river is like a portion of such a heap discharged from the confined breech of a gun.*

morning of the 4th, when the surrounding country presented the extraordinary appearance of one immense sheet of water. The tops of the embankments were alone visible in the adjacent grounds, and on these a few sheep and two ponies had taken refuge. But even there the water was fast rising, and at about four o'clock they were swept away. Nine of the sheep and one pony were drowned, and the rest, being carried by the current towards a steep bank, were saved with great difficulty. The greatest height attained by the river, opposite to Park, was 13 feet above its usual level, but this was at a point where the breadth of the inundation was not less than half a mile. Mr. Moir had 300 lineal yards of embankment, and two acres of land, swept away. He estimates his damage of all kinds at about £1000, and, as he says that he is induced to believe himself the greatest sufferer on Deeside,* we have some criterion for judging how much greater the destruction of the Findhorn and Spey was than that of this river.

A good deal of damage was done on the Duke of Gordon's property of Durris, on the right bank; but the greatest injury was sustained on the farm of Nether Balfour, where about 140 acres were inundated 4 or 5 feet deep, by the bursting of an embankment. As this ground formed a kind of bay, a great deal of wreck was drifted into it by the north wind; and, amongst other things, some very large trees. The crops suffered severely, and much soil was carried away from the turnip fields. About 4000 stones of hay were floated off; and, though much was saved by the bold exertions of the farm servants, who waded in and threw ropes around the ricks, yet it was utterly spoiled. The tenant's loss here was £400.

A farmer, residing about a mile and a half from the Church of Mary-Culter, said that there would be a great deluge of rain, for that he had not, for twenty years, heard the church bell so distinctly as he had done on Sunday the 2nd. This proved a greatly increased density in the atmosphere, which is the very reverse of what we should have looked for, previous to a great discharge of rain. But a variety of observations have long ago proved that the formation of rain sometimes takes place at a great height above the surface of the earth, and quite independently of the state of the lower strata of the atmosphere. But to explain why this increased density should have become a sure prognostic of rain with this farmer, we must take into account the effects produced by certain winds, which we know often raise the barometer, though followed by rainy weather, as was indeed very much the case on the late occasion. But the rain at Mary-Culter was, in fact, by no means so great as to lead anyone to anticipate a flood of any great magnitude. The height of the flood in

* *Deeside is the name applied to the country extending from about the Pass of Cambus-may to the sea.*

this neighbourhood was from 13 to 16 feet above the ordinary level. The crop was much damaged; and the fishing station at Inch-Culter, one of the best in the river, was so completely ruined that, it is believed, not a salmon was taken there for the whole season afterwards. Mr. Boswell of Kingcausie remarked that the weight and rapidity of the stream was so great that trees and boats passed downwards with the velocity of the *"chute of Alpnach."*

Colonel Duff of Fetteresso's farm of Milltimber, on the left bank, had 60 acres flooded, with much destruction of crop and deposition of sand and gravel. Mr. Thurburn's farm of Mains of Murtle, and Deebank, belonging to Mr. Andrew, suffered much, especially the latter where a stream burst through a bulwark, and cut up a haugh. The river also broke a strong embankment, and covered 60 acres of the Haugh of Pitfoddels, belonging to Mr. Menzies, doing not less than £500 damage. Many other farms have suffered, but these may serve as a sufficient sample of the extent of the destruction wrought on the banks of this part of the river.

About five o'clock on the morning of the 4th, the inhabitants of the quay at Aberdeen were roused from their slumbers by the noise of the flood, sweeping along under their windows, and, on looking out, they were astonished at the magnificence of the scene that presented itself. The Dee rushed from the narrow pass opposite the rocky eminence called the Craiglug, as if from a gigantic mill-dam, the sluice of which had been newly opened. From thence the waters spread themselves from side to side, filling the whole space of nearly a mile in breadth. At this hour the tide was subsiding, and it continued to do so until ten o' clock, the harbour exhibiting the anomalous appearance of a receding tide, and a rising flood. At ten o'clock it was dead low water, but the stream opposite to the town was then fully eighteen inches above the average elevation of spring-tides. At low water at the bar, the current ran at the rate of 9½ knots an hour, as ascertained by actual experiment. So powerful was the stream, that the *Duke of Wellington*, steam-vessel, in attempting to struggle against it, ran aground. The channel of the harbour was completely scoured of its mud. Thirty feet of the quay at the lower basin was undermined, and a portion of the *Raik-dike** was carried away.

* *Publisher's Note: something of the multi-national influence on the language of the Scots is seen in this expression, used by Sir Thomas without further explanation. It seems not to be used now in the dialect of the coast folk of the North East, but its derivation is apparently from the Old Norse* ***reik****, meaning 'to go a journey, or walk', and the Dutch word* ***dijk****, meaning 'a wall', and still in common Scots parlance. Putting the two words together, in the context of Sir Thomas's remarks, we would have, literally, a 'walk-wall', from which we would assume a reference to a sea-wall with a parapet suitable for walking. There is today a road in Aberdeen, near to the harbour, called 'Raik Road'.*

CHAPTER 26

A FEW OF THE MORE PROMINENT RAVAGES OF THE RIVERS NORTH AND SOUTH ESK, TARFF, LUTHER AND BERVIE

THE rain began to fall at Montrose about eleven o'clock on Sunday evening, the 2nd of August, and the inhabitants declare that the deluge was beyond all former precedent. The North Esk was in high flood, and the consequences to all the lower grounds were most disastrous. The Tarff carried away its bridge, and inundated the Reverend Peter Jolly's house at Lochlie to the depth of three feet. All the neighbouring bridges were injured. The new wooden bridge at Dalhesney was entirely swept away, and the fine suspension bridge, recently erected at Slateford, was also utterly demolished, as well as a small bridge in Glen Esk. The strong northerly wind came in squalls, and blew down many noble trees. At Gannachy Bridge, the flood rose to within a foot of the keystone. At the junction of the North, West, and Cruik waters, the scene was extremely grand. The large haugh above the Bridge of Marykirk was completely flooded, and the sheep that fed on it were extricated with the greatest difficulty.

The North Esk overspread the large bleachfield at Craigie Mills, belonging to Messrs. Maberly & Company, which was covered with cloths and yarn. It rose to the height of 3 feet in the mill and, if it had not been for a rampart raised by the people at the gainshot*, by risking their lives, the whole works might have been swept away. Mr. Carnegy of Craigo, the proprietor, measured the height of the water at the gainshot of the mills, and found it 7 feet 2 inches above the ordinary level. It rose to its greatest height about five o'clock on the morning of the 4th, and was not observed to subside till eight o'clock. A small unfurnished brick building at the Logie Mills was the only one that suffered. The loss of Messrs. Maberly & Company, in bleaching materials and yarns swept off, was considerable; and that of Messrs. Aberdeen, Gordon, & Company, at the Logie Mill, was still greater. The spinning-mill of Kinnaber, possessed by Messrs. Duke & Alexander, was deluged to the top of the lower flat of the mill. Mr. Mitchell of Nether Careston had fifty or sixty sheep carried away. Much agricultural produce was lost, but no land of any consequence was removed by the North Esk, and the damage it created altogether was so trifling, in comparison with that I have detailed as produced by any of the other rivers, that I notice it chiefly for the purpose of marking the difference.

This observation also applies to the South Esk, and the rest of the streams mentioned in the title to this article. The suburb called

* *Publisher's Note:* ***gainshot****, (Scot) the late eighteenth and early nineteenth century word used for the cover of the water inlet to a mill-wheel.*

the Nether Tenements in Brechin was flooded, and the inhabitants were confined to the upper part of their houses during the greater part of the day. The South Esk also swept away a great quantity of yarn from the Inch bleachfield; and sheep, hay, labouring utensils, wood, and other articles, were seen floating down. The Luther and the Bervie overflowed their banks, and the latter carried off the lesser bridge of Mondines, on the road between Laurencekirk and Stonehaven, but this is all I have to record regarding these streams.

CHAPTER 27

Concluding Remarks

MIRACULOUS as many of the circumstances of the foregoing narration may appear, I have stated nothing that cannot be vouched by unquestionable authority. On the contrary, I feel conscious that all my endeavours must fail to convey any just idea of the wonders of the flood, or of the fearful nature of its devastations.

It would be improper to dismiss the subject without shortly noticing the general effects which these have produced on the ancient province of Moray, the chief theatre of their operation.* To form a just estimate of that blow which its rising prosperity has lately experienced, it is necessary to know something of its previous state, and this knowledge will be best acquired from a brief sketch of the rapid progress of its improvement since the beginning of the present (nineteenth) century, which we may consider as the era of its commencement.

With a surface exhibiting every variety of wild and rich scenery, and possessing an early and productive soil, Moray is blessed with a climate of greater amenity, and proverbially drier, than its mere geographical position might warrant its enjoying. It is a well-known fact that the crops, in its best situations, are always ready for the sickle nearly a fortnight before those of any other part of Scotland. But, at the period I speak of, with all these natural advantages, it was still many years behind the southern parts of Caledonia, so far as regarded most of those things which man could do for it. The great thoroughfares, though naturally firm and hard in substance, were unnecessarily winding in line, waving in level, and rough in surface. The crossroads were impassable by any wheeled carriage except the light carts of the country, which are rudely constructed and altogether without iron, and with the exception of a very few bridges, there were no means of passing the many deep and rapid rivers, but by ferries and fords, always troublesome, and frequently fatal. Something, indeed, had been done to increase, by the cultivation of a few waste spots, the original quantity of the arable soil, for which Moray had been anciently celebrated, and much had been added to the extensive plantations already made. But many of the estates wore a meagre aspect; most of the mansion-houses were poor in

* *The ancient province of Moray is thus geographically described by old Lachlan Shaw: "This country lieth in the 57th degree of north latitude, and Speymouth is about 35 minutes east from Edinburgh. With regard to the neighbouring countries, the Moray Firth and the River Farar separate it from Ross to the north; and from Speymouth towards the south-east, the south, and south-west, it bordereth upon the Enzie, Strathdovurn, Strathdone, Braemar, Athol, Rannoch, and Lochaber."*

external appearance, as well as in their internal accommodation; and although the greater part of them possessed gardens substantially valuable in produce, their environs were, with a few exceptions, utterly destitute of those ornamental accompaniments which Taste now so largely demands from Art, for the decoration of a gentleman's residence. In those times, the post from Edinburgh came only thrice a week, and took about three days and a half to effect the journey. There was no mail-coach, or public coach of any kind, to the north of Aberdeen; and two days, or more, were required for posting between Aberdeen and Forres. In short, the whole complexion and circumstances of the country were such as to show that its powers were yet asleep.

But its energies were soon awakened, and their strength and rapidity of exertion largely compensated for the length of that slumber in which they had previously indulged. Magnificent bridges were built over the Spey at Fochabers, the Findhorn near Forres, the Nairn, and other large rivers. The grand iron bridge of Craigellachie, of 150 feet span, was projected and executed; and innumerable bridges of lesser importance were constructed. Many piers and harbours, both private and public, were formed, Turnpike Acts were obtained, and the country was everywhere intersected by great lines of communication. The ancient parochial roads, hitherto little better than tortuous indications of a primitive track worn over the undulating surface of the country, which had never been deviated from since they were first sketched by the sledges that originally discovered them, were now superseded by well-lined and well-constructed highways; and the circulation of the country being thus quickened by its own exertions, a daily post was established, which, by the gradual improvement of circumstances, ultimately reached Forres in little more than twenty-four hours from Edinburgh. The mail-coach ran north and south through the province, keeping up a direct line of intercourse between Dover and Wick. Two stage-coaches, one with three, and the other with four, horses, passed north and south every day, Sunday excepted;* and the posting between Aberdeen and Forres soon became easily practicable in nine or ten hours. A corresponding improvement in the breed of draught horses, as well as the introduction of a better description of carts, were the natural consequences of these happy changes, whilst the labourers who had been employed in constructing these roads gradually acquired a degree of knowledge and skill which brought the art of road-making, and of executing all other works of the same kind, to the highest perfection. During the short period I have referred to, many wide wastes of unprofitable moorland have been

* *The flood has so completely broken up the communication, that the arrangements regarding the coaches have been overthrown, and the time of the mails rendered quite precarious.*

divided among the conterminous proprietors who had common interest in them, and immediately cultivated or planted. Extensive lakes and morasses have been drained, the sea has been excluded in some places and rivers have been confined by expensive embankments in others, and large tracts of valuable land have been reclaimed from beneath deep depositions of drifted sand, which had buried them for ages. In short, it would be no easy matter to discover a possession which had not made some considerable addition to the extent of its useful soil; while many farms, and even some estates, could be found which have doubled the quantity of their arable land. Plantations have been increased to an extent almost incredible, and the woods alone, which cover the country in a manner almost continuous on either side of the river Findhorn from Dulsie to the sea, are roughly calculated to amount to 16,000 or 18,000 acres. Handsome mansion-houses have been built by many proprietors, and gentlemen's residences have had all the adornment of ornamental grounds, shrubberies, walks, and drives bestowed on them, in some instances on a scale not always to be paralleled in the more southern parts of the kingdom.

But these were not all the felicitous consequences resulting from this powerful spirit of improvement, for the great mass of the farmers, rising in intelligence, as well as in opulence, as they grew learned in agricultural science; and even the industrious cottagers, enabled by their increased skill in labour to earn a more regular, as well as a more liberal subsistence, began to participate in the taste which had already so widely spread itself among the higher ranks.

The face of the country was thus rapidly receiving that polished attire which dresses Nature, without either obscuring or caricaturing her native graces, and which nothing but refined civilization knows how to bestow. It may, therefore, be easily imagined that the ravages which it has been my unpleasant duty to record, were greatly more calamitous in their effects when occurring in such a country, than if they had taken place either where improvement had not yet commenced, or where the earth's surface had been long brought to a state of comparative perfection, for, in the recent case, both the subject and the capital with which existing individuals had so recently created it, were at once annihilated. The great and expensive works forming a part of the vast arterial system of national communication, the district and parochial branches giving life and energy to every estate and every farm, many of them created by proprietors at immense cost, and, in many instances, by incurring deep pecuniary engagements, and, finally, the very extensive and dear-purchased private improvements, executed both by landlords and tenantry, have all been more or less ruined, wherever they lay within reach of the direful ravages of these floods. It is quite vain to attempt to calculate the sum-total of damage; for the result of any calculation formed on the data which have as yet been collected would be greatly short of the truth, and the printing of it would be only the registration of a fallacy. Every day discloses additional injuries, overlooked at first from being less obvious, but adding fearfully by their number to the weight of the mass of loss. Nowhere has any work been left perfect, for even where rivers or rills ran not in ordinary, temporary torrents were established which tore up everything before them, and wrought incalculable mischief, so that it was difficult to walk many yards in any direction without beholding some of the footsteps of this dreadful deluge. The march of amelioration over this hitherto thriving country has thus received a severe check, and its rising prosperity has undergone a terrible prostration. Making every allowance for the advantages acquired from dear-bought experience, we cannot hope that it will be restored to the same high state it stood in previous to August last, in anything like the same short space of time in which it formerly attained it, for, alas! the same means of reproduction no longer exist. In circumstances so unprecedented, therefore, the wisdom of Government would be well displayed, and its funds well appropriated, in giving aid, at least so far as to restore the more important public works, and so to heal those wounds which have a tendency to affect the national health; for it is obvious that an interruption of free circulation cannot take place in any part of the national system, more than it can in the natural body, without more or less injuring the constitution of the whole. If patience under affliction may in any way strengthen a claim for commiseration, the suffering inhabitants of Moray may well look for sympathy, for, heavily as the dispensation has descended on people of all ranks, neither complaints nor murmurs have been heard to arise.

The operations of the flood are striking when brought singly and successively under our review; but there is an ideal survey which may yet be taken of them, that will probably appear to many as the most sublime of all. To enjoy this, let us lift ourselves, in fancy, to a height sufficiently commanding to overlook all their various actions at one glance, and let us then endeavour to imagine the effect. Behold the short-sighted emmets* of the earth, drudging on at their daily tasks as if they and their works were to endure for ever. Observe them building, planting, toiling, to make scratches on the surface, and their pride in their achievements. Fatigued with their important labours, they seek repose in the full confidence of safety, and they dream of their own greatness and power. But the deluge comes! It pours down the furrowed sides of the mountains in a thousand cataracts, like the mighty host of God's destroying angels, each separate cohort commissioned for its own especial career of

* *Publisher's Note:* ***emmet****, an ant (Old English).*

destruction! The numerous valleys are filled at once with the accumulated waters, and the riches of all are swept off to the ocean in different directions at the same moment. Throughout the whole windings of each respective strath all is sudden dismay, clamour, and dread. Some are struggling to escape with life from the devouring waves; some are pent up in their tottering dwellings with the shadow of death around them; others are hanging to their crazy and toppling roofs, suspended over the depths of eternity; whilst bold hearts are stirred up to do daring deeds, and all the finer feelings and magnanimous virtues of humanity are excited and called into activity. A few hours ago all was peaceful abundance, and smiling happiness, and proud exultation: now all is turmoil and terror, or daring determination. Anon the floods disappear, and gaunt Famine sits brooding over the new-born wastes, and, as in the overthrow of some huge ant-hill, the wild hurry of surprise and consternation arises, without concert, and utterly without benefit, either to the general body, or to the individuals composing it.

We cannot doubt that so terrible a judgment was sent by the Almighty Governor of the Universe for some great and beneficial purpose, and the mercy that has been mingled with the chastisement may well teach us the love of that Heavenly Father, from whose hand it comes. Amidst all the terrors and dangers of this unexampled calamity, where thousands of lives were placed in jeopardy, the instances of Providential deliverance were so numerous and so extraordinary, that, throughout so great an extent of flooded rivers, we have only the loss of eight human lives to deplore! Then, how delightfully has it served to develop those moral excellencies, which, though not altogether extinguished beneath the dross of human nature, do yet require some great stimulating cause to bring them into play. But, above all things, we ought not to neglect this awful admonition to a sinful land, nor refuse to lay it to our hearts. I know that many individuals of all ranks have deeply felt this warning; so that, if the temporal and physical effects of the flood have been severe, we may hope that the spiritual and moral fruits resulting from it will be but the more abundant.

APPENDIX 1

ABSTRACT STATE OF THE FLOOD FUND AND ITS APPLICATION

I AM indebted to Mr. Isaac Forsyth, of Elgin, for the following Abstract of the Subscription Flood Fund, which, being particularly appropriated to the destitute sufferers in the county of Elgin, was very much increased by his charitable zeal as Secretary to the Elgin Central Committee of Management. His labours have been unremitting and unwearied, and cannot fail to secure to him a yet more honourable, though, perhaps, less extended fame than rewarded his deceased brother, Joseph, as Author of the admirable and scholarlike *'Tour in Italy'*. Small as has been the relief afforded, yet the liberality of those who contributed, and especially of the London Morayshire Club who so promptly set the example, will be long warmly remembered by those who participated in it.

Subscribed between 20th August, 1829, and 20th February 1830.	£1470 10 1
Distributed between 10th October, 1829, and 27th February, 1830.	£1429 9 6
Allotted to be bestowed in honorarv rewards to the boatmen on the Findhorn and Spey, who risked their lives to save others, on the 4th August	£ 20 0 0
Expenses incurred in the management	£ 19 12 6
	£1469 2 0
Balance on hand, 3rd March, 1830,	£ 1 8 1

APPLICATION OF THE FUND.

Total amount ***distributed*** as above £1429 9 6

To	Speymouth	18 Cases	£52 10 0
	St Andrew's	7 Cases	16 0 0
	Spynie	19 Cases	42 5 0
	Forres	140 Cases	100 4 0
	Dyke	95 Cases	142 14 0
	Edinkillie	33 Cases	65 5 0
	Rothes	148 Cases	352 12 6
	Knockando	28 Cases	87 5 0
	Abernethy	33 Cases	106 5 0
	Duthil	25 Cases	82 0 0
	Dallas	41 Cases	70 14 0
	Elgin	21 Cases	44 5 0
	Drainy	2 Cases	10 0 0
	Alves	1 Case	2 0 0
	Boharm	3 Cases	7 0 0
	Urquhart	8 Cases	21 5 0

APPENDIX 2

COPY OF CIRCULAR BY THE CENTRAL COMMITTEE

ELGIN, 20th April, 1830.

SIR, The Central Committee for managing 'THE FLOOD FUND' so freely and generously supplied by Morayshire men and their friends, to an extent hitherto unparalleled in the North of Scotland, and which has averted the misery of absolute want from upwards of 3000 individuals; having often, during their investigations of the numerous cases of distress laid before them, had their attention drawn to the important services of the boatmen on the Rivers Findhorn and Spey, think it is a duty (before closing their labours), which they owe these brave men, to place their conduct and merits fairly before the public.

On the awful morning of the 4th of August last, these two rivers had swollen so much beyond all former precedent, as to assume the appearance of inland seas. The houses in their neighbourhood were surrounded and invaded by the inundation to such a height that all were endangered, some severely injured, and many were wholly swept away. The lives and safety of the inhabitants, and their cattle, being thus placed in the most imminent peril, a degree of alarm and excitation, which became almost agonizing, was created in the minds of all. At this painfully interesting and critical moment, at the very dawn of the day, animated by one common but generous feeling for the deliverance of their fellow creatures, at whatever personal hazard, five boats' crews started from the town of Findhorn, and several cobles from the west side of that river, proceeding in all directions, over hedges and embankments, and through every obstacle, to the objects in view. Their laborious and dangerous exertions were crowned with the most gratifying success: not one life was lost; though, without this noble, disinterested, and unsolicited assistance, many must have perished. On the Spey, at Rothes and at Garmouth, the same generous, prompt, and effective spirit was shown, with the same gratifying results. Several lives were saved, though at the most fearful risk to their brave deliverers. From the accounts already received by the Committee, forty of these warm-hearted brave fellows were engaged in that perilous work of mercy. Considering the Fund confided to their direction as a sacred trust for a specific object, the Committee, although deeply impressed with the merits of these brave men, and the propriety of some reward, could not venture to deviate from the principle they laid down for their own government in this matter, farther than by appropriating £20 as the foundation of a small fund for the purpose which they now beg to recommend to your patronage.

Instead of a present in money, which would be soon dissipated and forgotten, the Committee have thought that a preferable mode of remunerating such services would be by an *Honorary Reward*; and that a Silver Medal* to each man, with his name and services engraven on it, which, with an honest pride, on festive or solemn occasions, could be displayed by himself and his descendants as a proof of his merit, and of the public approbation; and hence become a stimulus in the little circle of his connections and acquaintance, to emulate his good conduct, and thus, in a certain degree, to elevate the character of this class of the people, would best accomplish their idea.

Having consulted artists in London, they find that something between £50 and £60 in all will be necessary to produce the requisite number of medals in a style worthy of the occasion, and as an object of pride and care to the receivers. Of course, £40 must be raised by the kindness and subscriptions of those who approve of this mode of rewarding these deserving men; in whose praise it can be truly stated that not one of them has ever made the most distant application to the Committee for reward, or allowance of any kind; and all of them are at this moment completely ignorant of such an application in their favour.

The Committee have adopted, as an appropriate design for this medal, a view of the Bridge of Spey, after the destruction of the two northern arches, by which the ruins of this noble structure are seen standing amidst the raging flood, emblematical of the devastation it occasioned, and also of those important services intended to be commemorated by the medal. On the obverse side will be an inscription of these services and the name and residence of each individual separately engraven. They hope that, although their countrymen have come forward in so unprecedented a manner to the relief of the sufferers by this awful calamity, that yet this humble appeal to their feelings in favour of those bold and fearless men who perilled their lives in the cause of humanity, will also meet their approbation and support. Any small contribution towards this object, from a crown to a guinea, will be thankfully received, and faithfully applied, if paid in to the persons mentioned below. I have the honour to remain, Sir, your obedient humble servant,

J. FORSYTH,

Convener of the Central Committee.

Subscriptions received, in London, by Messrs. SMITH, ELDER, & COMPANY, booksellers, 65, Cornhill; in Edinburgh, by Dr. WILLIAM RHIND, Broughton Place, and by Mr. A. BLACK, bookseller, North Bridge; in Elgin, by the CONVENER of the CENTRAL COMMITTEE

* *Publisher's Note: This Medal was indeed struck, and some examples still survive and are available for public viewing. The Falconer Museum in Forres, the Findhorn Heritage Centre and the Fochabers Museum all have original Medals on display.*